DATE DUE

AN AMERICAN DISSENTER

KENT & GRETCHEN KREUTER

An American
Dissenter

The Life of
Algie Martin Simons
1870-1950

UNIVERSITY OF KENTUCKY PRESS
LEXINGTON 1969

ACKNOWLEDGMENTS

We are indebted above all to the Colgate Research Council of Colgate University for its generous support and encouragement. A grant from the Littauer Foundation to the Colgate Research Council made possible a summer of research in the Simons Papers, and subsequent aid enabled us to examine other relevant collections.

A number of librarians contributed in a variety of ways to our work. Most helpful, interested, and tireless was Eric von Brockdorff, formerly reference librarian at Colgate University. Others who answered our queries and hunted up material were Warren Albert, American Medical Association; Emilie Al-Khazraji, Josephine L. Harper, Biagino M. Marone, and Judith Topaz, State Historical Society of Wisconsin; J. Frank Cook, University of Wisconsin Library; Michael Gieryic, Colgate University; Virginia R. Gray, Duke University Library; Helen S. Mangold, Huntington Library; Theodore Mueller, Milwaukee County Historical Society; and James W. Snell, Kansas State Historical Society.

Among those who offered ideas and information about Simons and the American socialist movement or who read parts of the manuscript were Merle Curti, James C. Davies, Marcus Franda, Gerald Friedberg, Jackson Giddens, Terry M. Hopkins, Dorothy Sickels, George H. Spargo, David Stern, and Karl von Loewe.

Special thanks are due Robert Huston of Ball State University, who began to collect material on Simons in the early 1950s, when a number of Simons' relatives and friends were still available for interview. Professor Huston was most helpful to us, both in his encouragement and in his warnings of the problems to be encountered in tracking down the writings of a man who was, for much of his life, a fugitive journalist.

We are grateful to the McKnight Foundation for awarding a McKnight Prize in American history and biography to the manuscript of this book.

CONTENTS

ILLUSTRATIONS

INTRODUCTION

Americans are a sentimental people, full of nostalgia for lost causes and vanishing frontiers. Few, however, have ever become nostalgic about the vanished hopes of the Socialist party of America. Often ridiculed in its heyday for its seemingly endless quarrels and controversies, and despised for its attacks on much that Americans held dear, the socialist movement in this country has since been dishonored by its supposed kinship with communism. Many of the old Socialists themselves repudiated their radicalism and gratefully joined what they once had called "the interests."

Algie Martin Simons was one of the leaders in that great lost cause. He began a twenty-year career as a radical on the very left edge of the movement. When he quit the party in 1917 he became a moving force in the ultrapatriotic Wisconsin Loyalty Legion and for the duration of World War I assailed some of his onetime colleagues. After a foray into international diplomacy he returned to America to pursue a new vision of social justice, a vision based not upon the teachings of Karl Marx but upon the theories of Frederick Winslow Taylor and the disciples of scientific management. The Great Depression destroyed that career, and he spent the last active years of his life writing books and articles on health insurance for the American Medical Association.

To characterize Simons as merely an apostate Socialist is to ignore both his historical importance and the intrinsic interest of what he had to say about America. The very range of his ideological experience brought him into touch with many of the movements and personalities of his time. As a propagandist and historian he wrote the first Marxist survey of American history, and he disseminated his ideas about the role of economic forces in American development to a wide audience. As a journalist, he furnished Upton Sinclair with much of the material used in *The Jungle*, and as a party politician Simons was a leading force in unifying the party, in establishing the Industrial Workers of the World (IWW), and in trying to make socialism an acceptable alternative for the American voter. As a theoretician he maintained important links with the leaders of European socialism. From his days as a settlement worker on Chicago's South Side through his years as a teacher and writer on industrial relations, he sought to come to grips with the major problems that face industrial society in the twentieth century.

The renewal of radicalism that has taken place in America in the 1960s does not have its roots in the socialism that A. M. Simons espoused. The black revolution, the New Left, and the student uprisings of recent years are all responses to problems that were, for the most part, unknown to the Socialists of the early twentieth century. Yet in the careers of Simons and his contemporaries, one may see exemplified the problems faced by many men who try to resolve the tension between their sense of social injustice and their desire for the good life for themselves and their families.

For many black Americans and for some draft-resisting youth, the two go hand in hand—there can be no good life without the righting of social wrongs. But for large numbers of today's radicals, essentially middle class in background and expectations, there is an abundance of such tension. In a larger sense, then, Simons' life may suggest something of the meaning and importance of a certain kind of radicalism in the American past, and illuminate the burdens that radicalism has customarily imposed upon many of its followers.

CHAPTER ONE

On Native Ground

A slim, dark-haired youth, with a mustache that made him look older than his years and more distinguished than his origins, gathered up his luggage and hurried off the train as soon as it ground to a stop.[1] Algie Martin Simons joined the crowd of young people who made their way up the platform and into the station on that autumn day in September 1891. The train had taken him to Madison, Wisconsin, but his journey had been brief. He had come from Baraboo, in Sauk County, and it had been little more than an hour since he had said goodby to his family and friends.

In a different sense, the journey was far longer than any member of Simons' family had taken in the course of several generations. None of them had had either time or money for the luxury of higher education. His people were farmers, descendants of English and Scottish stock who had settled in America in colonial times and had moved westward through succeeding generations. Algie's grandfather had gone west from Ohio to Illinois and thence to Minnesota, where the accustomed hardships of homesteaders were augmented by a severe climate and hostile Indians.

To Simons' forebears, prosperity never came. After the farm in Minnesota had failed, Grandfather Simons moved his family to the fertile Sauk Prairie of south-central Wisconsin. There his son, Horace, was to spend the rest of his life trying to earn a living. The land near the village of North Freedom was both unusual and fruitful. At the north end of the small prairie rose the Baraboo bluffs, part of the spectacular scenery of the nearby Wisconsin Dells. The Wisconsin River carved the rocky dells and then meandered through the grassy prairie southwestward toward the Mississippi, and along its banks were hundreds of Indian mounds, effigies of animals and birds made by an unknown people of an unknown culture that left its mark along the river systems of the American interior.

Horace Simons married in 1869, and a year later his first child, Algie Martin, was born.[2] It was good, the new father thought, that the baby was a boy, for boys were useful on the farm, and Horace needed help on the quarter section he worked. Times were not easy. To make ends meet Horace sometimes worked in the small shingle mill that his father-in-law operated on a nearby farm, but this often meant that his own chores went undone.[3] Sons were valuable indeed, for they could do the work that took endurance instead of skill—the kind of endurance that kept youngsters following a moldboard plow hour after hour or hoeing corn under a midsummer sun. It was a hard life, and because the schooling of farm children was limited to an occasional term when farm duties were light, it customarily meant also that young men and women early received a life sentence to till the soil.

Algie Simons had other ideas. He was not a robust youngster, but he was a bright and bookish one, and by the time he was old enough to be of help to his father he had found other uses for his time. He read omnivorously, and his Grandmother Blackmun, who lived nearby, encouraged him, giving him his first books and urging him to go to school as long as he could. His grandfather, a determined Baptist, went to services each Sunday in North Freedom, and because the services were held in German, his young grandson, who often went along, early acquired a smattering of knowledge of the language.[4] Horace Simons had to have two more sons before he had the farmhands he needed. His eldest boy was more interested in reading than

[1] Physical description of Simons is based upon the Anthropometric Record, made in his senior year at the university, deposited in the Algie M. and May Simons Papers, State Historical Society of Wisconsin, Madison, Wis.—hereafter cited as Simons Papers.

[2] Genealogical material compiled by Ada Simons Bunker, Simons Papers.

[3] Interviews of Robert Huston with C. A. Lange, an uncle, and Clarence Simons, a brother of A. M. Simons, Aug. 1951. Cited in Huston, "Algie Martin Simons and the American Socialist Movement" (unpublished Ph.D. dissertation, University of Wisconsin, 1965), 2.

[4] Interview, John Harmon with A. M. Simons, 1947, cited in Harmon, "Algie Martin Simons" (unpublished A.B. thesis, Princeton University, 1947), 4.

in hoeing.[5] It was a familiar problem, for a whole generation of fathers was watching its sons chafe against the dull, crabbed existence of pioneer farming and cast about for other ways to spend their lives.

Before long young Algie had read, as he recalled years later, "everything on heaven or earth that could be found within miles" of home.[6] He went off eagerly to public school, and by the time he was 19 he had obtained the equivalent of a tenth-grade education. He had missed a few terms, for even reluctant labor was needed at home, but in the legendary manner of nineteenth-century youth, he had persevered.

The schools he had gone to were still well insulated from the social and economic realities in which they were set down. In Sauk County, as in a thousand other rural counties in America, were the one-room schools of fond memory and faint distinction. The chief concession they made to environmental reality was to adjust their terms to the growing season of whatever crop the countryside was raising.[7] They were ungraded and poorly taught; the subjects of instruction were the traditional three R's, and recitations averaged ten minutes per subject per class. Discipline, a major preoccupation of the day, was stern and often unreasonable. Not unusual was the principal who forbade the students in his school to move their heads in class. "Why," he inquired rhetorically, "should they look behind when the teacher is in front of them?"[8]

Still, young Simons was fortunate in some respects. A free high school bill, passed when he was only five years old, offered state aid to any district in which a majority of the voters wanted a local high school.[9] Before this legislation, any youth who expected to qualify for college or university work—and Simons was early convinced that he wanted to go to the university—had to spend some of his family's

[5] Interview, Huston with Clarence Simons, in Huston, "Algie Martin Simons," 5.
[6] Harmon, "Algie Martin Simons," 4.
[7] Conrad E. Patzer, *Public Education in Wisconsin* (Madison: University of Wisconsin Press, 1924), 124.
[8] Quoted in Lawrence A. Cremin, *The Transformation of the School* (New York: Knopf, 1961), 5.
[9] William Raney, *Wisconsin: A Story of Progress* (New York: Prentice-Hall, 1940), 431.

money to attend a private academy. That would have been out of the question for the Simonses.

There was no high school in North Freedom in 1890, so Simons was obliged to go ten miles to the county seat at Baraboo.[10] Here, too, the curriculum was limited—German was the only foreign language offered, and bookkeeping the only course that made even a gesture in the direction of "vocationalism." The pedagogy was primitive; book study and memory recitation were the principal habits of instruction. There was a certain wisdom in the method, for the teachers often had no more than third-grade county certificates. They were on safer ground hearing recitations, one eye on the text, one eye on the class, and ears attuned for the principal's step down the hall, than they would have been in taking a more creative role in the instruction of their young scholars. Simons finished the two-year course in half the allotted time. He was older than most of his classmates, and he was restless and eager to leave Sauk County.

His ambitions were vague. He knew only that he didn't know enough and that his family could do no more on his behalf than give him his freedom. He knew, too, that he had a talent that the common schools of Wisconsin, despite their vagaries and defects, had given him a chance to develop. It was a gift for oratory. In the years that he had scanned the McGuffey Readers, he had gained abundant experience in declamation. The great orations of American history had been memorized and delivered by generations of stumbling students, but young Simons had performed the task articulately and with relish. The florid rhetoric of Webster, Clay, and Calhoun, the bold utterances of the Lincoln-Douglas debates, had flowed from the tongue of this slight, Wisconsin farm boy who was coming to love the sonorous language of deep conviction—even other people's conviction. At his high school commencement, he had a chance to deliver a speech of his own. Its theme, "The Progress of Electricity," was less grand than the paeans to liberty and union he was accustomed to declaiming, but his hometown newspaper considered the address eloquent.[11]

[10] Patzer, *Public Education*, 83.
[11] Sauk County *Democrat*, June 18, 1891; see also Baraboo *Republic*, June 4, 1891.

Eloquence was not an inconsiderable gift in nineteenth-century America, for oratory was one of the art forms of democracy. The man who could speak well and animate a crowd had plenty of opportunities to do so. There were elections, legislative sessions, lyceums, and law courts in every hamlet across the nation, and at each an eager public waited. The favored style of oratory was not subtle: "Pump yourselves brim full of your subject until you can't hold another drop," one successful orator-preacher characteristically advised, "and then knock out the bung and let nature caper."[12] It was a style that permeated a great deal of American culture. Education, religion, politics, and literature all felt the impact of audiences that wanted to be aroused and exhorted, and nature "capered" on a thousand public platforms.[13]

For a youth of ambition and limited means, oratory was a way of gaining early public notice, and for Simons this was its first reward. Jake Van Orden, banker and lawyer of Baraboo, had lent money to several local young people so that they might advance their educations; in the spring of 1891 he offered to lend Simons $100 a year so that he might attend the University of Wisconsin, and Simons readily accepted.[14] He would have to work part time, he knew, for $100 would pay less than one-half of his expenses at Madison, but the prospect did not dismay him. He would be the first member of his family to be given a chance to get a university education.

As Simons searched for a place to stay, registered for courses, and ambled around the hilly, tree-shaded campus, he felt that he was in an exhilarating new world. It was an exciting time to be at the university. Like almost everything else in the America of the 1890s, it was undergoing great and rapid changes. Although the University of Wisconsin was essentially a school for the sons and daughters of the

[12] Lyman Beecher, quoted in Daniel Boorstin, *The National Experience* (New York: Random House, 1965), 320.
[13] The significance of oratory in nineteenth-century America is treated at length in Boorstin, *The National Experience*, 307–24.
[14] Jake Van Orden's role in Simons' education was described in interviews conducted by Robert Huston in 1951 with C. A. Lange and in 1953 and 1955 with Miriam Simons Leuck. Cited in Huston, "Algie Martin Simons," 8.

middle class—the rich still sent their children east—the university encouraged people of modest means like Simons to work their way through. Partly because of such encouragement, the enrollment had doubled over the past six years; in 1891 nearly a thousand students were in school.[15]

Some things were particularly striking to the farm youth who was only lately removed from the common schools of Sauk County. The university was, ironically enough, less an ivory tower than were the one-room schoolhouses on the frontier. There was in Madison no single-minded devotion to classical studies, no polite, perfunctory nod toward the genteel art of bookkeeping. On the contrary, the university developed the most thoroughgoing sense of social responsibility attained by any American university of its day. It was not afraid to be useful, and it was not afraid to teach its students to be useful. It believed that a state university had certain obligations toward the state and the people who supported it, and it fulfilled these obligations nobly.

The firstfruit of the "Wisconsin idea" might have helped Horace Simons, if it had come earlier. An agricultural experiment station had been established at Wisconsin in 1883, and it had developed a variety of innovations that made possible the success of dairying in the state. Such accomplishments as better ways of curing cheese, combating tuberculosis in animals, and feeding livestock made dairying far less risky than the haphazard planting of crops. The improbable millennium toward which every small farmer worked—a bumper crop from his own fields and a slender harvest from enough others so that market prices would be high—would never come to the Simonses. The kind of expertness that the university developed would one day bring prosperity to Wisconsin. It was a lesson young Simons never forgot.

For now he spent little time dwelling on the meager results of all his family's efforts. He found a teacher who had quite another way of looking at the kind of people from whom he had sprung. Frederick Jackson Turner had come to Wisconsin only the year before, and

[15] Merle Curti and Vernon Carstensen, *The University of Wisconsin* (Madison: University of Wisconsin Press, 1949), I, 659.

Simons became one of the young historian's advisees. It was two years before Turner was to present his "frontier thesis" before the American Historical Association, but he had long been developing the ideas he articulated in 1893. Teacher and student were kindred spirits. As Simons listened to Turner's lectures, he found that they lent a new value to his own experience and to the history of the American nation. The schools of the middle western farming frontier were still teaching of the supposed Teutonic origins of democratic institutions, or propounding the theory, as Simons remarked, "that New England created the world."[16] To thoughtful students like himself such notions, though hallowed by long acceptance, didn't jibe with experience. He had seen the wilderness transformed—had even helped a little himself—and he had watched the institutions and organizations of civilized life emerge from the developing environment. "I had the pioneer feeling all the way through," he once mused as he reminisced about his early days at the university. "I helped dig out a farm in the woods of Wisconsin. It was godawful work."[17]

As Turner saw it, the people who had done that godawful work were the backbone of the nation and its most important product. His was not the traditional mythology of rural life that had long focused on the joys of pitching hay with a song in the heart or kissing the milkmaid with tossing curls. That image instantly appeared false to anyone who had been raised on a small farm in nineteenth-century America. What Turner did was to show that the combination of free land to be broken and a people willing to acccept its challenges had created the characteristic traits of the American citizen and the distinctive institutions of democratic society. It was a romantic view in its way, but it was a heady and therapeutic antidote to the kind of history that had gone before.

Because of Turner's convictions about the importance of environment, he taught his American history course quite differently from other teachers. Turner's history didn't dwell upon supersized statesman-heroes or upon sacred documents like the Constitution. It concentrated instead upon social and economic forces that were always shap-

[16] John Harmon, "Algie Martin Simons," 3.
[17] *Ibid.*, 8.

ing and reshaping the individuals and groups they acted upon. This, too, was persuasive to Simons. He had seen no supermen in North Freedom, but he had seen some men grow rich and others poor through the accidents of environment. He had heard Fourth-of-July orators recall the nobility of the Declaration of Independence, but it seemed to him that life, liberty, and the pursuit of happiness depended more upon weather, soil, and railroad rates than upon the sentiments of eighteenth-century lawyers.

In his first year at Wisconsin, Simons came to know Turner well. He was a frequent guest in the historian's home, and through the winter he picked up some needed cash by firing the furnace there.[18] He took courses in German and French, mathematics and biology, but the new horizons that Turner had revealed to him were the most exciting and influential experiences he had.

In his sophomore year, Simons transferred into the School of Economics, Political Science and History in order to pursue his new interests further. The school had been established only that fall, but it had an instant claim to distinction because its director was the well-known economist and founder of the American Economic Association, Richard T. Ely. Ely had been lured from Johns Hopkins, partly at Turner's behest,[19] by the offer of an unprecedentedly high salary and the promise of fellowships, assistants, and large sums of money for books. Ely wanted the new school to serve as a kind of West Point for civil life; it was not only to teach its students the rudiments of the nascent social sciences but also to offer its students training for public careers.[20] It was quite in harmony with the "Wisconsin idea," and Ely's department promised to give Simons training in economics and sociology that was available in few other universities of the day. Contemporary social issues were to be the meat of Ely's courses, and social action the anticipated result.

Simons soon found that most of his classmates did not share his enthusiasm for this sober fare. The interests and expectations of the

[18] *Ibid.*, 5.
[19] Richard T. Ely, *Ground Under Our Feet* (New York: Macmillan, 1938), 179.
[20] *Ibid.*, 181.

undergraduates had changed since the 1850s and 1860s, when university students had assumed they would hold positions of civic responsibility upon graduation. In those decades debating and literary societies had served as forums for the discussion of the issues that would confront the responsible graduate. By Simons' day fraternities, for which he had neither time nor money, had usurped much of the prestige once held by the societies, and football games seemed more exciting than public debates.[21]

Though most of the students were natives of a state overwhelmingly committed to agriculture, they showed scant interest in the agrarian unrest of the late nineteenth century. Neither the Grangers nor the Populists were admired by the undergraduates of the state university. In the campus literary magazine in 1891 a student warned, "The one thing which tends toward disaster in the political world is radicalism."[22] And among the part-time jobs that indigent students took to defray their college expenses was strikebreaking.[23]

The fear of radicalism expressed within the student body was but a reflection of the fears of the middle class in general. These were troubled times in the nation, times of economic and social discontent in which even wise men found it easier to blame "foreign ideas" for civil disorder than to probe the fundamental causes of distress. In such an atmosphere, freedom of inquiry seemed an invitation to anarchy. After President Cleveland sent troops against striking railroad workers in Chicago in 1894, even Johns Hopkins forbade the open and public discussion of the president's decision and its implications. Social questions, said the trustees, are such important subjects that only the ablest and wisest men of the university should be permitted to talk about them.[24]

Richard Ely soon became a victim of this kind of fear and conservatism at the University of Wisconsin. Simons was a junior and one of Ely's research assistants when the first attacks were made. The accuser, Oliver Wells, state superintendent of public instruction,

[21] Curti and Carstensen, *The University of Wisconsin*, I, 659, 682.
[22] Quoted in *ibid.*, 682–83.
[23] *Ibid.*, 663.
[24] *Ibid.*, 510.

charged that Ely was guilty of defending strikes and boycotts and of attempting to give moral justification to attacks on life and property. The charges attracted nationwide attention, and before the affair had ended, Ely had been obliged to defend himself before hearings of the board of regents.

He kept his job, but he based his defense not on his right to think and teach whatever he liked, but rather on the claim that his social ideas were essentially conservative and growing more so all the time.[25] That was probably true, though it seemed a pale assertion of academic freedom. He made the same claim to conservatism in the book that he published in the year of his "trial," *Socialism and Social Reform*—a book that Simons had worked on as one of Ely's assistants.[26]

To help with such a volume, however conservative its intent, was a useful part of the young economics major's education in social thought. The work described and evaluated the most prominent contemporary efforts at social reform. Ely's view of socialism was an unsympathetic one, but his was not the conventional half-informed criticism made by nervous businessmen and strikebound industrialists. He admired the intelligence and perception of major socialist theorists, and he attempted to convince his readers that such thinkers were neither wildmen nor visionaries. At the same time, he made it clear that he was not sympathetic with the more apocalyptic predictions of continental Socialists, or with the all-embracing materialism of Karl Marx.

What socialism could do, Ely asserted, if it did nothing else, was to make people aware of the whole spectrum of social ills that existed in America. "Nothing in the present day," he wrote, "is so likely to awaken the conscience of ordinary man or woman . . . as a thorough course in socialism. The study of socialism has proved the turning point in thousands of lives, and converted self-seeking men and women into self-sacrificing toilers for the masses."[27] In Algie Simons,

---

[25] *Ibid.*, 516–24.
[26] See Richard T. Ely, *Socialism and Social Reform* (New York: Crowell, 1894), x, for acknowledgment of Simons' help.
[27] *Ibid.*, 145.

who was learning for the first time about socialism, Ely had an apt pupil.

Though his means were limited and his interests more intellectual than athletic or social, Simons achieved considerable distinction among his fellow students. He did so by exercising the talent that had first brought him notice back in Sauk County: his talent for public speaking. As a sophomore he joined Hesperia, a literary society that was, in fact, more oratorical than literary. He participated often in its weekly meetings, which featured debates, addresses, and the discussion of social issues; and in his senior year he became president of the society.[28] His course work with Turner and Ely was beginning to give him convictions of his own, and Hesperia gave him practice in articulating them. He was beginning to develop the style of a debater along with the habits of intellectual inquiry that a good university engendered. In many respects it was this style that made the man.[29]

Each year, the University of Wisconsin sponsored a joint debate between two of the campus literary societies. It was always a major event. Though football might engage the student body more completely in the autumn, the joint debate was held in January, and the loyalty and enthusiasm devoted to gridiron prowess was temporarily transferred to this more cerebral pastime. Late in his sophomore year, Simons was chosen captain of the team for Hesperia that would engage Athena the following winter. Athena chose the subject: "Would the national ownership and operation of the railroads in the United States be preferable to ownership and operation by private corporations?" Hesperia chose to argue the affirmative.[30]

---

[28] Huston, "Algie Martin Simons," 12.

[29] Lucian Pye, drawing upon the work of Erik Erikson, has observed that "a major dimension of personality formation . . . is learning a craft or skill and developing proficiency in manipulating particular tools, instruments or symbols." Pye, "Personal Identity and Political Ideology," in *Psychoanalysis and History*, ed. Bruce Mazlish (Englewood Cliffs, N.J.: Prentice-Hall, 1963), 164.

[30] Curti and Carstensen in *The University of Wisconsin*, I, 435, claim, after surveying the list of men who participated in the joint debate over a sixty-year period, that "it is doubtful whether any other list of students compiled on the basis of their participation in a particular activity would contain as large a percentage of men who attained distinction after graduation."

In succeeding months Simons and his two teammates worked hard to prepare their defense. Simons did most of the research. He read dozens of books on the "railroad question"; he pored over government documents and scholarly monographs. With two years of French and several of German under his belt, he tackled stacks of material on the operation of railroads in western Europe. "When we finished that debate," one of his teammates Guy Stanton Ford observed, "we were both qualified for the Interstate Commerce Commission."[31] Ford and Simons had contacted Henry Demarest Lloyd, who was then writing *Wealth Against Commonwealth* and who generously invited the two young students to his home to look through his files for material they might use. Ford went alone. Lloyd was a man of means, who lived in comfort and elegance in Winnetka, Illinois. Hesperia's captain feared that his own background was too humble to make him anything but uncomfortable and embarrassed in such surroundings.[32]

Library Hall was crowded to capacity on that January evening in 1894. Many stood throughout the contest, and cheers and applause greeted each debater as he finished his performance.[33] It was inevitable, perhaps, by the terms of the debate, that the case for the affirmative should be put with so much more indignation than the negative. Athena's debaters needed only to describe the beneficent effects of a condition that already existed, while Hesperia sought to arouse its audience to a consciousness of evil. Simons was the anchor man for the affirmative and also gave the final summation, and his speeches bristled with ire. The railway corporations had dragged "legislatures and executives and courts through the mire of corruption."[34] The corporation heads were "often the most unscrupulous financiers of our day."[35]

[31] Guy Stanton Ford to Eric Goldman, April 11, 1952, quoted in Huston, "Algie Martin Simons," 14.
[32] *Ibid*. Ford gave essentially the same account of the debate in "The Reminiscences of Guy Stanton Ford" (Oral History Research Office, Columbia University, 1956), 87. A typed transcript of these oral reminiscences is on deposit in the University of Minnesota Archives, Minneapolis, Minn.
[33] "Athena Again Triumphant," *Daily Cardinal*, Jan. 20, 1894.
[34] *Aegis* (Joint Debate Number), Feb. 2, 1894 (Madison, Wis.), 145. *Aegis*, the campus literary magazine, reprinted the full text of the debate.
[35] *Ibid.*, 141.

They had carried on careers of "corruption, discrimination and extortion unparalleled in the commercial history of the world."[36] The struggle between corporate owners and corporate users of the railroads was a contest in which "avarice upon the one hand, is arrayed against demagoguery upon the other."[37] Simons even hinted once at bad faith on the part of one of his opponents: "He . . . made a great deal of the fact that the chart on accidents presented by my colleague did not give the rate of accidents per mile. But he knew and every member of the negative knows that the *results* would have been the same had he given the rate per passenger mile."[38] All this was well within accepted debate practice, but for Simons it was a manner of discourse he was to use time and again in the years to come. Many an opponent was to be similarly accused and was to find that the manner of accusation won him friends that his arguments had not.

The judges of the joint debate deliberated only five minutes. Wagering on the debate had been heavy. Bettors with an eye for the realities of the day and a knowledge of who the judges were—a state official and two federal judges—should have known where the smart money belonged. Hesperia and public ownership went down to defeat, and the Athenians were carried from the hall on the shoulders of their cheering classmates.[39] "Our arguments," Guy Ford declared, "skipped right over the bald heads of . . . the jury."[40]

The defeat was by no means crushing to Simons or to his campus reputation as an oratorical giant. He continued to speak regularly in Madison, and in March 1895 he was chosen to represent the university at the Northern Oratorical League contest.[41] A genuine source of anxiety, however, was his precarious financial position. It cost him about $250 a year to stay in school,[42] and this meant that even with the loan from his benefactor he had to earn $150 annually by himself. To do so he took on a variety of part-time jobs: he worked on the

[36] *Ibid.*, 142.
[37] *Ibid.*, 141.
[38] *Ibid.*, 140.
[39] "Athena Again Triumphant," *Daily Cardinal*, Jan. 20, 1894.
[40] Ford to Goldman, quoted in Huston, "Algie Martin Simons," 17.
[41] Huston, "Algie Martin Simons," 18.
[42] *Catalogue of the University of Wisconsin, 1891–1892*, p. 134.

university farm, tutored, washed dishes, and did German translation at which he was by now quite adept.[43] Then in his junior year his financial problems multiplied. Jake Van Orden was bankrupted by the aftermath of the disastrous panic of 1893, and Horace Simons lost the family farm.[44]

Simons managed to make ends meet by taking on two new jobs. He began to cover campus events for one of the local newspapers, the Madison *Democrat,* and he served as the Madison correspondent of the Chicago *Record.*[45] Although these jobs involved only straight reporting, they were a good deal more desirable than dishwashing. More important, they developed in Simons the useful skills that day-to-day journalism demands: clear, concise, and constant writing, and the ability to meet deadlines.

Through it all, Simons made a distinguished academic record at the university. In his senior year he was obliged to prepare a scholarly dissertation to satisfy the degree requirements. With the vast researches of the joint debate already done, he chose to write on "Railroad Pools," and his work was good enough to be published in the *Transactions of the Wisconsin Academy of Sciences, Arts and Letters.* Compared to the fire and indignation of his performance in the joint debate, it was a curiously temperate piece of work. The subject itself was provocative, as the debate the year before had amply shown. It was particularly so to a youth like Simons who had grown up in an environment where individual success or failure was often determined by the rates the railroads charged farmers for carrying their crops to market. The subject was also one upon which Simons' mentor Richard Ely had strong feelings: he had long argued in favor of government ownership of natural monopolies.

Simons made no such recommendation in his senior thesis. He merely presented a restrained discussion of the various effects of railroad pools upon rates, discriminations, and monopolies. He made

---

[43] A. M. Simons, Typescript biography for civil service examination, 1916, Simons Papers.

[44] Interviews, Robert Huston with Clarence Simons and Miriam Simons Leuck; Huston, "Algie Martin Simons," 9.

[45] Simons, Typescript biography for civil service examination, 1916, Simons Papers.

it clear that the issue of pooling as a step toward government ownership lay beyond the scope of his paper. He accepted the premise that
railroads were natural monopolies and declared that the fundamental
question—one he chose only to raise, not to answer—was whether
traffic should be apportioned by competition or by authority.[46]
To be this prudent was probably sound. Simons could satisfy the
demands of the dissertation requirement in this way without becoming embroiled in controversy that might hold up his degree. The Ely
"trial" might have made him wary of acting the role of firebrand in
what was primarily an exercise in scholarship. He was not trimming
his convictions—if, indeed, the sentiments he had expressed for purposes of the debate had been his own. He was merely fulfilling a
different kind of obligation. He would never entirely lose the habits
of research that he had demonstrated at the university, but he was
soon to grow restive under the restraints of scholarship. Before long
the passionate debater would begin to struggle with the sound
scholar, and what was to emerge would be an amalgam of both.

In June 1895 Algie Simons received his bachelor's degree with
special honors in economics. He received awards in oratory and debating and his overall average was sufficient for admission to Phi Beta
Kappa.[47] In addition, he was chosen by the faculty to speak at the
commencement exercises, and in the oration he revealed that his
intellectual distinction was now coupled with a growing sense of social
commitment. The young man who four years earlier had discoursed
upon "The Progress of Electricity" now spoke soberly upon "The
Church as a Social Factor."

To his mentor, Richard Ely, and to most of the educated members
of his audience, the ideas Simons expressed were not new. Ely's
writings were filled with the canons of Christian socialism and with
reminders of the great distance unrestrained capitalism had traveled
from the ideas of Christ. Most Americans were willing to call a man
Christian if, though rapacious for six days, he were pious on the

[46] A. M. Simons, "Railroad Pools," *The Transactions of the Wisconsin
Academy of Sciences, Arts and Letters*, XI (1896–1897), 66–77.
[47] The University of Wisconsin was not awarded a Phi Beta Kappa chapter
until 1913. At that time Simons was admitted.

seventh. To Simons, however, the ideas were still new and disturbing, and his own concern was reflected in his address.

The Golden Rule, he said, was being forgotten in the struggle for wealth. The cities of America, which ought to be forums for the advancement of human brotherhood, had become something quite different. They were arenas of pitiless struggle, where the strong took every advantage of the weak, and where the children of the meek inherited not the earth but a lifetime of poverty. Christ's law, Simons insisted, had been cast aside in favor of the law of competition: "Men . . . have defined [competition] as the supreme principle of civilization. Its sway was at first confined to the market place. Competition in commodities became competition in flesh and blood— and the gory altars of this nineteenth century Moloch were erected in the mines of Cornwall, the New York tenement, and the London sweatshop."[48]

Humanity's only hope, Simons claimed, lay with the Christian church; it was the "mightiest force for social regeneration." But the church needed to put its own house in order before it could fulfill its function as the conscience of society. It had to abandon dogma and give up its exclusive preoccupation with the life everlasting in favor of efforts to approximate more nearly Christ's kingdom on earth.

What Simons had to say was only faintly controversial. Few people in late nineteenth-century America believed that the church was solely a theological institution, and no one claimed that the Golden Rule had been fulfilled. Still, there was a great difference between taking such evident truths for granted, and believing that they were worth talking about. Simons did not suggest just how the reforms in church and society might be brought about, but he had begun to ask himself such questions.

There was a certain abstractness about the young graduate's address. His remarks about the baleful effects of urban life were certainly not drawn from his own experience, for he had never lived in a city larger than Madison. They were a blend of what he had learned in Professor Ely's courses and the traditional farm-bred dislike and

[48] Quoted in "U. W. Commencement," Baraboo *Republic*, June 26, 1895.

distrust of the wicked city. To the middle western farmer of the late nineteenth century, the city stood for what was most hated—the moneychangers, whose mysterious dealings amplified the farmer's economic insecurity—and for what was most envied—the comforts and conveniences that were absent from rural life.

The city was not long to remain an abstraction to Simons. He had accepted a special fellowship to the Associated Charities in Cincinnati and was to begin work and study under the widely respected leader of the charity organization movement, Philip W. Ayres.[49] Simons had decided to become a social worker.

His years at the university had been fruitful ones, and when he graduated at the age of 25, he took with him qualities of character and intellect that he would never lose. He had come as a farm boy who spoke well. He left with some notion of which things were worth speaking about. He had come to Madison with an intellectual curiosity that had ranged over the books that happened to be near enough to borrow. At the university he had learned how to find out what he wanted to know, and he had met scholars who respected him for the vigor of his mind and the determination that kept him at his work. And despite the demands of work and study, he left the University of Wisconsin with a reputation as a formidable debater. He was to be a debater for the next fifty years.

The train that carried Simons eastward to Cincinnati crossed a land held tight in the grip of depression. It was a land where men of talent and ambition had long dedicated themselves to exploitation and self-aggrandizement. The country could use the energies of those with other values.

---

[49] Ayres to Ely, Jan. 14, March 10, 1895; C. M. Hubbard to Ely, June 4, 1895, in Richard T. Ely Papers, State Historical Society of Wisconsin, Madison, Wis.—hereafter cited as Ely Papers.

CHAPTER TWO

Poverty and Philosophy

Algie Simons moved into the Cincinnati Social Settlement in September 1895. During the day he worked as an investigator for the Associated Charities of the city, and in the evenings he took part in the regular activities that the settlement house provided for the surrounding area. When he had time, he talked with students from the University of Cincinnati who came down to the settlement to help out with its clubs and classes, he wandered about the ugly, crime-ridden neighborhood, and he pondered the effects of the great depression of the 1890s. It was a busy life, but a worthwhile one, he thought.[1]

His job was bringing him in touch with the two main instruments that were being used in the 1890s to cope with urban social and economic problems: the settlement and the charity organization movements. Both were English innovations, and both were free from any trace of radicalism in origin or intent. Almost in spite of themselves, however, both served ultimately to deepen Simons' understanding of social ills.

The charity organization movement was originally intended to promote efficiency in administering alms to the poor. What made it acceptable to many Americans who would otherwise have been chary of helping those who did not help themselves was that it promised to reduce the amount of money spent on the indigent. It was assumed that the high cost of charity was partly due to waste and to gullibility on the part of well-meaning but naive philanthropists. If the work of all alms-giving organizations were coordinated, then presumably aid would be given only to those who were truly deserving, and duplication of effort would be avoided.[2]

Initially, the Associated Charities of Cincinnati furnished no financial aid to the needy. It merely served as a bureau of information and administration. Young Simons and other investigators like him were sent out to find the "worthy poor" among those who had applied for help. It was almost inevitable that the thoughtful investigator should find himself questioning some of the prevalent nineteenth-century assumptions about poverty. The belief, hallowed by long acceptance, that the individual was always at fault was hard to sustain when one found men eager to work but confronted by closed factories or restricted production. Simons was predisposed to doubt that individual defect was the reason for economic difficulty. He had seen too many hard-working, temperate farmers reduced to total dependence by natural disasters and by the exactions of a distant and often mysterious market, to believe that a man's destiny was in his hands alone. His own family had worked grimly and single-mindedly for years and had still lost all. Now he was discovering the urban conditions that produced the same unhappy results.

The quest for accurate information, a central aim of the charity organization movement, also proved to have more far-reaching consequences than its founders had anticipated. Investigators were obliged to look into the housing and working conditions of their clients, as well as into the personal habits of those who sought aid.[3] Such conditions were often shocking, and doubly so to the sons and daughters of the middle-class, who made up the bulk of charity organization workers. These were the very people who had been most thoroughly indoctrinated with Spencerian notions of the "survival of the fittest" and Protestant assumptions about the union of wealth with virtue.

Cincinnati was beset with the same economic and social problems that were evident in all American cities in the 1890s. It had grown too fast, had chosen to ignore the problems posed by incoming immigrants and expanding industries, and had suffered its share of greedy hands in the municipal treasury. Simons had little time, however, to

[1] Simons to Ely, Dec. 6, 1895, Ely Papers.
[2] The best account of the charity organization movement and its contributions to the understanding of poverty in America is in Robert Bremner, *From the Depths* (New York: New York University Press, 1956), 50–55.
[3] *Ibid.*, 55.

assimilate these conventional ills, for he soon left Cincinnati for a city that made his previous post seem almost like the New Jerusalem by comparison. Philip Ayres had gone to Chicago to head its Bureau of Charities, and he asked Simons to join him.[4]

Even with his brief Cincinnati experience, Simons could not have helped but find Chicago deceptively exhilarating. The traffic of half a continent passed through the city, and on the street corners of the Loop one could hear the incessant roar of trolley cars and drays and the elevated trains that shook the iron framework. Beside the crude exhibition of the Eden Musée, where one could view wax figures of the nation's most notorious murderers, there was the opulence of the State Street department stores, from Siegel Cooper's on up to Marshall Field's—all capable of dazzling the farm boys who came fresh from the austerity of rural America to seek their fortunes.[5]

Simons was coming on a more somber mission, for the luxury of State Street and the vitality of the city were making the nineties gay for only a small fraction of Chicago's population. The Bureau of Charities, for which he was to work, had been formed in the bitter winter of 1893–1894, when economic depression had begun to crush the life out of much of Chicago. The Columbian Exposition had drawn people, money, and jobs the summer before and had made the city an island of apparent prosperity in the midst of growing distress elsewhere in America. But the fair closed at the end of October, and economic distress steadily darkened memories of the White City.

Workers who had come to Chicago while the fair was open were left destitute when it closed. Few had the resources to go back where they had come from, and had little reason to think their prospects would be better there anyway. Each night crowds of tramps and vagrants swarmed about the precinct police stations of the city, where the homeless were allowed to sleep on the benches and stairs and in the hallways.[6] Every day throughout the long winter, groups of

[4] Hubbard to Ely, Nov. 4, 1895; Ayers to Ely, Nov. 4, 1895, Ely Papers.
[5] Carl Sandburg, who first came to Chicago at nearly the same time as Simons, describes his impressions in *Always the Young Strangers* (New York: Harcourt, Brace, 1952), 378–80.
[6] Jane Addams, *Twenty Years at Hull House* (New York: Signet Edition, 1960), 122.

hopeless men and women milled about the Cook County Agency, where outdoor relief was dispensed to the worthy. When a case of smallpox was discovered among the waiting throng, and the Cook County Agency was closed for a day or two in consequence, the crowd outside did not even disperse, but waited grimly for the office to open again. They had to eat.[7]

City and county agencies provided only a small percentage of the relief needed. Private agencies and individuals—churches, unions, and ladies bountiful—attempted to do most of the charity work. In this welter of groups and organizations some coordinating agency was necessary, and it was this function that the Bureau of Charities had been organized to perform. The bureau was to find out, first of all, how many people in Chicago could not supply themselves with one or more of the basic necessities. Once this was known the bureau's agents were then to organize and coordinate the effects of existing private organizations in a way that would best use the resources of each. No one believed any longer that even the most ambitious and efficient administration would reduce the relief burden of the city.

When Simons arrived in November, Chicago was beginning its third winter of profound economic depression, and in many areas of the city the organization of relief work had not even been started. The Stockyards District, on the southwest side, had barely been touched by the bureau's efforts, and privation there was acute. It was to this area that Philip Ayres assigned Simons.

Though he was new to the city, the young social worker already knew something about the packing industry which dominated the life of southwest Chicago. The Union Stock Yard, destined to become perhaps the most notorious industrial complex in America, had been in operation since the end of the Civil War. In the 1870s and 1880s, the fortunes of Armour, Swift, and Morris had been made with the combination of imagination, ingenuity, and immorality that often marked the growth of industry. In the 1890s, the process of economic concentration had been accelerated and, again in a familiar course of events, smaller and less efficient packers had been crowded out. Si-

[7] Julia Lathrop, "Cook County Charities," *Hull House Maps and Papers* (New York: Crowell, 1895), 158–61.

mons had learned, in the research he had done for the joint debate at the university, something of how this was done. The manipulation of railroad rates by the large-scale packers had been as disastrous to their competitors as the similar favors done to Standard Oil had been to the small refiners of Pennsylvania.

Criticisms of the yards and their methods had been raised from the start. Some came from groups that clearly had reason to hope for the failure of the packing industry. The Butchers National Protective Association publicized the supposed dangers of eating meat that had been shipped long distances and urged a boycott of Chicago beef. More disinterested groups, like the Humane Society, charged the yards with cruelty to animals, and sanitation experts were troubled by the plagues of bluebottle flies that swarmed through the yards and into the surrounding neighborhoods.[8]

For the most part, public attention was focused upon the marvels of ingenuity and efficiency that were said to characterize the Chicago stockyards. In 1892, for example, P. J. O'Keefe, a writer for the *New England Magazine*, had shared with his readers some of the marvels of this great new industry. "Everything," Mr. O'Keefe wrote admiringly, "is arranged with a view to cleanliness and nicety, and the thousands of pounds and the miles of sausage links which are the product of a day's work form a wonderful sight." The author found a moral in it all, too: "The fact that nature intended nothing to go to waste is well exemplified in this case."[9]

Within rather severe limits, Mr. O'Keefe was right: nothing went to waste in the stockyards, except human beings. These, as Simons was soon to find to his disgust, were hired, used to the limit of their endurance, and discarded with an almost Oriental prodigality. Newly arrived immigrants, hardly able to speak a word of English, were employed in the yards at starvation wages. They lined up each morning in front of the packing plants, hoping to be chosen for a day's work. The kinds of work demanded were often crippling and

[8] For a discussion of the rise of the packing industry in Chicago and of some of the early opposition to the stockyards, see Bessie Pierce, *History of Chicago* (New York: Knopf, 1957), III, 108–44.
[9] P. J. O'Keefe, "The Chicago Stockyards," *New England Magazine*, n. s., VI (1892), 367, 368.

nearly always brutalizing. Some men spent their working lives crushing the skulls of cattle and hogs, while others stood all day, ankle deep in water and blood, in freezing temperatures.

When disease and accident struck, there was no help short of charity for the stricken person and his family. Workmen's compensation was unknown in the 1890s in virtually every industry. Occupational diseases were ignored in America by employers, employees, and the medical profession alike. Before 1910 the American Medical Association had never held a meeting on industrial illness and injury, and though European medical journals were filled with articles on the kinds of poisoning, disease, and debility that were met in the stockyards, American journals included only an occasional nod toward the subject.[10]

The neighborhoods around the yards provided as fragile an existence as the packing plants themselves. The stockyards worker was not customarily a tenement dweller. He was likely to "own" his own single-family home—he had, that is, paid some money down on a small wooden house near his work. If he missed even one payment, he was likely to be evicted instantly. Through the streets flowed the sewage from the packing plants and killing houses, and overhead hovered the dense, black smoke which carried the unmistakable stench of the industry.[11]

These were the stockyards in good times. Times were, however, far from good when Simons was assigned to organize the relief efforts of the area. Unemployment was high. There had been a strike in 1894, which the packers had dealt with simply by firing the rebellious employees and bringing in trainloads of Negroes from the South. When the strike had been settled to the packers' satisfaction, and the newly formed unions totally destroyed, the Negroes were promptly fired—without, of course, being given the means to leave Chicago.

[10] According to Alice Hamilton, *Exploring the Dangerous Trades* (Boston: Little, Brown, 1913), 3.

[11] For a report on housing conditions in the stockyards district as it existed in 1900, see Robert Hunter, *Tenement Conditions in Chicago* (Chicago: City Homes Association, 1901), 12, 181–82. Hunter and his investigators found that while adequate light and ventilation were more prevalent in the yards area than elsewhere in the city, the general filth of this district was unparalleled.

They remained, a floating pool of unemployed people, victims of the hatred of half-starved white workers and of the indifference of the packers. Economic hardships were intensified by social disorganization, and a legacy of hatred was left for succeeding generations. In 1896 families that had only begun to recover from the effects of the strike were once again enduring wageless weeks and months. Many had invested their meager savings in down payments on their homes. Unable to keep up the mortgages, they faced the prospect of homelessness without resources of any sort.

Simons had three jobs to do without delay. He had to find out who needed assistance among a population of from 125,000 to 175,000 people, and what kinds they needed; he had to find out where the various forms of charity might be obtained; and he had to organize ways of distributing the supplies once they had been gathered. It was a staggering undertaking, especially for a young man whose experience in such matters consisted of some courses he had taken in social welfare at the University of Wisconsin and a few months as an investigator in Cincinnati.

He began at once. He brought together volunteer and professional help and solicited donations from a variety of private organizations. He began to gather information about the district in order to find out where the most serious needs existed. Within a short time he had united a group of some fifty "friendly visitors," who went among the poor to distribute relief and to help the destitute in the best use of charity. Some of these visitors were volunteers, with little to aid them in their work except a charitable heart, and some lacked even that. Others, like Simons, were new members of a new profession, given their social consciousness and their knowledge of social conditions by men like Richard Ely at Wisconsin and Albion Small at the University of Chicago. Harmony between the two groups was not always easy to achieve. The volunteers tended to think of charity as a personal obligation, performed by people of comfortable means and unimpeachable character, and bestowed out of mercy upon those of little means and doubtful character. As late as 1899 the standard guidebook to aid the friendly visitor in the performance of charitable duties warned against straying from "that safe middle ground which recognizes that character is at the center of the problem."[12] Those who had absorbed such ideas did not readily accept the professionalization of good works. They often resented social workers the way a doting mother might resent the child-rearing advice of a spinster schoolteacher.[13]

Despite the friction Simons managed successfully to administer his battalion of visitors who went down into the stockyards district throughout the raw, bleak winter. And if their advice about temperance and virtue fell on uncomprehending or incredulous ears, the tangible relief they brought was welcome.

Simons also took an active part in the fact-finding aspects of his job and in efforts to raise the needed funds. He walked through the residential streets back of the yards, watching children at play beside the rivers of raw sewage that ran past their houses. Sometimes in those early months, until he realized the futility of the attempt, he spent hours at the Chicago Health Department trying to arouse its officials to do something about this obvious menace to life and health.[14] Sometimes he went into the packing plants and watched the fortunate minority—those who were able to find employment at all— doing the tedious, enervating labor that earned them enough to keep their families together and their wives and children at home.

On Sunday evenings, Simons spoke in the churches of Chicago, pleading before Protestant and Catholic congregations for relief aid to his district. He described the conditions that were destroying human lives in a country that claimed to be the promised land. To parishioners who cherished notions of an invisible hand guaranteeing justice and equity, he described the workings of the Illinois law on damage suits: families whose breadwinner had been killed in the yards were guaranteed lifelong employment for all other family

[12] Mary E. Richmond, *Friendly Visiting Among the Poor* (New York: Macmillan, 1899), 8–9.
[13] See A. M. Simons, Typescript biography for civil service examination, 1916, Simons Papers, for description of his work in organizing the friendly visitors. See Bremner, *From the Depths*, 52–54, on the growing professionalization of social work in the 1890s and the friction between volunteers and professionals.
[14] Simons, *Packingtown* (Chicago: Charles Kerr, 1899), 27.

members if they agreed not to bring damages against the company. At the end of two years, they found that the bargain was off, for the Illinois period of limitations for damage suits was two years.[15]

To churchgoers who imparted the virtues of hard work and thrift to their children, Simons described the hard-working and thrifty children of the stockyards: small boys, for example, who operated dangerous machines, in order to hold jobs for their fathers, who had been disabled by those same machines.[16]

These were unpleasant stories, and many who heard them or read them in the brochures and pamphlets that Simons turned out from his office at the Bureau of Charities gave generously of time and money to alleviate the miseries of the district. In terms of what Simons set out to do during that winter he was remarkably successful. In a few months he had united the church relief societies into an efficient organization that lasted many years. He had prepared a budget for stockyards relief and apportioned financial responsibility among the many private societies that furnished charitable aid to the area. He developed an administrative staff of both unpaid volunteers and trained professionals and managed to keep peace between them, and through his tireless writing and speaking he succeeded in raising additional sums of money.

So successful was he that the stockyards district was the only one in Chicago which made no general appeal to the city for help. It was the only slum from which no case of extreme unrelieved distress was reported in the Chicago newspapers that winter.[17] All this had been accomplished in an area that was traditionally among the most difficult relief problems, and by a young man of meager experience and limited training. It was a personal achievement in which Simons could take legitimate pride.

In a larger sense, even the comparatively great resources he had managed to muster on behalf of Packingtown were minuscule compared to the problems and the needs of the area. To keep a man from

[15] *Ibid.*, 20.
[16] *Ibid.*, 21.
[17] Simons, Typescript biography for civil service examination, 1916, Simons Papers.

starving was a hollow triumph if blood poisoning, from a scratch incurred in the yards, was to take his life a few months later. To clothe a child against a cold winter was useless charity if, when summer came, the youngster was to contract some crippling illness bred in the filth around his house. If one could begin to get at the underlying causes of problems like these, then there would be real cause for pride.

In the summer of 1896, when some of the most urgent problems of the stockyards district had subsided, Simons began to make a systematic study of poverty in Packingtown and adjacent Englewood. He set out to discover, and to represent with statistical impartiality, the exact number of individuals and families who depended on charity, and the reasons that they did so. Above all he wanted to find out, if he could, how much poverty was actually due to individual defects and how much could be attributed to circumstances beyond the control of the indigent.

It could hardly be supposed that Simons began his study with an entirely open mind. What he had seen during the winter had given him some suspicions about what he might find in the dispassionate survey he set out to make. Yet the task he set himself was a common one among the young social workers of the late 1890s; and most had come to it with the same preconceptions as he. If they had not done so, it is doubtful that such undertakings would even have been started. As long as everybody believed that the individual was entirely to blame for his economic and social condition, there was nothing to ask questions about. One merely went among the poor, preaching the lessons of moral uplift and distributing what largess one commanded. As a result, nobody even knew how many needy Americans there were, until very late in the 1890s. When Richard Ely had tried in 1891 to determine the number of paupers in the country he discovered that no accurate records were kept, either by the state or federal government, of how many people were in public institutions or receiving relief.[18]

Such inadequacies not only made for inefficiency in the administra-

---

[18] Bremner, *From the Depths*, 72.

tion of charitable assistance but also spared the public from knowing the dimensions of economic and social problems in America. The "tramp question" was endlessly discussed in the popular magazines of the 1890s because tramps were the visible poor, whom even middle-class and wealthy Americans saw without going slumming. It was alarming to discover so many homeless vagrants on the roads and village streets of the nation; in the absence of any documented and widely disseminated knowledge about poverty and homelessness, it was also quite surprising.[19]

Gradually, however, the gaps were being filled. The settlement houses were a leading force in the effort to get a better grasp of the social maladjustments that became so pronounced during the Depression of the 1890s. They began the careful block-by-block investigations of poor neighborhoods that revealed the conditions of homes, health, and finances of the families that lived near the settlements.[20]

It was this kind of investigation that Simons started in 1896. He began by listing the manifold causes of poverty, determining the most prominent cause in each case he found, and then adding up the number of occurrences of each cause to discover which were the most important. It was a simple method, but an important one, for it clothed a highly controversial subject with the respectability of science. What Simons documented was what might have been concluded by any observer who had watched the milling crowds of men that gathered about the packing plants each gray morning: by far the most prominent cause of indigence was unemployment, pure and simple. This, Simons found, contributed three times as many "units" to the total sum of distress as any other single cause. It contributed more than any other four causes combined.[21] It was, moreover, unemployment caused not by the sloth or intemperance of the would-be breadwinner, but by too many people for too few jobs.

More important, Simons found that the causes of poverty were

[19] See *ibid.*, 142–45, for a discussion of some of the major articles and books written in the 1890s on vagrancy.
[20] *Ibid.*, 149.
[21] A. M. Simons, "A Statistical Study in Causes of Poverty," *American Journal of Sociology*, III (March 1898), 617.

complex and interrelated, and that oftentimes an ever-widening web of misfortune ensnared the families who became objects of charity. Unsanitary housing might bring illness, compelling the wage earner to let his son substitute on the job. This in turn might finally drive the son from home, as an untrained and uneducated vagrant who might turn to charity or theft or worse in his efforts to survive.[22] Simons also concluded that the social causes of poverty far outnumbered those that could be blamed upon the individual.[23] Intemperance was rarely the initiating factor in any chain of poverty; improvidence was seldom a cause of degradation in families that had nothing to be improvident with.

None of these conclusions could have been wholly unexpected to Simons or, in fact, to the readership of the *American Journal of Sociology*, where he published the results of his work. The number of such studies with such conclusions was growing. Oftentimes, however, fact gathering served as a substitute for action. A few eyes were opened by the monumental nature of the problems, but then those same eyes refocused on more pleasant and profitable subjects. For Simons this was only the beginning. Once he had what he considered irrefutable proof that American society suffered from more serious problems than working-class intemperance, he began to seek out the avenues of reform. He began to look for solutions that would be more enduring than the dole.

Nearest to hand was the settlement house. Here was an agency that sought to alter the quality of both the individuals and the environment in which they were set. Simons lived in two of the best, Hull House and the University of Chicago Settlement. He came to know many of the famous ladies of settlement work—Jane Addams, Julia Lathrop, Alice Hamilton, and Mary Richmond—and he took part in a host of settlement activities.

The University of Chicago Settlement, located within the stockyards district, was concerned with finding solutions to the problems that Simons knew most about. It carried on a constant campaign for

---

[22] *Ibid.*, 614.
[23] *Ibid.*, 616.

adequate building laws and sanitary regulations, and it sought to make the inhabitants of the area themselves agitate for such services. It campaigned for an end to the system whereby the packing plants kept thousands of people on hand as a pool of surplus labor. The settlement sponsored a variety of educational activities, designed to prepare the immigrants and their children for civic responsibility, to teach them manual skills and good health habits, and to provide wholesome places to gather and work or play.[24]

Yet nothing that the settlement could do seemed to touch the problems of the area in any fundamental ways—problems, for example, like the city garbage dump. Years after the University of Chicago Settlement began efforts to have it removed, the city garbage dump remained, breeding the diseases that killed great numbers of babies each August in the stockyards district. Campaigns of education and enlightenment, however energetically pursued, could do little to alter conditions that would cost money to remedy.[25] It made people feel good to give to "charity," but to be told that they had an obligation to pay for the righting of social injustice was quite another matter. It was not long, therefore, before Simons began to doubt that the settlements could become agents of important reform.

What the settlements lacked, of course, was effective, coercive power. In some respects, as Simons would soon begin to point out, they served the interests of businessmen and industrialists: they performed tasks that should have been the employers' responsibility but that helped to keep employees healthier and more contented. In another respect, however, the settlements were a more radical force than they were ever intended to become. Their very existence provided focal points around which clustered young men and women like Simons who were troubled by the misery and greed they saw and who were beginning to seek effective ways of coping with them. Intent upon performing "educational" functions, the settlements sponsored lectures and meetings that might familiarize people with the alterna-

---

[24] Robert A. Woods and Albert J. Kennedy, eds., *Handbook of Settlements* (New York: Russell Sage Foundation, 1911), 69–72, describes the work of the University of Chicago Settlement.
[25] *Ibid.*, 69.

tives of social reform. And because radicals of all shades and varieties were abroad in the land in the 1890s, it was inevitable that such groups as Hull House's Working People's Social Science Club should hear radical speakers from time to time.[26]

For the immigrants who lived along Halsted Street or back of the yards, such speakers seemed like a touch of home amid alien surroundings. They spoke an ideological language that was almost as familiar to the European immigrant as his own mother tongue, and as reluctantly abandoned. These were the years when socialism and anarchism still spoke almost entirely in foreign accents, and when most Americans, even those of tender conscience and large heart who went into the urban slums of the 1890s, found it hard to believe that foreign ideas should furnish keys to the solution of American problems. As Jane Addams observed, "The residents of Hull House discovered that while the first impact with city poverty allied them to groups given over to discussion of social theories, their sober efforts to heal neighborhood ills allied them to general public movements which were without challenging creeds."[27]

To rely upon "general public movements" in that decade was more easily said than done. In some cases they simply were not in existence. Jane Addams had tacitly admitted that, in the winter of 1894, when she had had to create jobs like streetsweeping in a feeble effort to assume a responsibility that government might more logically have performed. And if by public movements she meant public agencies and officials, there was little to be hoped for there. The police of Chicago were hardly sympathetic to the aspirations of working-class immigrants and were all too willing to seize upon any excuse to commit violence against them.[28] Other agencies that were presumed to operate in the public interest were, in fact, operated at the behest of whoever could offer the fattest bribe.[29]

---

[26] Jane Addams, in *Twenty Years at Hull House*, 135–37, describes the club, its speakers, and its reputation for radicalism.

[27] *Ibid.*, 144.

[28] Several lurid examples of police brutality are given in Alice Hamilton, *Exploring the Dangerous Trades*, 76–81.

[29] Ray Ginger discusses some of the more notorious Chicago scandals in *Altgeld's America* (New York: Funk and Wagnalls, 1958), 6–7, 12.

For a time in 1896 it looked as though there might be a "general
public movement" for social and economic reform that had a chance
of success on a national scale. The Democratic party had gathered up
the scattered threads of reform, put them in the hands of young
William Jennings Bryan, and sent him before the nation to campaign
for the presidency against William McKinley. It was a sorry struggle.

Simons observed the campaign from South Chicago. He watched
while the bosses of Packingtown equipped their employees with ban-
ners and canes and sent them downtown to join the parade on behalf
of the Republican party. He watched as Tom Carey marshaled his
voters on election day, certain of victory, for he held the key to these
men's continued employment in the yards. Civil service reform had
diminished the political spoils at the command of unscrupulous politicians, but other kinds of spoils were available. When Gustavus Swift
expanded his stockyards operation in the winter after the
Bryan–McKinley campaign, each employee who was hired to help
construct the new facilities bore with him a letter from Tom Carey.[30]

To see all this, and then to heed the advice of Jane Addams and
her compatriots in the settlement movement, was a difficult matter.
For Simons it was impossible. He made a final effort in 1897, after
another devastating winter of poverty, depression, and unemployment in Chicago. He journeyed to the National Conference of Charities and Correction in Grand Rapids and listened one more time to
the arguments of those who talked of caution, character, and fact
gathering. By this time his patience was at an end. To Richard Ely he
wrote, "I look back on my work with the Bureau of Charities with
feelings not unmixed with disgust. . . . Perhaps I am wrong, but I
believe that Charity Organization is fundamentally wrong in theory
as well as impossible of application in practice."[31] When the convention ended he came back to Chicago and joined the Socialist Labor
party.

Some time after he had joined the socialist movement, Simons set
down the reasons why he had become a member. It was a common
enterprise at the time for various organs of the socialist periodical

[30] *Packingtown*, 25–29.
[31] Simons to Ely, March 13, 1897, Ely Papers.

press to print the conversion experiences of new and promising members of the faith. Such articles were the more compelling because American Socialists so often came to their ideological convictions after a series of lurid experiences of injustice and inequality. Socialism in this country was not absorbed by the individual at his mother's knee, as he absorbed his religious faith or regional and national loyalty. For most native Americans, it was grafted onto the mature man, and this was not always a source of strength for the movement. Sometimes the organism rejected the graft.

As Simons described his conversion in the pages of *Comrade*, he linked family tradition and personal experience to explain his new allegiance. He was, he said, a son of the rural proletariat whose family had for generations been driven westward by the greed and oppression of capitalist landowners. Now that the last frontier was gone and there was no place further to flee, it was almost inevitable, he said, that he should seek to change the economic system that could no longer be escaped. His education at the University of Wisconsin had acquainted him with the literature of socialism, and Frederick Jackson Turner had shown him that the substance of American history was the struggle between economic classes. His experiences in Cincinnati and Chicago had made him aware that country people were not alone in their hardships and suffering. Greed, misery, and injustice were equally familiar in the cities of America, and only a radical transformation of society could bring a good life to the working people, urban and rural, of the nation.[32]

The article was a good piece of socialist propaganda. In linking the interests of rural and urban workers and in attributing the westward movement to the dynamic of capitalism, it sounded themes that Simons would elaborate for years to come. As an explanation of why Simons had become a radical, it was highly superficial. Not every son of migrating parents went into the socialist movement when he thought the frontier was closed, not even every bright and talented son. Other Wisconsin farm boys went in quite different directions. Hamlin Garland became a writer, John Muir a naturalist, and Si-

[32] A. M. Simons, "How I Became a Socialist," *Comrade*, I (Aug. 1902), 254–55.

mons' own brothers never strayed far from the Republicanism of their elders. Not every student of Ely and Turner became a radical. Not every visitor to Chicago's South Side was appalled by what he saw there, and Simons could not explain why he had seen wretched human beings in Packingtown while P. J. O'Keefe saw only remarkable machinery.

This much is certain. For a man of intelligence, industry, and a certain amount of optimism about human affairs, socialism offered and demanded a great deal. It promised to transform human nature while it transformed industrial life; it offered an interpretation of the actions of all men and all nations; and it demanded for those who were intellectually as well as emotionally committed to it, knowledge about a great many things. All these factors drew Simons to the movement. With relief and enthusiasm he felt that at last he could do more than bind up the wounds of a diseased society.

Guy Ford, who visited his friend in Chicago shortly before Simons became a Socialist, thought he saw another reason. As he watched his classmate at the Hull House lectures and the socialist discussions they attended together, he noted that Simons, despite all his experience as a debater, was tied in knots by the arguments of the Marxists he encountered. He was being beaten at his own game.[33] He needed better arguments, as well as a more effective way of trying to cope with America's social and economic ills.

Simons did not enter the socialist movement alone. He went home to Baraboo in June 1897 and married a former high school classmate, May Wood. Together they would help to carry out an exhilarating mission—the reformation of society. "I can still see him at his desk," one of Simons' colleagues wrote of those last days before the wedding, ". . . aglow as he told of the wonders of his loved one—her beauty, her charm, the quality of her mind, her abilities, their dream plans for the future—lives dedicated to a cause."[34]

[33] Ford to Goldman, April 11, 1952, cited in Huston, "Algie Martin Simons," 33.
[34] Herbert E. Phillips to Miriam Simons Leuck, Jan. 12, 1951, Simons Papers.

CHAPTER THREE

Many Mansions

Simons returned to Chicago with his bride shortly after the wedding, and together they began working to bring the Cooperative Common-wealth to pass in America. On the face of it this seemed a rather curious enterprise for one of May Wood's background. Her parents were Presbyterians, and May had, until recently, given every indica-tion that her interests were thoroughly religious. As a girl, she had been a delegate to the convention of the Christian Endeavor, and when she graduated from high school she delivered a commencement address on "Missionary Enterprise in India."[1]

Her ambition was to become a medical missionary, but her family was of modest circumstances and lacked the resources to finance their daughter's education. Therefore, like many another young lady, May became a schoolteacher. For two years she taught in Sauk County and put money aside with the expectation that she would one day continue her education.

The opportunity came in 1893. May's sister had in-laws who were on the religion faculty at Northwestern University, and they ar-ranged for her to live in a cooperative cottage dormitory while she pursued her studies. Tuition was modest, and in the fall of 1893 she enrolled as a student in the College of Liberal Arts. While her future husband was being introduced to economics and social theory at the University of Wisconsin, May was encountering some ideas that proved unsettling to one of orthodox religious belief.

Two years after she had begun her studies, she left Northwestern and returned to Wisconsin. The alleged reason for her early depar-ture was inadequate funds, but there was more to it than that. A combination of circumstances had left her deeply troubled and had ended her desire to become a Christian missionary.

There was, first of all, the matter of Darwinism, which could not accommodate the beliefs of a rural Presbyterian. Then there were the books that young Simons urged her to read—those that had set him thinking in new directions.[2] There was also a petty and bitter theological dispute that had involved her sister's relatives at Northwestern. Quarreling over the accuracy of a translation of the Gospel of John, these theologians showed little evidence of Christian charity or piety.[3]

Finally, there was the sense of her own differentness, the realization that she was a small-town girl of very limited means set down in an environment that was strange to her. She pledged Pi Beta Phi in her sophomore year, but the companionship of her sorority sisters did not make her feel any more comfortable in Evanston than she had been from the start. The shyness and sense of social inadequacy that had led young Simons to send someone else to the home of the well-bred Henry Demarest Lloyd were no less marked in the girl he married; they helped to make her first effort at higher education a painful experience.

For two more years May Wood taught school in Sauk County. When the term ended in June 1897 she and Simons were married in her parents' home at Baraboo, by the local Presbyterian minister.[4] Her faith may have been shaken, but filial piety at least demanded that much.

Simons had not yet left his job with the Bureau of Charities or ended his association with the University of Chicago Settlement. When May returned with him to Chicago she joined in the activities of both. She too became a visitor to the poor of the stockyards district,

[1] Sauk County *Democrat*, June 18, 1891; Baraboo *Republic*, Oct. 8, 1890, June 4, 1891.
[2] No correspondence between Simons and May Wood during this period survives. Miriam Simons Leuck believes that her parents destroyed many of their papers before they left Evanston in 1944. Typescript comments, Simons Papers.
[3] May Wood Simons, "How I Became a Socialist," *Comrade*, II (Nov. 1902), 32. Information about May Wood's early years was supplied by Miriam Simons Leuck in interviews with Robert Huston, "Algie Martin Simons and the American Socialist Movement" (unpublished Ph.D. dissertation, University of Wisconsin, 1965), 29–31.
[4] The foregoing is based upon interviews of Robert Huston with Miriam Simons Leuck, in Huston, "Algie Martin Simons," 29–31.

and she too soon came to feel the sense of outrage and helplessness that had led her husband into the socialist party. "Professing 'sincerity' in their efforts to assist the laborer," she wrote bitterly of the social and settlement workers, "they cannot see that they form a constant hindrance in his way, as they help to perpetuate the system that binds him."[5] The girl who might have become a Presbyterian missionary put aside the old faith and, like her husband, took up one that seemed more relevant to the needs of the twentieth century.

Socialism had few miracles of which to boast, but it had its sacred writings, its holy men, and above all, its promise of redemption. To join a socialist party, as a colleague of Simons once wrote, was nothing to be undertaken lightly: it was "like joining a church. One must have had experience in grace, [and] one must show that one has come out from the tents of the wicked."[6] For the Simonses, the tents of the wicked were those that sheltered the charity movement and social work, and as soon as they were able, they abandoned both.

If socialism was churchlike in many respects, there was nothing Christlike in its quest for political recruits and disciples. From its first appearance in America, Marxian socialism was subject to a variety of interpretations, each with a devoted following. Each sought membership in the raucous manner of frontier villages competing for the new railroad. Each was certain that its own distinctive virtues would bring the greatest prosperity, and each was eager to belittle the prospects of its neighbor. Quarrels over doctrine and discussions of alternative species of Marxism were so central a part of the socialist movement in America that subsequent historians have often written of little else.[7] The Socialist Labor party (SLP), to which the Simonses pledged their allegiance, was the strongest and the most contentious of all. Its

[5] "Ethics of Socialism," *Workers Call*, July 29, 1899. See also May Wood Simons, "How I Became a Socialist," 32.

[6] Charles Edward Russell, *Bare Hands and Stone Walls* (New York: Scribner's, 1933), 196.

[7] This is especially true of David Shannon's, *The Socialist Party of America* (New York: Macmillan, 1955) and Daniel Bell's long essay, "Marxian Socialism in the United States," in *Socialism and American Life*, ed. Donald Drew Egbert and Stow Persons (Princeton: Princeton University Press, 1952), I, 215–405.

membership, consisting largely of German and Jewish immigrants, had risen and fallen with the economic fortunes of the country. Throughout the 1870s, Lassalleans, who believed in political action, and Marxists, who emphasized union organization and class consciousness, had contended within the party for leadership and control of policy. A brief period of harmony in New York had nearly resulted in the election of Henry George as mayor. Once the campaign was over, the Lassalleans were expelled and, in due course, the Socialist Labor party came under the leadership of the brilliant and vitriolic radical Daniel DeLeon.[8]

As a speaker and editor of the party's chief English-language weekly, *The People*, DeLeon disseminated his own brand of Marxism. He had nothing but contempt for the kind of unionism represented by the American Federation of Labor (AFL). DeLeon believed that unions should be used to heighten class consciousness, not to plead for crumbs from capitalism's table. The revolution that would liberate the working classes could come only from a proletariat that understood the inevitability of class struggle. When it came, however, the revolution would be peaceful: American workers had the ballot and could vote for a socialist state once they realized that was where their interests lay. The creation of a class consciousness, said DeLeon, was primarily a task of education.

There was always much about American socialism that was ironic. But few aspects of the movement were more ironic than the fact that the warfare against capitalism was never as bitter as the struggle of one Socialist against another. Daniel DeLeon was a master of insult and invective, and party members who strayed from his path found themselves attacked mercilessly.

The Chicago local of the SLP was far from the scenes of combat in New York where DeLeon fought against evil capitalists and labor fakirs. Algie and May Simons, filled with zeal for the cause, were not disturbed by the vehemence with which DeLeon attacked those who threatened the party's success. There was a certain simple logic to its official position. It was clear on every hand that the working class

[8] Howard Quint, *The Forging of American Socialism* (Indianapolis: Bobbs-Merrill, 1953), 3–71, 142–74.

greatly outnumbered its employers. The American proletariat needed only to gain a sense of its own power, prepare itself to command and control the instruments of production, and vote itself into power. Education and discipline were the tools by which the proletariat would be brought to the degree of wisdom already possessed by its leaders and teachers.

No one had more reason than Simons to have confidence in the power of education and discipline. Education had been the means by which he had broken the chain of circumstances that had bound generations of his family to the land. Discipline had been the quality that had enabled him to do distinguished academic work while he held down the jobs that he needed to stay in school. Surely these qualities could be the instruments for transforming society as they could transform the lives of individuals.

The defects in DeLeon's reasoning and in his own seem more apparent today than they did then, but even Simons' personal experience might have made him wary. Confidence in the ballot box as an instrument of social revolution was wishful thinking if the votes of the impoverished majority could be bought, as some were in the elections of 1896. Education was also a two-edged sword, for in America its benefits had customarily induced men of humble background to leave the proletariat. There was little reason to believe that even an education in Marxist theory could impart a sense of class solidarity: it had not even happened to Simons. Never again would he be as close to working men and women as he had been in the years before he became a Marxist.

Whatever the flaws of logic in the party's position, they were invisible to Simons as he embarked upon his first tasks. He began writing articles that were published in DeLeon's paper, *The People*. He wrote about what he had seen in the stockyards. His descriptions anticipated the work of the muckrakers, but Simons gave them a distinct ideological framework on which were hung the horror and greed of Packingtown.[9]

Anxious to try his hand at educating the working classes, Simons did an article on "Socialism and Its Objections," designed to convince

[9] *The People*, May 29, 1898.

the proletariat that its interest lay with the followers of Daniel
DeLeon.[10] The reading of the treatise could hardly have been anything but a painful experience—painful to laboring men because the
article made no concession to their educational shortcomings; painful,
too, because Simons was still the stylist of the *American Journal of
Sociology* and the *Transactions of the Wisconsin Academy*. Even his
zeal for the socialist cause could not make him instantly abandon the
evidence of his learning, so dearly bought. He would not descend to
the role of popularizer but would make his readers struggle upward
to grasp what he had to tell them.

The socialist daily and periodical press was still resisting the lure of
yellow journalism, which offered circuses, not bread, to its mass
audience. The socialist papers were deadly serious, and in the decade
of the 1890s they were still in the hands of party leaders, not
professional journalists or business managers. They sought to emulate
the intellectual distinction of an E. L. Godkin rather than the rabble-
rousing of a Hearst.

This meant trying to attract a mass audience, as the Hearsts and
Pulitzers were doing in the respectable press, while using the techniques of the Godkins, who were steadily being sentenced to journalistic oblivion or the polite exile of little magazines. As if this were not
difficult enough, the publicists of the Socialist Labor party complicated their task by persistent attacks against all who would promise
the working class immediate, tangible gains. By denying the proletariat any hope of improvement in their condition until the socialist
millennium, they set themselves against both the material appeal and
the psychological truth of bread-and-butter unionism. The Socialists
asked the proletariat to cultivate a quality that is the very essence of
middle-class psychology, the ability to defer present desires in favor
of future satisfaction. For a movement that claimed a profound
comprehension of class differences, this was a fatal lapse of understanding.

If Simons was aware of the problems that confronted him and his
new comrades, his awareness did not diminish his confidence. His
socialist activities took up an increasing share of his time, and he

[10] *The People*, July 10, 1898.

plunged into them relentlessly.[11] He was reading Marx and the Marxists in order to master fully the ideology that had won his allegiance. He was also combing the scholarly journals and monographs for the best information on contemporary economic and social theory and practice.[12] He longed to leave the Bureau of Charities, but family responsibilities kept him at his work there, for in March 1898 a son, Laurence Wood, was born to the young couple.[13]

The chance to escape social work finally came in the spring of 1899. The Chicago local of the Socialist Labor party decided to establish a weekly newspaper for the workingmen of the city, and Simons was named its editor.[14] The paper, *Workers' Call,* intended to present the news of the day through socialist eyes and at the same time to provide educational material that would give workers a better grasp of Marxist principles.

Such intentions almost at once caused problems for the new and comparatively inexperienced editor. The *Call* developed two major flaws, either of which could have destroyed even a more robust publication. First, events that were newsworthy and events that fitted the Marxist dialectic were not always the same. The workingman who bought the paper in the summer of 1899 might find discussions of the Spanish-American War, which had ended the year before—discussions that appeared there because the war was such a striking example of capitalist imperialism.[15] He then had to buy another newspaper in order to read the news of the day.[16]

[11] Simons to Ely, Nov. 4, 1898, Ely Papers.
[12] A. M. Simons, "Scientific Socialism," *The Social Crusader,* Jan. 1899, and "Socialism, a Philosophy of Social Development," *Appeal to Reason,* March 25, 1899. The published results of much of Simons' reading and study of this period appeared later. He was listed as cotranslator of two works by German Socialists: Wilhelm Liebknecht, *No Compromise—No Political Trading* (Chicago: Charles Kerr, 1900), and Karl Kautsky, *The Social Revolution* (Chicago: Charles Kerr, 1902).
[13] As early as March 13, 1897, Simons had written to Ely about his dissatisfaction as a social worker and asked him to suggest other possible occupations (Simons to Ely, March 13, 1897, Ely Papers).
[14] Huston, "Algie Martin Simons," 50.
[15] See, for example, *Workers' Call,* April 1, 8, May 27, Sept. 2, Oct. 28, Nov. 11, 1899.
[16] This defect in socialist newspapers generally is suggested by Charles Edward Russell, *Bare Hands and Stone Walls,* 204.

Second, a newspaper that was supposed to impart to its readership an education in socialist theory could not long hold itself aloof from the debilitating arguments about just what socialist theory was. The *Call* was only five months old when it was drawn into the ideological dispute that was tearing the Socialist Labor party apart.

The question at the root of the struggle concerned the policy that the SLP ought to observe toward the trade union movement. After failing to get control of the AFL some years before, DeLeon had abandoned the policy of "boring from within" and had established the rival Socialist Trade and Labor Alliance, which was to compete for membership with the AFL.[17] The party was to strive for political control, while the Alliance sought economic command.

The party was never united in its attitude toward the Alliance, and in December 1898 open rebellion had erupted in the New York *Volkszeitung,* a German-language paper of the Socialist Labor party. The editorial writer lamented the fact that DeLeon's policy had made the AFL feel secure against the assaults of socialism. Where once the AFL had been unaware of the socialist strength within its ranks and had had to contend with subversion, now it had only to observe the straightforward tactics of the infant Socialist Trade and Labor Alliance. There was, moreover, an undeniable attraction in belonging to a union like the AFL, which brought immediate small gains for the workingman, and at the same time in belonging to a movement which promised that the future would be strikingly better for him.[18]

DeLeon's response was entirely predictable. His indictment of the heretics began with attacks on their false ideology and quickly branched out into scurrilous personal assault. One of the *Volkszeitung*'s defenders was characterized as "a semilunatic, a freak, with more kinks in his head than the average, well-balanced man could ever begin to think of, and more mental dishonesty in his make-up than could be traced with a thousand x-rays."[19]

---

[17] For an account of the career of the Socialist Trade and Labor Alliance, see Quint, *The Forging of American Socialism,* 162–68.

[18] The first statement of this position appeared in the *Volkszeitung* of Dec. 14, 1898. See Quint, *The Forging of American Socialism,* 332–33, for the paper's arguments against the Alliance.

[19] Quoted in Quint, *The Forging of American Socialism,* 334.

The Chicago local at first tried to assume a mediating role in the dispute. It suggested that a referendum be held on the issue of moving the executive committee of the party from New York to more neutral ground. It suggested that all sections of the party withhold recognition from both the dissidents and the DeLeonites until a national convention could be held to resolve the differences. In the pages of the *Workers' Call,* Simons urged temperance and neutrality until the points at issue could be settled.[20]

Neutrality with Daniel DeLeon was impossible. Whoever was not with him was against him, and he erupted anew at the suggestion of disloyalty within the Chicago SLP. It was not long, therefore, before Simons was added to the list of DeLeon's enemies. The columns of *The People,* which had so recently welcomed Simons' contributions now accused him of the vilest characteristics that could be possessed by a Marxian Socialist: personal ambition, in one who professed concern only for the elevation of the masses; religious belief, in one who claimed devotion to the materialist conception of history; and ignorance, in one who sought to educate others.[21] "This A. M. Simons, Editor," DeLeon fumed, "really is as much of a simpleton as he is a fraud."[22] And one of DeLeon's allies accused Simons of "unit[ing] in himself the subtlety of the Jesuit and the naïveté of a child."[23] It was a testament, either to the unexceptionable nature of Simons' personal life or to the purity of socialist journalism, that these attacks, which included everything else, did not cast aspersions upon his actions as husband and father.

Simons was not a man to turn the other cheek. He abandoned his efforts to calm the troubled waters and mounted an attack of his own. What DeLeon was really upset about, he insisted, was that the *Workers' Call* was doing so much better than DeLeon's own paper, *The People.* It was an old story, said Simons. DeLeon had tried to cut the throat of every party paper that threatened the success of his own, and now, despite his professed interest in the purity of socialist

[20] July 22, 29, 1899.
[21] *The People,* July 30, 1899.
[22] *Ibid.,* Sept. 24, 1899.
[23] *Ibid.,* Oct. 22, 1899.

doctrine, he was out to destroy the *Call*.[24] When some of DeLeon's supporters tried to organize a rival socialist labor group in Chicago, Simons called the effort a "contemptible farce," reaching a "depth of hyena-like ghoulishness in political tactics never touched by any bourgeois politician."[25]

Throughout the summer and fall of 1899, the conflict between the two factions raged in party newspapers, convention halls, and on street corners. Both sides devoted themselves to personal invective and individual fisticuffs.[26] It was not an auspicious time for a movement that expected soon to take over and govern the nation.

An observer with a sense of history might have been struck with the resemblance between this small but vicious struggle and the wider but equally vicious strife that characterized political journalism in the early national period in America. In the first years of the nineteenth century, when tempers had flared over politics, economics, and public personalities, Alexander Hamilton had been one of the most notable defenders of the practice of transforming ideological differences into personal attacks.[27]

The reasons for the excesses of both periods were similar. The socialist editors of 1899, like their short-tempered progenitors of the previous century were, first and foremost, pamphleteers, eager to convince or destroy. In addition, the allegiances of both were recently come by. The Socialists had been born into the world of capitalism and had rejected it; the Federalists and anti-Federalists had been colonials and now had won independence. Both groups needed constant affirmation that they had made the right choice, and both reacted violently against any suggestion that they were mistaken in their acquired convictions. And because both groups believed that political power was within their grasp, they decided it might be worth the scramble, however unbecoming, to be in a position to receive the rewards of the true believer when they were handed out.

[24] *Workers' Call*, Aug. 26, Oct. 21, 1899.
[25] *Workers' Call*, Sept. 9, 1899.
[26] Daniel Bell, "Marxian Socialism," 257–58.
[27] Frank Luther Mott, *American Journalism* (New York: Macmillan, 1962), 170.

Simons was not willing to jeopardize the party's existence. After a few weeks of rebutting DeLeon's arguments and sounding some shrill blasts of his own, he began to look for more temperate alternatives. In the pages of the *Workers' Call*, he urged that the Socialist Labor party seek to form alliances with the Social Democrats, a group that had been organized by Eugene Debs and Victor Berger in 1898.[28] If the differences between these two organizations could be resolved, the socialist cause would be much the stronger, and the influence of DeLeon might be decisively crushed.[29] Simons had not joined the socialist movement just to be a debater.

Then, in the midst of this effort personal tragedy struck the Simonses. Their 18-month-old son Laurence found his way to the medicine cabinet at the home of friends. He swallowed a lethal dose of poison and died within minutes.

The future that once had appeared so promising was suddenly darkened. It was the Christmas season, and the bereaved parents rode sadly home to Wisconsin for the holidays, bearing with them the body of their son, who was buried in the small churchyard at Baraboo. When the funeral was over, and there was nothing left to do but wait for time to heal their sorrow, the Simonses returned to Chicago to take up the cudgels once more. They found, however, that they had no heart for the struggle. The terrible accident had broken May's health, and her husband, though deeply saddened by the death of his son, was now more concerned for her recovery than for his own bereavement. To the readers of the *Workers' Call* he confided, "There are times when, try as we may to prevent it, personal facts dominate all else."[30]

Fortunately, the Simonses had friends who were as kind as their enemies were bitter. Their old colleagues in social and settlement work—Herbert Phillips, William English Walling, Mary McDowell, and Jane Addams among them—quickly raised a fund to enable Simons to take his wife abroad for the early months of 1900. Perhaps

[28] A summary of the Social Democratic party platform of 1898 appears in Daniel Bell, "Marxian Socialism," 265–66.
[29] *Workers' Call*, Nov. 18, Dec. 9, 1899, Jan. 6, 1900.
[30] "Personal," *Workers' Call*, Dec. 23, 1899.

a new century and a new continent would help work a cure and restore their zeal for the cause.[31] Simons resigned his editorship and left Chicago.

Though their journey was undertaken to help them escape their sorrow, yet it turned out to be both stimulating and rewarding. They carried letters of introduction to prominent Socialists on the continent and in England, and in the course of their trip they made contacts that they were to maintain for more than a quarter of a century. As editor of the *Call*, Simons had published a great deal of material on the progress of socialism abroad,[32] but here he had a rare opportunity to see at firsthand how more advanced socialist movements were coping with problems that might soon become as real in America.

The unity sought by American Socialists appeared to be equally elusive in Europe. Within many nations Socialists were only enemy brothers with a common parent in Karl Marx. Adding to controversy everywhere was the fact that Marx seemed to have been significantly wrong in some of his major conclusions about capitalism and the working class. In the most highly industrialized nations of the western world, Germany and England, the middle class was not disappearing. The capitalist system showed few signs of collapse, and the lot of the working class altogether was improving, not growing more wretched.

These observed conditions, together with a relaxation of repressive measures against Socialists generally, brought them into existing parliaments all over Europe. In 1899 the first Socialist had entered a bourgeois government—Alexander Millerand became a minister in the cabinet of Waldeck-Rousseau in France, a cabinet that included a general who had helped to suppress the Paris Commune in 1871. In the same year, Italian Socialists officially declared necessary and pru-

[31] Interviews, Robert Huston with Miriam Simons Leuck and Herbert E. Phillips, cited in Huston, "Algie Martin Simons," 93; *Workers' Call*, Dec. 30, 1899.
[32] See, for example, *Workers' Call*, May 20, June 3, July 8, Aug. 12, and Oct. 21, 1899.

dent the tactics of alliances with nonsocialist parties and govern-ments.[33]

Perhaps violent revolution, which had seemed inevitable earlier in the century when workingmen had absolutely no other access to the machinery of power, could now be avoided. Perhaps the goals of Marx and Engels could be fulfilled gradually and without the shed-ding of blood.

The European debates about the continued relevance of Marxian socialism were familiar to Algie and May Simons even before they went abroad. In Germany in 1899, Eduard Bernstein had published *Evolutionary Socialism*, a major work of revisionism, and in America, during the fight within the SLP, DeLeon had accused his opponents of being under the thrall of Bernstein's ideas. To the orthodox Marxist, this was equivalent to consorting with the powers of darkness.

The Simonses considered themselves orthodox. In the same year that Bernstein's book appeared, May Simons had translated Karl Kautsky's book on Engels,[34] and in general both she and her husband had always seemed to be more in sympathy with the ideas of Kautsky, who was Bernstein's most articulate opponent, than with any kind of revisionism. Kautsky did not think that violent revolution was neces-sary to destroy capitalism. He did believe that the reins of govern-ment must be wrested from the bourgeoisie and handed over to the proletariat. This, he thought, could be done through democratic means, but until it was, the misery of the working class would in-crease. Even though the worker might achieve a middle-class income, he could not truly be a member of the middle class as long as he was employed and exploited by the controlling class of society.[35]

An aspect of Kautsky's thought which was particularly persuasive to the Simonses was his denial that industrial concentration was going to decline and that the individual producer and small industries could

---

[33] George L. Mosse, *The Culture of Western Europe* (Chicago: Rand McNally, 1961), 188–89.
[34] *Friedrich Engels, His Life, His Work and His Writing* (Chicago: Charles Kerr, 1899).
[35] Harry W. Laidler, "European Socialism Since 1848," in *Socialism and American Life*, ed. Donald Drew Egbert and Stow Persons (Princeton: Princeton University Press, 1952), I, 72–73.

survive. The Chicago Socialists' own experience made them certain of the inevitability of monopoly and the extinction of the small producer at the hands of capitalist exploiters. Both in rural Wisconsin and in the stockyards of South Chicago they had seen these forces at work.

Algie and May did not visit Germany, but in France they found that the struggle between orthodoxy and revisionism had taken similar forms. Simons talked with both Jules Guesde, veteran of the Paris Commune, and Paul Lafargue, son-in-law of Karl Marx, and from both he heard the "treason" of Millerand castigated bitterly. There could be no compromising with capitalism, they insisted, for to do so meant to give up all the gains, both material and ideological, that had been won through half a century of struggle.

More compelling to Simons than these discussions of theory was the evidence he saw that the class struggle was being fought valiantly both in Paris and the provinces. He attended the funeral of a Russian Socialist exile, Pierre Lavroff, and heard the cries of "Vive la Commune" from the throngs of workingmen who came to pay their last respects. He watched the hordes of police swarm in upon the mourners and tear away the red flag that had been raised for a moment in the midst of the crowd. In the bookstores of Paris he found stacks of socialist books and pamphlets, prominently displayed on the shelves and in the shopwindows, not hidden under the counters like obscene matter destined for the eyes of an occasional crank. In the village of Roubaix, not far from Lille, he found a government of revolutionary Socialists who had fed and clothed the children of the workers, and sent them to schools that would prepare them for leadership in the socialist society of the future.[36]

In England the Simonses came in touch with other variants of the orthodox-revisionist dialogue. In the land their ancestors had left more than a century earlier, they found much that seemed familiar. For a week they traveled about the English countryside with H. M. Hyndman and Keir Hardie, noting the transformations that industrialism

---

[36] Simons told of his European experiences in a series of letters published in the *Workers' Call*. For his impressions of French socialism see "An Event in Paris," March 3, 1900, and "Something Now," March 24, 1900, *Workers' Call*.

had worked. Hardie had been a miner and had first gone to parliament as an independent labor member in 1892, and as he and Algie and May journeyed through the dreary mining villages, they saw the men and boys who went down in the shafts at daybreak and came up at dusk. The lives of these people were little different from the lives of the families of Packingtown. The threat of death and disease hung over both; they were equally insecure in their lives and in their jobs; and both groups were distant from the economic and political forces that shaped their existence. The miners of Cornwall, like their working-class brethren in southwest Chicago, had little reason to like free enterprise. They were ripe for the doctrine of class struggle.[37]

Hyndman, head of the Social Democratic Federation, was a man much admired by Simons. Like Simons, he was a pugnacious intellectual who devoted much of his life to disseminating Marxist theory and who made many enemies doing so. In 1881 Hyndman had published a book on Marxism, *England for All*, in which he made no mention of Karl Marx. He considered this a sound and necessary tactic, in view of the British antipathy to Marx. Hyndman believed that ideas which could change the lives of miners in Cornwall and industrial workers in Sheffield and Leeds and a hundred other grimy warrens deserved a fair hearing. Understandably, Hyndman earned the lasting enmity of Marx and Engels for his pains.[38]

Simons addressed a rally of workingmen while he was in England, and he promised them that one day America, the most highly advanced industrial society in the world, would lead the international socialist movement. It was a promise that betrayed more than a shadow of nationalistic pride in a man who, like the movement to which he belonged, deplored patriotism.[39]

[37] *Workers' Call*, April 7, 1900.
[38] Laidler, "European Socialism," 76. Miriam Simons Leuck, in general comments appended to her father's correspondence, claims that Hyndman came nearer than anyone else to being a "hero" to Simons. There is, however, nothing in surviving correspondence to suggest so strong an admiration, though letters between Simons and Charles Edward Russell, exchanged shortly after Hyndman's death, indicate that both men believed his passing was a great loss to the socialist movement.
[39] *Workers' Call*, April 7, 1900. For Simons' attitude toward national loyalty see *ibid.*, Nov. 4, 1899.

His speech was evidence that as he talked to socialist leaders abroad, he became increasingly aware of the distinctive modifications that each country made to basic Marxist theory.[40] Certain themes were repeated everywhere. All Socialists talked about the role of labor unions, the wisdom of contributing socialist ministers to bourgeois governments, and the nature of the revolution. But each country had also developed its own characteristic responses to these questions—responses that reflected a national style or a particular form or stage of industrial development. In France, for example, there was Syndicalism; in England, Fabianism. This, Simons realized, was something that had not yet happened in America. Marxism was very much an imported ideology that was only beginning to adapt itself to American conditions.

As he reflected upon his growing knowledge about European socialism, he thought again of Frederick Jackson Turner and his belief in the preeminence of environment in shaping social institutions. The frontier had made American democracy; perhaps it could also make an American socialism. It was an idea worth thinking about.

Meanwhile there was still much to learn abroad. If the Simonses felt most at home in England, they found the most to admire in Belgium. Nowhere else was adaptation to environment so obvious or so ingenious. "One constantly feels when studying the socialist movement in Belgium," Simons wrote, "as if he were examining a sort of miniature sample world."[41]

A socialist party had existed in Belgium since 1879, and a labor party since 1885. These were not, however, indications of a generous attitude on the part of the Belgian government toward the working class. Quite the contrary: workingmen had been denied the franchise until the 1890s, and even then universal suffrage was supplemented by a system of plural voting. Citizens who owned property or had a certificate of higher education were awarded more than one vote.[42]

---

[40] He had first suggested this while editing the *Workers' Call*. See "No Side Issues," *Workers' Call*, Aug. 12, 1899.

[41] "Belgium's Capital," *Workers' Call*, March 31, 1900.

[42] Rene Hislaire, "Political Parties," in *Belgium*, ed. Jan-Albert Goris (Berkeley: University of California Press, 1945), 100–103.

Labor unions had been forbidden until 1867, and thereafter working-men, though allowed to join unions, were punished with fines or imprisonment if they went out on strike or in any other way tried to force employers to alter wages or working conditions.[43] Thus denied political participation on the national level or the right to exert economic pressure, Belgian socialism had developed along the only lines left available to it—self-help in the form of cooperatives and mutual aid societies, and municipal reform in industrial cities where they gained control from time to time. Belgian Socialists, under the guidance of Emile Vandervelde, had also had considerable success in organizing agricultural labor, and in their propaganda they cultivated specialized appeals to each economic group; a weekly newspaper devoted to the agrarian movement had been established and was apparently flourishing. The Belgian farmer was beginning to be persuaded that his welfare could best be improved by the triumph of socialism.[44]

It was strange indeed that two Americans who had recently claimed to be pure Marxists should find so much to praise in a movement that clearly contradicted much of Marx's teaching. The reformism of Belgian socialism was extolled[45] by a man who only a few months earlier had deplored the reformism of progressive American politicians like "Golden Rule" Jones and Hazen Pingree.[46] The alleviation of slum conditions in Belgium was hailed by the same person who one year earlier had attacked slum clearance as a device for making the working class content with its dreary lot for just that much longer.[47]

In part, what made the difference was that in Belgium the reformist measures were directed by the Socialists themselves—not, as was so often the case in America and elsewhere, by the enemies of socialism who wanted to appease the discontented. Belgian Socialists insisted

[43] Max Gottschalk, "Social Legislation," in *Belgium*, ed. Jan-Albert Goris (Berkeley: University of California Press, 1945), 188–89.
[44] "Socialism at Work," *Workers' Call*, April 7, 1900.
[45] *Ibid.* See also A. M. Simons, "The Belgian Political Situtation," *Independent*, LIV (April 24, 1902), 970–73.
[46] *Workers' Call*, May 27, June 3, Aug. 19, Oct. 7, 1899.
[47] *Ibid.*, April 7, 1900; March 25, 1899.

that they had not given up their desire for the eventual overthrow of capitalism; their measures were, in fact, strengthening the physical and mental condition of the proletariat, so that they would be better prepared for revolution when the proper moment came.[48]

The most powerful reason that the Simonses admired the Belgian socialist movement was somewhat different: nobody argued about reformism or orthodoxy in Belgium; nobody discussed the ideas of Eduard Bernstein or quibbled about what Karl Marx had really meant. They devoted their energies to doing practical things, instead of haggling over theory and insulting one another. "We have been . . . often asked," the Simonses wrote to the readers of the *Workers' Call*, "to explain some of [Daniel DeLeon's] remarkable arguments of the mudslinging style but have invariably declined on the ground that it had no connection with Socialism." But, they could not resist adding, "If [DeLeon] desires to retain a reputation for sanity, now that about everything else is gone, he should certainly drop all his European exchanges or subscriptions."[49]

The unity that seemed to characterize Belgian socialism was decidedly attractive to these American visitors who were fresh from the lists of 1899. To people like the Simonses, who had come to Marxism out of a sense of moral indignation, the paralysis of American socialism was especially trying. They had come from charity and settlement work, which tried to do small things, to a movement that promised one day to bring perfect justice to society. They found, however, that the movement was able to do nothing to prepare for that day because its members quarreled endlessly. It may seem paradoxical, in the light of their desire for real action, that they should have given their allegiance to the kind of Marxism that denied any ameliorative measures until the revolution sounded the death knell of capitalism.

This paradox is more apparent than real, for there seemed to be no realistic alternatives to the Socialist Labor party. The Social Democrats were still talking about colonization plans in the 1890s. They wanted to take the wretched faithful west and set up a socialist colony

[48] *Ibid.*, March 24, 1899.
[49] April 7, 1900.

in Wyoming or Idaho. The whole utopian tradition, a strong compo-
nent of American socialism, emphasized escaping from the problems
of industrialism instead of trying to solve them. Algie Simons knew
enough economics and history to believe that efforts to turn time
backward were doomed.

Marxist orthodoxy, which accepted the industrial revolution as an
inevitable and ultimately desirable historical development, offered
another satisfaction to Algie and May Simons: it provided a justification for not being able to accomplish much in the way of social and
economic betterment in the here and now. It also explained that the
misery and distress which existed within the proletariat was, like
industrialism itself, an inevitable stage in the dialectic of history.
Therefore, one need not feel discouraged when, despite herculean
effort, human misery did not vanish.

What, then, could be more appealing than what the Belgians
seemed to have attained—a movement that boasted a class-conscious,
revolutionary proletariat, together with the promise of decent living
in the present, to be achieved through self-help. This was not the
bread-and-butter unionism of the AFL, because it was done without the
aid and cooperation of employers and because it sought the ultimate
overthrow of the capitalistic system. Though not all Belgians agreed
upon the timing or the form of the revolution, they were able to
submerge their differences sufficiently to get on with the tasks at
hand.

Algie Simons had no illusions that the successes of Belgian socialism could be precisely duplicated in America or that industrial conditions were sufficiently similar to permit the development of a successful cooperative movement in this country. The degree of unity
achieved by the Belgians, however, was highly attractive. In his final
word as editor of the *Workers' Call*, before he had left Chicago, he
had pleaded for an end to discord and an attention to the social
purposes for which socialism stood. "The revolt of labor," he had
written in the *Workers' Call*, "is a movement . . . that goes on
regardless of names, nations, or parties. The task of the socialist is to
remove the friction and further the progress of that movement. . . .
A united party would mean that the guidance, direction and assistance

given to the socialist movement would be intelligent . . . instead of blind, discordant, contradictory and weak."[50]

It was early summer when the Simonses returned to Chicago. Hardly anything had changed but the weather. Unity, for which Simons had pleaded before he went abroad and in his dispatches from Europe, was still not a reality. The desire, however, was sharper, for 1900 was a presidential election year. American Socialists wanted to run a candidate of their own, in order to measure the national strength of the movement and to gauge the degree of discontent in the country. Such an effort was impossible unless the members could stop bickering among themselves long enough to agree upon a candidate. With his personal sorrow put aside, Simons returned home to join his comrades once again in the struggle for solidarity and a socialist America.

[50] Jan. 6, 1900.

CHAPTER FOUR

Spreading the Word

Unity seemed distant in 1900, but not unattainable. In the struggles that finally resulted in the creation of the Socialist party (SP) of America in 1901, Algie Simons personified both the aspirations and the contradictions of the movement. He wanted revolution and success, but he also wanted to see the triumph of the essential ideas in which he believed. He was already a professional radical, seasoned by party conflict and made wiser by what he had learned abroad, but he was still young enough to point his career in other directions if it should appear that socialism was destined to remain only a well-chewed bone fought over by small groups of powerless malcontents. If success and peace with principles still intact should seem possible, then Simons, like so many others, was prepared to fight on.

The first efforts at socialist unity were made early in 1900 when the Simonses were still traveling in Europe. The dissidents from the Socialist Labor party, led now by Morris Hillquit, had held a convention in Rochester, New York, and had chosen Job Harriman, a California lawyer, as their presidential candidate. Overtures were made almost at once to the Social Democrats, in the hope that a united ticket could be formed. Eventually it was done. Eugene Debs would run for president, Harriman for vice president.[1]

The joint ticket was by no means a reflection of inner harmony. Years of wrangling and insult had left wounds that could not be healed overnight, and throughout the campaign there was backstage scuffling among the factions that was only muffled by the oratory of Debs. Apart from all this was Daniel DeLeon and his Socialist Labor party, trying to believe that its recent purge, like a therapeutic blood-letting, was going to restore it to robust health.

For all intents and purposes the patient died, and the new socialist coalition danced on the coffin. When the campaign was over, and William McKinley had been returned to the White House, the Socialist Labor party found it had polled only 33,000 votes. The Debs-Harriman ticket, on the other hand, had polled 97,000. It was still a long way to Washington, but the gain in the total socialist vote between 1896 and 1900 was impressive indeed, for Socialists had received only 36,000 votes in all in the preceding presidential election. Marxists, convinced that capitalist decline was inevitable, took the results of the 1900 election as a sign that the decline was beginning at last. As they girded themselves for the coming contests, unity seemed more imperative than ever before. The coalition of 1900 must be nourished into a robust and unified political movement.[2]

The convention that was to accomplish this miracle met in Indianapolis in the summer of 1901, and Simons was one of five Chicago Socialists sent as official delegates.[3] His editorship of the *Workers' Call* had made his name familiar, and his capacity for work had made him welcome.

Simons' prestige had also been enhanced by his recent trip abroad, and upon his return he became editor of Charles Kerr's *International Socialist Review*, a periodical designed to familiarize the American worker with current European socialist thought. He had also been nominated by Cook County Socialists as a congressional candidate from the Fourth District of Illinois. According to the official tabulations, he received 710 votes.[4]

Simons had no illusions about the dimensions of the task that was to be undertaken in Indianapolis. He feared that the wrangling which had always marked conventions of Socialists would not be put aside. If it were not, he believed, socialism might lose its greatest opportunity for success in America. If "petty exhibitions of jealousy" were not put aside, he wrote, "then we shall have failed to meet the demand, and must stand aside until we have learned our lesson."[5] There was

[1] Ira Kipnis, *The American Socialist Movement, 1897–1912* (New York: Columbia University Press, 1952), 81–98.
[2] *Ibid.*, 99–100.
[3] *Workers' Call*, Aug. 3, 1901.
[4] *Social Democratic Herald*, Dec. 8, 1900.
[5] Editorial, *International Socialist Review*, I (July 1901), 75.

prophetic irony, as well as a whiff of classical economics, in his admonition.

He did not want the convention to wrangle, and he did not want it to be inefficient. A movement that sought the allegiance of all reasonable men should be rational in its deliberations. A movement that deplored waste in life and resources should not waste the time of its members in haggling over details. Simons wanted the convention to formulate a brief statement of principle that would have "no shadow of compromise, no concession to capitalism in any form."[6] Still, he could not forget how hollow had been DeLeon's victory in achieving an uncompromising party. The answer as Simons saw it was not to drive dissenters away, but to iron out differences through free—but succinct—democratic discussion.[7]

Simons made these recommendations to American Socialists in general, but they included warnings that were clearly applicable to himself. Having initially joined the Socialist Labor party, he found it as difficult as anyone to regard the SLP's chief rival, the Social Democrats, as serious radicals. In spite of the Social Democratic party's motto, "Pure Socialism and No Compromise," they were not the tough-minded Marxists that Simons thought the movement needed. Filled with converts who had deserted the Populist standard after the election of 1896, the Social Democratic party reproduced much of the Populist platform in its own right. From the day of its founding in June 1898 the Social Democrats had been quarreling over agricultural demands. The left wing said that efforts to propitiate farmers were foolish. Farmers were simply small capitalists who would have to surrender private ownership of land as soon as the Cooperative Commonwealth was brought to pass. The executive board, on the other hand, insisted that the demands for farmers were entirely consonant with the principles of international socialism; besides, it would be nice to have the farm vote.[8]

Until his falling out with Daniel DeLeon, Simons had publicly

---

[6] *Ibid.*
[7] "New Tendencies in American Socialism," *International Socialist Review*, II (Aug. 1901), 151–56.
[8] Kipnis, *The American Socialist Movement*, 69–73.

ridiculed the meanderings of Social Democratic theory. In the pages of the *Workers' Call* he had as often tested his lances against the periodic convulsions of the SDP as against the evils of capitalism.[9] As the conflicting groups prepared for the Unity Convention in Indianapolis, Simons recommended peace with honor.

Peace came, at last, after exhausting battle. Simons himself was in the frontlines throughout the campaigns waged in the Masonic Hall in the midst of a steaming middle western summer. He was elected to the most quarrelsome and important subgroup there: the platform committee, which was supposed to work out a program to which all American Socialists could subscribe.

From the beginning of the convention Simons was the leader of the "impossibilists"—those who wanted the party to waste no time getting people to subscribe to immediate demands, but to hold out for the day when capitalism would collapse utterly and the nation would be completely transformed. There was an iron logic to the position, which lent Simons the tenacity to argue it. If the capitalistic system were indeed on the verge of collapse, it was foolish for the Socialist party to come out for piecemeal reform. While editing the *Workers' Call* Simons had often proclaimed the imminent demise of capitalism. Every strike, every bit of violence that might smack of class conflict, was seen as a turning point.[10]

The conclusion was fatally defective, and older Socialists told him so. Those who had watched the whole sobering parade of labor-management struggles in the last quarter of the nineteenth century knew that both capitalism and the system of government that kept it in power were far more resilient than Simons thought. It was a shallow reading of history that predicted a nearing crisis of capitalism, but it was not entirely uninformed.

Simons thought revolution was imminent because he assumed that economic opportunity had ended with the closing of the frontier. No longer could the workingman entertain even the hope of westward migration as an escape from poverty. Forced to remain a member of the proletariat, the industrial worker would surely be eager to cast off

[9] See, for example, *Workers' Call*, July 15, Aug. 19, 1899.
[10] See, for example, *Workers' Call*, April 22, June 3, 17, Oct. 28, 1899.

the bonds of capitalism. Therefore the Socialist party ought to prepare itself to receive him. It should not become an accomplice of middle-class reformism.

Simons tried to hammer his ideas home to his colleagues on the platform committee. It wasn't just a matter of which position was better theory, he insisted. It was a question of which would win the dedicated support of the American proletariat. As Simons argued and entreated the delegates, he tried to make them see the workingman as he had seen him in Cincinnati and Chicago and the farm fields of Wisconsin. Working people didn't want a "better" life later; they wanted the good life here and now. They didn't want the balm of the settlement-house reformers or the escapist fantasies of utopian socialism; they wanted revolution now, and they could have it, Simons vowed, if they could look to a political party that would show them how. Again and again he argued his position: class consciousness and class struggle were the rocks upon which he would build the party.

The majority felt otherwise. There would be "immediate demands" in the platform of the new Socialist party of America, and when Simons saw that his passion would not carry the day he cast his own vote for them. It was more important that socialism should present a united front, he decided, than that his own disagreement should be registered.[11]

On only one other issue did Simons disregard his own advice about harmony. He brought up the troublesome matter of farmers' demands. There was still discontent in rural America, and a persuasive program put forward by Socialists, he thought, might win over the men who had once voted for Bryan or Weaver or cursed "the interests." The farm population needed to understand that it was more like the proletariat than like the bourgeoisie. Simons' own experience and his reading of European and American writers on agriculture had made it seem clear that the farmer was exploited no less than the wageworker. In terms of what he owned of the "tools of production" the farmer was much like a miner. The miner owned his own pick but

[11] *Minutes of the Socialist Unity Convention*, Indianapolis, 1901, p. 213, in the Socialist Party Collection, Duke University, Durham, N.C.—hereafter cited as Socialist Party Collection.

worked for those who controlled the crucial means of production—the mine and its equipment. So too the farmer was in bondage to the banker, the railroad, and the owner of storage facilities.[12]

Once again he failed to convince the convention. He was, however, named to a permanent committee that would study the problems of the farmer's relationship to the socialist movement and make recommendations to future conventions.

Despite his personal losses, Simons was well satisfied at what the Indianapolis convention managed to accomplish. A platform had been constructed, a constitution drawn up, and a national secretary, Leon Greenbaum, chosen. As Simons stood with the other delegates at the closing session, spiritedly singing the Marseillaise, the song of revolution, he burned with eagerness to get at the job that lay ahead. Around him were the delegates who had come as enemies and who would leave devoted to a common cause. Old Populists and labor leaders, Bellamy Nationalists and immigrant Marxists, Christian Socialists and conscience-stricken millionaires sang together lustily, their private visions submerged for now into a common dedication to the class struggle.

America's best-known Socialist, Eugene Debs, who had no taste for intraparty conflict, stayed home in Terre Haute. Perhaps he was still pondering a recent dream he had experienced, in which he struggled in vain to pull a strange ungainly animal out of a bog.[13]

For Simons the die was cast. This was to be an American movement. No longer was socialism to be the affair of homesick immigrants. It had broken away from its sectarian origins, had put aside many of its quarrels, and had become at last a legitimate political force. Once it had taken on a distinctly indigenous flavor there was every reason to expect continued success. The native American Marxists, Simons exulted, would provide the "stiffening" for the movement. They were the "descendants of that race of hardy fighting

[12] Simons' farm position at this time appeared in *Socialism and Farmers* (Chicago: Charles Kerr, 1900).
[13] The dream is recounted in Ray Ginger, *The Bending Cross* (New Brunswick, N.J.: Rutgers University Press, 1949), 212.

pioneers who have been fighting the wilderness for a century, and now [find themselves] confronted with social conditions more pitiless than the wild beasts or the native Indians."[14]

As Simons returned to Chicago, his head still filled with echoes from the Masonic Hall, he considered how he might most effectively serve the movement. Agitation and education were most needed. Workers had to be educated to their true interests and given a sense of their own power. For decades America had rung with platitudes about the nobility of profitmaking and the virtues of businessmen and industrialists. The very greatness of the nation had been attributed to its entrepreneurs and risk-takers, while the working men and women of the nation had been casually taken for granted as losers in the great Darwinian race for survival. If workers were to be enlisted in the socialist cause, they had to be convinced first that the achievements of capitalism had been vastly overrated and that their own capacities were undervalued—perhaps even by themselves. Simons longed to give the American proletariat a new view of its own past, a sense of pride in what it had accomplished, and a realization that its next great accomplishment ought to be the withdrawal of economic and political power from the minions of capitalism.

Simons also knew that working people needed a special kind of education that would prepare them for service in the Cooperative Commonwealth. He believed that he could fill the gaps that a capitalist education had left all too purposely. He could dispel once and for all the fantasies that had long inhibited the growth of class-consciousness in America: the myth that through hard work one could ultimately become an entrepreneur, or that one could escape to the West when hard times came.

Always brimming over with plans and programs and ideas, Simons was now more than ever convinced that hard work and dedication could bring the Cooperative Commonwealth to pass in his lifetime. What if it did not? This was a question that he had not yet begun to ask himself. Already, however, there were indications that if the

[14] "A New Milestone for American Socialism," *International Socialist Review*, II (Sept. 1901), 235.

question should begin to press in upon him, it would be a painful one to answer, for not only had he decided to dedicate his own most productive years to radicalism, but he had dedicated his family's life as well to a cause shunned by respectable Americans. There was no money in the enterprise and, if Simons' estimate were wrong, there would be little power. He was not indifferent to these considerations, nor was he the kind of radical who could so completely lose himself in his work that he cared little for his private life. Fortunately his wife shared his commitment to the socialist movement. Their mutual dedication minimized the painful fracture that men of ambition commonly experience between their public and private lives. There was, however, already some reason for concern. Perhaps in the midst of the tumult and trials of Indianapolis he had forgotten, but back home in Chicago, the realities of his personal life intruded again.

A second child, Miriam, had been born to the Simonses shortly after their return from Europe. It soon became clear that the shock of losing their son had exerted a profound enduring impact upon May, and it was seen most vividly in her concern for their new child. She faced parental responsibility with a deep sense of anxiety. Determined that no harm should come to Miriam, she insisted that either she or a member of the family must be with the child every moment. When May Simons went to socialist conventions both in America and abroad, her daughter went too, and when May addressed socialist meetings or Chatauqua audiences a small voice could sometimes be heard calling out, "Come on, Mama."[15]

In other ways, too, May Simons displayed discomfort and anxiety that troubled her husband. Her health was precarious, and she worried and brooded over each public appearance for days, sometimes weeks, before it occurred. She was plagued with attacks of what she called "nervous indigestion," which always increased in intensity as the time for a speaking engagement neared. Worst of all, nothing could quite put from her mind the constant recollection of little Laurence, the "dear and beautiful" child she had lost.[16] Sometimes, she confided to her diary, it seemed that she could not go on living

[15] Diary of May Wood Simons, Feb. 22, 1903, Simons Papers.
[16] Ibid., Jan. 16, 1903.

without a glimpse of the boy whose picture stood beside that of Miriam in their Chicago apartment.[17]

She countered these times of depression by working harder than ever. She was writing, studying, translating, and doing research nearly as much as her husband was. She enrolled at the University of Chicago to finish the degree she had begun at Northwestern, and she did well there. But none of her efforts gave her any deep sense of accomplishment or fulfillment. They were merely weapons in a war against what she regarded as her weaker self.[18]

The way in which she chose to cope with these anxieties was both therapeutic and constructive, but it suggested a fragility about her commitment to the socialist movement. Perhaps if this cause gave hint of failure she would need to move quickly to another. It was not this possibility, however, that troubled her husband, but her prolonged grief and anxiety. Still, they were young in years, and perhaps their common dedication to each other, to their daughter, and to the movement could make them young in spirit again as well.

In the beginning was propaganda. For the time being nothing was more important to the onward rush of socialism than spreading its message of promise throughout the country. "Soapboxers" appeared on the street corners of America's cities to besiege the passerby with visions of the nation that could be, and socialist worthies crisscrossed the prairies in the summer, bringing the wisdom of Marx and Engels to the patrons of the Chatauqua circuit.

Both Algie and May Simons set out often on these journeys of persuasion. Time was of the essence. Simons' reading of history had made him well aware that third parties, under the American system of government, had virtually no chance for survival. Only the Republican party of the 1850s had succeeded in displacing an existing major party, and it had done so within the space of a very few years. The Socialists would have to re-create that marvel. They would have to set in motion a tide of such proportions and with such momentum that

---

[17] *Ibid.*, March 23, 1903.
[18] This is clear from her diary, in which she invariably moves directly from grief and reminiscence to the determination to work harder.

the weaker of the major parties would crumble before it. In small, second-floor meeting rooms in cities like Chicago, Minneapolis, and Kansas City they urged their message upon all who would walk a flight of stairs to listen. In towns of the Middle West they addressed what Simons considered the most important audiences of all—those he thought most "American" and whom, he believed, were potentially the most dangerous citizens if left unconverted. The labor disturbances of the 1890s had often been put down by militia or national guard drawn from small towns and villages. The newspapers that reached these areas were almost exclusively in the hands of the enemies of socialism.[19] The campaigns of the 1890s, however, had proved that there was unrest aplenty in the Midwest and Southwest, and if it could be channeled into the Socialist party then there would be votes and funds where there were now only vaguely informed enemies. Who could be better equipped to bring the gospel of socialism to these areas than a man and woman who themselves spoke in the accents of rural America and who knew firsthand the grievances of the farming frontier?

These were no lavish expense-account excursions. Despite the adherence of an occasional eccentric millionaire, the socialist movement was never distinguished for its opulence. Its grand ambitions had to be modestly financed. On most trips the Simonses had to depend upon the hospitality of the faithful for food and lodging along the way. After spending an afternoon or evening in a steaming tent, before a sea of waving fans and programs, they might be bedded down for the night on a couple of folded horse blankets. There they could ponder the gains of the day while slapping at the infinite variety of insect pests that plagued the prairies. The following morning they could consult their notes on the next encampment while waiting for their host to hitch up the horse and wagon that would carry them to that day's engagement, or for the train that would jolt its way a few miles closer to the millennial promise. Through North and South Dakota, Nebraska, Minnesota, and Illinois the Simonses brought the message

[19] "Call for Organization," *International Socialist Review*, III (April 1903), 686.

of socialism. Sometimes they appeared before audiences in several towns in a single day. They spoke in Madison and Aberdeen, South Dakota, and Fargo, North Dakota on one summer day, and in Rockford, Freeport, Rock Island, Galesburg, Quincy, Jacksonville, Peoria, Springfield, Decatur, Bloomington, and Joliet, Illinois on another.

Conviction and success were powerful solvents of discomfort, and Algie Simons had his share of both. He was a highly persuasive public speaker with a knack for bending an audience to his will. He was not the master of warmth and sentimentality that Eugene Debs was, nor the eloquent scholar that Norman Thomas was later to become, but he was an exciting man to hear. His piercing eyes and fiery delivery could, temporarily at least, make a prairie farmer more excited over socialism than dollar wheat. Simons had a temper to match his delivery, and the presence of hecklers or skeptics in any gathering only heightened his enthusiasm. Though his colleagues might urge a discreet retreat when the verbal fireworks threatened to get out of hand, or when it seemed that debate might escalate into hand-to-hand combat, Simons would ignore them and plunge ahead.[20]

His confidence in the face of antagonism was built both by his mastery of Marxian dialectics and by long experience in the rugged art of invective. Just as socialism was an ideology that embraced the whole of life, so Simons was a man who threw every ounce of his energy into the cause that he sought to advance. Like most young men, he held nothing in reserve.[21]

Neither Algie nor May had any illusions about the long-term effect of this sort of propaganda. They did not suppose that the spell of oratory and exhortation was sufficient to make dedicated Socialists out of even their most attentive listeners. Lectures and public polemics

[20] On Simons' debating and oratorical skill and manner, see Ford to Goldman, April 11, 1952, and interviews, Robert Huston with Miriam Simons Leuck and Herbert E. Phillips, cited in Huston, "Algie Martin Simons and the American Socialist Movement" (unpublished Ph.D. dissertation, University of Wisconsin, 1965), 103.
[21] On some of the Simonses' speaking tours and itineraries, see the Chicago *Socialist*, Aug. 16, 1902, Dec. 5, 1903, Sept. 10, Oct. 15, Nov. 5, 1904, Jan. 7, 1905, March 21, April 28, Sept. 22, 1906.

could arouse interest, but other means had to be found to furnish the solid matter of fact and ideology that could replace temporary enthusiasm with permanent conviction.[22]

To provide instruments of socialist education was, however, no simple matter. Here, as in every other direction of socialist effort, the attempt had to be launched in the face of the powerful tides of the establishment, none of which was more powerful than education, whether pursued on the elementary, secondary, or university level. Public education since the days of Horace Mann had been one of the chief instruments by which the young were inculcated with the values of society. In the decades before and after the turn of the century the schools skipped to the tunes of business and strove to produce graduates who would either yearn to climb the ladder to financial success or fit promptly into a productive chink in the economy.

Child labor had been an accompaniment of industrialism from the beginning, but now, through the medium of industrial education, even the child who was able to attend school often found himself on a make-believe assembly line learning industrial discipline from pedagogical models of Henry Clay Frick. May Simons, who was particularly interested in public education, investigated vocational training programs in the technical high schools of Chicago. At Lane High School she encountered shop teacher Ernest Andrews, an avowed admirer of the logic of Herbert Spencer, who believed that he should be a foreman, not a gentleman, to his students. She met the principal at Lane, Mr. Bogan, whose deepest regret was that vocational training was not begun in the kindergarten. At Crane Tech she learned

[22] See, for example, A. M. Simons, "After-Election Work," *International Socialist Review*, V (Nov. 1904), 306. Simons' own knowledge of socialist ideology was acquired first at the University of Wisconsin where he read Marx and Engels for Ely's courses. As Ely's assistant, he probably became familiar with most of the Socialists and reformers Ely discussed in *Socialism and Social Reform*. Simons' knowledge of European socialism can be judged from his editorship of the *International Socialist Review* and from his translations of the works of German Socialists. For example, in 1903 he translated, with Marcus Hitch, Wilhelm Liebknecht's *No Compromise, No Political Trading* (Chicago: Charles Kerr, 1903), and in subsequent years he translated, with May Simons, Karl Kautsky's *Social Revolution* (Chicago: Charles Kerr, 1908) and *The Road to Power* (Chicago: S. A. Bloch, 1909).

that the student was taught, along with industrial skills, the evils of trade union organization.[23]

The schoolchild who had only lately been liberated from the classical curriculum was now being fastened in the technical and vocational schools to a bondage far more ominous—a bondage of both mind and body. During the great Chicago teamsters' strike of 1905, many schoolchildren struck with their fathers. A chorus of criticism was immediately raised. Children, it was said, cannot possibly understand the issues at stake in such a strike and therefore should not become involved. Simons was quick to point out the irony of such objections: "These same moralists," he observed, "do not object to the use of the public schools to teach lessons of 'patriotism,' servility and submission to the system that means enslavement for the laborer's child the moment he leaves the school."[24]

The Simonses were surrounded by articulate people in Chicago who were looking for new directions in American education.[25] John Dewey had come to the University of Chicago in 1894, and two years later he and his wife had established their laboratory school. The purposes of the school sounded refreshing indeed to those who had seen the operation of both the old-style curriculum and the business-blessed industrial programs. Dewey wanted to discover how a school could become a cooperative community and at the same time permit individual children to realize their own capacities and satisfy their own needs. He wanted a kind of education that would be committed to cooperative effort and scientific methods. In this way, he believed that the schools could direct the course of social progress.[26]

In years to come educational theorists of many persuasions were to find in Dewey's writings and teachings support for their own predilec-

[23] May Wood Simons, "Industrial Education in Chicago," *Pedagogical Seminary*, XVII (1910), 398–418.
[24] "School Strikes in Chicago," *International Socialist Review*, V (June 1905), 749.
[25] Robert L. McCaul, "Dewey's Chicago," *School Review*, LXVII (April 1952), 258–80, discusses the educational ferment that permeated both the university and the city of Chicago at this time.
[26] For a brief discussion of the Dewey Laboratory School in the context of the educational reform efforts of the day, see Cremin, *The Transformation of the School* (New York: Knopf, 1961), 135–42.

tions. Few could do so with more justifiable cause, however, than the Socialists. They could easily believe that Dewey had seen the same vision as they: an America that combined a sense of community and interdependence with individual self-fulfillment. Visions, however, are notoriously indistinct. In the Socialist party's years of great expectations it was hard to imagine that American educators would one day draft Dewey's philosophy to the service of the establishment.[27]

Algie and May Simons sometimes talked with the faculty of the Dewey School—with first-rate teachers like Katherine and Anna Camp who were filled with excitement about what the laboratory school was trying to accomplish. It seemed that here, without question, was the model of the socialist education of the future. True freedom—the freedom of self-realization—together with a genuinely cooperative spirit learned from the kindergarten years on, in John Dewey's exciting educational experiment, were the goals of the socialist society.[28]

For the time being, the Socialists could not hope to capture the public schools by direct attack. Neither did they have reason to expect much success at the college or university level. Algie Simons, under different circumstances, might have become a scholar-teacher associated with some major university. His interests were broad, and though his writings sometimes displayed the haphazard research that men of many interests often indulge in, that research was always in scholarly sources. He criticized academic writing because he believed it abhorred both partisanship and generalization, but he always tried to find out what the trained minds of the day had to offer on a particular subject.[29]

The citadels of American scholarship at this time dared not tolerate the kind of dissent that Simons represented. He had seen at Wiscon-

[27] William English Walling, who, like Simons, went from the Chicago Bureau of Charities to the socialist movement, discusses Dewey's theories and their relevance to socialist education in *The Larger Aspects of Socialism* (New York: Macmillan, 1913).
[28] See especially May Simons, "Education and Socialism," *International Socialist Review*, I (April 1901), 600–607; "Democracy and Education," *ibid.*, III (Aug. 1902), 89–96.
[29] Simons gave his objections to the "scholarly approach" in a book review, *International Socialist Review*, V (May 1905), 698.

sin what could happen to a man like Richard Ely who uttered even the most temperate criticisms of the existing social and economic order. The year before Simons moved to Chicago, the University of Chicago ousted one of its tenured economists, Edward Bemis, an authority on cooperatives, utilities, and labor. Upon Bemis's removal the Chicago *Journal* soberly declared that the *pursuit* of truth was not the object of university teaching, and that the duty of a professor who is salaried by a university is to teach established truth.[30] William Raney Harper, first president of the University of Chicago observed, "It is all very well to sympathize with the working man, but we get our money from those on the other side, and we can't afford to offend them."[31]

If there was no place on American campuses for sympathy with the working class, there was certainly no room for a man who said that the working class ought to run the country. The colleges were, in the rhetorical conventions of socialism, tools of the interests. As long as they remained such, socialism had to create its own educational institutions and it had to do so without endowments or benefactors—in most cases without any means of support but the tuition fees of those they sought to enlighten.

One such school was Ruskin College. Founded in 1897 in Trenton, Missouri, it was intended by its founder and chief benefactor Walter Vrooman to be the American branch of the Ruskin Hall movement in England. Vrooman tried for awhile to run the town of Trenton on "socialist principles," but the experiment soon collapsed from internal dissension. Ruskin College, however, was not permitted to die so quickly. Without its benefactor, but with high hopes still, Ruskin College was moved to Glen Ellyn, Illinois, to make a fresh beginning.

It was there in 1903 that Algie and May Simons became associated with Ruskin. The school tried to provide its students with several things that they could not easily obtain elsewhere: a thorough grounding in "scientific socialism," a schedule of classes adapted to

---

[30] Quoted in Chester Destler, *Henry Demarest Lloyd and the Empire of Reform* (Philadelphia: University of Pennsylvania Press, 1963), 368.
[31] *Ibid.*, 372.

the hours of workingmen, and opportunity for full-time students to earn their room and board.

The faculty, which consisted exclusively of the Simonses, was conscientious in the desire to disseminate socialist theory to working-class youth. Charles Kerr, the socialist publisher and publicist announced that he could recommend the school "as one to which Socialist parents can send their sons and daughters from fourteen years up, with the assurance that their minds will not be perverted by the capitalistic atmosphere such as surrounds most colleges."[32] Kerr also observed that May Simons' lectures on socialism were attended by nearly the whole student body, and that her presentation had a "marked effect in clearing their ideas."[33]

The Simonses were by no means sentimentalists about the nobility of the working class. They found it particularly irritating that the class which stood to benefit most from socialism should show so little interest in bringing the new society to pass. Simons could write snappishly that "until the laboring class are intelligent enough to vote for their own emancipation they do not deserve to be free and wouldn't know what to do with liberty if they had it."[34] For the earnest working-class students at Ruskin, however, the Simonses had nothing but admiration. Here were young people who, despite the rigor of their daily existence, still found time to read and study and hear lectures on economic and social theory and even, once in a while, to drop around after classes to chat about the material that had been covered.[35]

The obstacles to be surmounted by both students and teachers were great. The lack of library facilities was a major problem. The kinds of students the Socialists sought to instruct did not have funds to buy their own books. Charles Kerr's publishing house put out a great many inexpensive editions of socialist classics and propaganda pamphlets with bibliographies attached, and Simons wrote several of

[32] Charles Kerr, "The Real Facts About Ruskin University," *International Socialist Review*, IV (Sept. 1903), 192.

[33] *Ibid.*

[34] "Anarchy vs. Socialism," *International Socialist Review*, IV (Oct. 1901), 246.

[35] Diary of May Wood Simons, May 12, 1903, Simons Papers.

these.[36] Other materials could be obtained from the federal government at no cost. One of the favorite educational devices of the Socialists was to show capitalism condemned out of its own mouth. The decennial census report, for example, could be had for the asking. It was a useful text to the socialist economist who wished to show his students the "inevitable" processes of industrial concentration, farm to city migration, and other truths vital to comprehending the close proximity of the revolution. Simons also used the *International Socialist Review* as a vehicle for reproducing Marxist classics and other texts he thought his students should have. In 1905 he reprinted the whole of Turner's essay "The Significance of the Frontier in American History" for this purpose.[37]

In spite of efforts at ingenuity, there was much about this educational effort that was pedestrian. As in so many other aspects of the Simonses' activities there were very strict limits to their radicalism. Though they were greatly interested in what Dewey was doing at the laboratory school, and though May studied educational philosophy at Chicago, their teaching methods remained most conventional. There were lectures—which even the lecturer sometimes feared were "too dry"[38]—and occasional discussions. Correspondence courses, offered both through Ruskin and through the *Appeal to Reason,* provided printed versions of the same thing: exposition of subject matter,

[36] A. M. Simons, *Packingtown* (Chicago: Charles Kerr, 1899); *The Man Under the Machine* (Chicago: Charles Kerr, 1899); *Socialism and Farmers* (Chicago: Charles Kerr, 1900); *What the Socialists Would Do If They Won This City* (Chicago: Charles Kerr, 1901); *The Economic Foundations of Art* (Chicago: Charles Kerr, 1903).
[37] David Shannon, in *The Socialist Party of America* (New York: Macmillan, 1955), 18–19, cites Simons' reprinting of the Turner thesis as an illustration of how out of touch the editor was with his audience, without apparently being aware that Simons used the *Review* as an ingenious way of providing low-cost texts for his students. Correspondence between Simons and Turner proves this was the purpose of the reprinting. See Simons to Turner, April 1, 1903; Turner to Simons, April 24, 1903; Simons to Turner, April 29, 1903; Simons to Turner, Oct. 21, 1905. All in Turner Collection, University of Wisconsin Archives, Madison, Wis.
Turner's essay appeared in the *International Socialist Review* of Dec. 1905. The delay was caused by Turner's reluctance to have the essay reprinted until he had decided whether or not to include it in a book.
[38] May Wood Simons, Diary, Feb. 8, 1903, Simons Papers.

bibliography for further reading, and the hoary teaching device of "study questions." The teachers relied wholly upon the intrinsic interest of the material and the style of their own elocution to get their message across. They deplored, it is true, the traditional socialist pedagogy which, as Algie Simons described it, consisted of the "application of German metaphysics to English economic history, with a French vocabulary."[39] At the same time, they believed that American accents and American illustrations were sufficient to arouse American interest.

Before long, Ruskin College closed in a tangle of disputes about its affiliate, the Chicago Law School.[40] Undaunted, the Simonses at once began another school of their own design, the Institute for Social Studies, and added two more members to the faculty: Ernest Untermann, who offered courses on biological sociology, and Jerome Raymond, who taught anthropology. This effort, too, collapsed within two years. Simons put away his dream of a school for worker education after that, but he never forgot it. Fifteen years later he returned to it, but by then his conception of its purposes had become quite different. At that time he wrote to the newly founded Rand School in New York and offered his lectures to the faculty there.[41] Rand, an institution much like Ruskin and the Institute, prospered for many years. It was nourished by a wealthy patroness, who was persuaded by her son-in-law George Herron that worker education was essential to the progress of the socialist movement.

The failure of his socialist schools did not exhaust Simons' inventiveness. He had still other ways of winning converts. Because he believed that success could come only if people were convinced that socialism was in the American grain, he devoted a great deal of his time to studying and writing American history. His work with Turner and Ely at the University of Wisconsin had convinced him

[39] "American Socialist Literature," *International Socialist Review*, III (March 1902), 697.
[40] Charles Kerr, "The Real Facts About Ruskin University," 192.
[41] Simons to Morris Hillquit, Oct. 6, 1905, Morris Hillquit Papers, State Historical Society of Wisconsin.

that the American past was quite different than the common school textbooks would have people believe. What Simons was determined to do was to replace the textbook view of American history with one that was closer to reality as he saw it and, at the same time, that could serve as a dynamic force in the socialist movement. If capitalism were to be overthrown at the ballot box, a majority of the voters had to be persuaded that their present form of government was not worth keeping and had, in fact, always been used by the few to swindle the many. The people had to be shown that the American traditions they had believed in were frauds perpetrated by the "ruling class."

In 1903 Simons wrote a ten-cent pamphlet, *Class Struggles in American History*, in which he tried out some of his ideas. By 1910, according to the publisher, 23,000 copies had been sold.[42] Two years later Simons issued a much-expanded and improved version of the work, and in between he did several articles for the *International Socialist Review* on the economic aspects of slavery in America.[43]

He did not consider this work as only propaganda. He wanted his history to be respected as sound scholarship. His research was continuous, and his ideas kept changing on the basis of new information.[44] Moreover, he sought scholarly evaluation of his work. In 1906, for example, he began the serial publication of "American History for the Workers" in the widely circulated socialist newspaper *Appeal to Reason*. He asked that Frederick Jackson Turner be put on the subscription list and then wrote to him explaining the purpose of his venture:

"I must . . . ask you to excuse some . . . faults in manner of

[42] Preface to 1910 edition, *Class Struggles in American History* (Chicago: Charles Kerr).
[43] "Economic Aspects of Chattel Slavery," *International Socialist Review*, IV (July, Aug., Sept., 1903), 25–33, 95–105, and 167–73.
[44] This is true, for example, of Simons' view of the Jacksonian period. In *Class Struggles* he described Jackson's victory as the victory of frontier over eastern capital. Ten years later, in *Social Forces*, he developed his own version of the entrepreneurial thesis and called Jacksonianism "The Democracy of Expectant Capitalists." Charles Grier Sellers discusses Simons in "Andrew Jackson vs. the Historians," *Mississippi Valley Historical Review*, XLIV (March 1958), 628–31.

presentation which are made necessary by the fact . . . that they are written intentionally for propaganda. I do not mean that I have ever consciously distorted facts—*au contraire,* I have tried to be as srupulously [*sic*] accurate as my knowledge will permit. . . . They are intended to set off the traditional prejudice of the conventional school history, and I have probably leaned occasionally too far to the other side. . . . I wish, however, if you discover any flagrant errors that you would tell me of them before they are finally placed in a more permanent form. I do not wish to mislead."[45]

Turner, for his part, regarded Simons as a serious historian, and one who was doing intriguing things. "The articles which you are writing," he had told the young Socialist back in 1903, "interest me very much. I can see that they are written rapidly for the purpose of hitting the man who will not read long articles. In this they seem to me peculiarly effective."[46]

The series on "American History for the Workers" was Simons' most ambitious effort to reach a substantial public and his most explicit attempt to counteract the platitudes of textbook history. "Nowhere," he declared, "throughout the thousands of American school histories is there even a suggestion that such a body as the working class ever existed. All that has been accomplished was brought about by the altruistic efforts of a few 'great men.' The moral which we are expected to draw from all this is that if the workers will but trust all to our benevolent rulers, 'everything will be for the best in the best possible of worlds.' " Simons believed that his history would show that quite the opposite was true: that the freedoms and privileges most cherished by Americans had been won by "organized, intelligent fighting on the part of the working class."[47]

He believed he could prove his case by using the recent works of professional historians—Libby's work, for example, on the geographical distribution of the vote on the Constitution, Turner's essays on frontier contributions to democracy, and the lesser-known textbook of

---

[45] Simons to Turner, Dec. 3, 1906, Turner Papers, Huntington Library, San Marino, Calif. Quoted by permission of the Huntington Library.
[46] Turner to Simons, March 30, 1903, Turner Collection.
[47] "The Appeal Study Club," Dec. 8, 1906, *Appeal to Reason.*

economic history by a Wellesley professor, Katherine Coman. "Many of our ablest historians," Simons explained, "are now . . . beginning . . . to publish the truth. Few or none of their conclusions, or the facts which they have unearthed, have as yet reached the school textbooks or have begun to influence 'public opinion.' "[48]

The *Appeal* at this time claimed a circulation of around 200,000, and Simons anticipated that 10,000 study clubs would be formed.[49] Much of the *Appeal*'s readership came from the villages and farms of the Midwest, where long winters and the absence of competing media made such expectations reasonable, but clubs were founded elsewhere too. Comrade Henry Allen wrote from Florida, "We are going after the wage slaves here by the forming of 'Study Clubs.' The comrades here have signified their approval of our plans, and in this way we can rope in the teachers and high school students and others who might be scared off by the name of 'Socialism.' "[50] From Chicago, the *Daily Socialist* reported a study club among members of the local postal clerks union.[51] By the end of 1906 Simons claimed that 5,000 such groups were in existence.

In the next nine months faithful readers were rewarded with a set of interpretations that were indeed quite unlike the pieties of traditional history. "A Civilization Founded on Lying," was the title of the first lesson, and it revealed the outlines of what was to come. In succeeding weeks, Simons promised, he would show that the patriot-heroes of the American Revolution were businessmen and entrepreneurs looking for higher profits. He would prove that the American Constitution, far from being divine revelation, was simply a devious construction foisted upon the separate states by rich men who wanted to get richer. He would show that the Civil War, supposedly fought

---

[48] *Ibid.*
[49] In April 1906, a circulation of 175,000 was claimed. "March of the Appeal," *Appeal to Reason*, Dec. 5, 1906. On Feb. 2, 1907, the circulation was put at 275,000 (*Appeal to Reason*). The actual circulation must remain a matter of conjecture, however, for the *Appeal* reported quite a different set of figures to Ayer's *Newspaper Annual:* in 1906 Ayers put the *Appeal*'s circulation at 276,000, in 1907 at 380,674.
[50] "Appeal Study Club," Dec. 22, 1906, *Appeal to Reason*.
[51] *Ibid.*, Dec. 29, 1906.

to free the slaves, was nothing more noble than a struggle between rival economic systems.[52] He was as good as his word. His American history was a saga of plunder and conspiracy whose victims were the real American heroes, the men and women of the working class.

Simons also lost no opportunity to point up the parallels between historical and contemporary events. Shays' Rebellion, suppressed, he claimed, by a militia supported by the private donations of wealthy men, was reminiscent of recent labor struggles in Colorado.[53] The Whisky Rebellion, crushed by federal troops, set the precedent upon which Cleveland acted in the Pullman strike.

All these ideas were to become staples of debate in the historical profession within a few years. Some of them had already been suggested by J. Allen Smith at the University of Washington. Some were to be elaborated by Charles A. Beard before the students of the Rand School. It was Simons, though, who first brought such interpretations into the homes of plain people and who tried to make them the subject of discussion between neighbors.

The influence of Simons' debunking of the American past cannot be measured. One cannot know how many of the *Appeal*'s subscribers actually read the articles on American history, or how many who did read them became convinced or converted, or how many converts actually put their new convictions to work in any way. It is surely true, however, that what Simons' history had to offer was a good deal more plausible to working men and women than the history they had learned in school. Farm families knew that contrary to textbook admonishments, it was possible to work diligently, abjure liquor, and still lose all through the operations of distant markets or fickle weather. Working-class families, where the breadwinner belonged to a labor union knew that the unions were as likely to be the victims of violence as its initiators.

Furthermore, the Socialists were not the only ones who, in the years of the century, were urging Americans to look critically at society's sacred cows. The era of the muckrakers was at hand, and in the magazines of wide circulation denunciations of greed, corruption,

[52] *Ibid.*, Dec. 8, 1906.
[53] *Ibid.*, Jan. 26, 1907.

and dishonesty had come to be commonplace. Ida Tarbell's *History of the Standard Oil Company* was serialized in *McClure*'s in 1903. Lincoln Steffens' *Shame of the Cities* appeared a year later, and shortly thereafter exposés were written of the life insurance trust, the beef trust, Wall Street, and the Senate of the United States. It began to look as though some of the Socialists' work of propaganda was being done for them. Perhaps the revelations of the muckrakers could help in the softening-up process that would prepare the electorate to cast their ballots for the Socialist party of America.

Simons soon found, however, that little could be expected from that pious hope. He became convinced of this in 1904, when the young novelist Upton Sinclair came to Chicago to write a book.

Sinclair had been a Socialist since 1902, and since his conversion he had tried his hand at writing exhortations and propaganda for the movement. Early in 1904, when a strike at the Chicago stockyards was broken by the packers, he penned a manifesto for the *Appeal to Reason* in which he urged the long-suffering employees to embrace socialism, the only thing that was able to save them from utter destruction.

In the same year, Sinclair had published a novel of the Civil War, *Manassas*. Like his earlier books, it had only meager success. Fred Warren, editor of the *Appeal*, read it through, and he suggested that Sinclair follow this novel of the struggle over chattel slavery with one on the struggle over wage slavery. It sounded like a promising idea. Warren agreed to a $500 advance for the serial rights, and Sinclair decided that the Chicago stockyards should be the locale of his new book.

One of the first people that he talked to when he got to Chicago was Algie Simons, for in 1899 Simons had published a propaganda tract, *Packingtown*, the first stomach-turning account of life in the stockyards district. There was little reason to suppose that conditions had changed very much since then. The strike of 1894, whose consequences Simons had described in his pamphlet, had been followed by the strike of 1904, another bitter conflict with scabs, blacklists, and all the rest. The accusations Simons had made about filth and adulteration would never have been denied by the American troops in the Spanish-American War. Seven million pounds of tinned "roast beef" had been shipped to the army, and soldiers came to gag at the very sight of a can of the meat. Embalmed beef, they called it, and though there was some furor about the quality of the product, the scorn and disgust settled upon the agents of the War Department who had purchased it, not upon the packers who had produced it.[54]

Simons liked Sinclair at once. The two men, though very different in tastes and temperament,[55] still had much in common: Sinclair had told Jane Addams, while dining with her at Hull House, that "the one useful purpose of settlements was the making of settlement workers into socialists."[56] It was the sort of candor that Simons enjoyed.

In short order, the preparations were made for Sinclair to enter the yards and begin gathering material for his projected novel. Simons introduced the writer to his friend and fellow-Socialist Herbert Phillips, and Phillips, who had relatives working in the packing plants, guided Sinclair through these infernal regions.[57] Finally, Simons gave Sinclair permission to use any material from *Packingtown*. Several of Simons' particularly lurid findings were therefore included almost verbatim in *The Jungle*—among them the tale of the worker who fell into the rendering vat and was processed along with the lard.

Sinclair returned home and in three months had written the manuscript. The final scene described a socialist postelection rally, where an orator addressed the crowd—an orator who "had been the head of the city's relief bureau in the stockyards, until the sight of misery and corruption had made him sick. He was young, hungry-looking, full of

[54] Margaret Leech, *In the Days of McKinley* (New York: Harpers, 1959), 298–300, 316–22.

[55] Comments of Miriam Simons Leuck, Simons Papers. She suggests that the two men might have met before 1904, but in the light of other evidence of Sinclair's activities between his "conversion" and his journey to gather material for *The Jungle*, this seems doubtful.

[56] Upton Sinclair, *Autobiography* (New York: Harcourt, Brace & World, 1962), 109.

[57] Interview, Herbert E. Phillips with Robert Huston, June 1954, and letter, Sinclair to Huston, Aug. 1, 1958; cited in Huston, "Algie Martin Simons," 47.

fire; and as he swung his long arm and beat up the crowd . . . he seemed the very spirit of the revolution."[58] It was Algie Simons.[59]

The novel's impact was instantaneous and immense. Simons' pamphlet, part of Charles Kerr's "Pocket Library of Socialism," had gone only to the socialist faithful and had caused virtually no stir. Socialists took it for granted that scandal, hardships, unemployment, and cruelty were the everyday four horsemen of capitalism. Sinclair's novel went as far as the White House, and before long federal commissioners were repeating the investigations that the author had made in *Packingtown*. When they had finished corroborating Sinclair's evidence, legislation was framed which purported to end the opportunities for crooked practices in the yards.

The storm of public outrage over the packing industry was in marked contrast with what *Packingtown* had aroused. In part, the difference was purely one of time. In 1899 America was still seeing life through nationalist spectacles. The country and its leadership preferred to solve the problems of the persons sitting in darkness across the seas than to confront the injustices of its own industrial economy. In part, the difference involved the personalities and ambitions of the two writers: Sinclair's work might have been serialized in the *Appeal* and then forgotten, if he had not been so determined to find a commercial publisher for the manuscript. He wanted above all to be a successful novelist, without compromising his ideological convictions, and so he took *The Jungle* from one publisher to another, until he found someone who would bring the book out.[60] Simons, on the other hand, moved on to other projects once he had written his

[58] Upton Sinclair, *The Jungle* (New York: Viking, 1946), 342.
[59] Sinclair stated this explicitly in a letter to Robert Huston, Aug. 1, 1958. However, in his introduction to the Viking edition of *The Jungle*, Sinclair makes no mention of Simons, but claims that the speech given by the orator is one that he himself made shortly before he left Chicago. This may well be true, but the description fits Simons much more nearly than it fits Sinclair— "Head of the City's Relief Bureau in the Stockyards." It is also possible that Sinclair put his own words in the Simons-figure's mouth in *The Jungle*, but the sentiments embodied in the speech are exactly those that Simons would have expressed at that time.
[60] See Sinclair, *Autobiography*, 114–16, for an account of the author's efforts to get the book in print.

exposé. He was then more interested in ideology than in audience, and he was bound more closely to politics and economics than to literature.

One thing is certain—the differences between the two men's success had almost nothing to do with literary quality. *The Jungle,* as a novel, was not much to boast about—even its author admitted that he was too exhausted toward the end to conclude the book properly.[61] The critical reader might have found evidences of one kind of exhaustion or another even earlier. *Packingtown,* even as a piece of propaganda, was pretty strident, and its readers must have been at least a little troubled by its shifting point of view. It asked, by turns, that people do something to remedy these dreadful conditions and that they accept the fact that it was all coldly, scientifically inevitable.

When the dust had settled and all the investigation and legislation had been concluded, the packers carried on their work under a new aura of respectability: federal inspectors were making sure that the consumer got what he paid for and that the meat which came to his table was clean and decent.

Seen from the point of view of either Simons or Sinclair, it was an ironic finish to the matter. The central focus of both had been the brutalization and impoverishment of the men, women, and children who depended upon the meat packing industry for their livelihood. The central focus of those who wanted to "reform" the industry had been upon the consumer. The only incident described in *The Jungle* for which Sinclair had been unable to secure either documented or eyewitness proof had been the tale of the hapless worker who was rendered into pure leaf lard. The packers who were questioned on this point denied that such a thing had ever happened: true, they said, men occasionally fell into the vats to their death, but the bodies were always fished out at once. No harm came to the product.

Simons greeted that comforting revelation with his customary mixture of derision and disgust. The whole notion of capitalism investigating itself was preposterous, and nothing could prove it more conclusively than to find a complex of issues reduced to a mere

[61] *Ibid.,* 114.

quarrel over whether the victims of industrial accidents did or did not diminish the quality of the product.[62]

Muckraking, it seemed, had a great deal of shock value, but, like the fact-gathering of the settlement house workers, it had little power to change men's minds.[63] People merely selected out of the mass of data those points that already fitted their stereotypes and predispositions. Propaganda had to be supplemented by a strong, well-knit political organization—one that would persistently and forcefully deny to people the comfort of their illusions, and one that would furnish a framework of radical theory upon which to build the evidence of social injustice in America.

---

[62] Simons, "Packingtown—The Jungle—Its Critics," *International Socialist Review*, VI (1906), 713.

[63] Simons elaborated upon his scorn for the muckrakers in "Roosevelt and the Muck Rake," *International Socialist Review*, VI (May 1906), 692; and in book reviews of muckraking literature in *ibid.*, III (May 1903), 698–99; V (June 1905), 758–59; and VI (Feb. 1906), 505.

CHAPTER FIVE

Politics

It was not the itch for office that had brought Simons into the Socialist party nor was it the desire for spoils. Once within the fold, however, and with some influence and a chance to be heard it was hard not to think of the possibilities that might open up within a few years. Simons was young, energetic, and American in heart, mind, and ancestry. If the party was truly to become a major force in American politics, then these were the qualities of a man to be reckoned with.

The Unity Convention of 1901 had marked his emergence as a figure of importance. He had a strong power base as leader of the Chicago local, and he had frequent and easy access to the socialist newspapers and magazines, which could make his name familiar to party members everywhere.[1] His 1900 campaign for Congress had been disappointing, but there was really no way of telling whether the vote recorded for Simons was an accurate reflection of the vote cast. More than once it had happened that socialist candidates made a strong showing in state and local campaigns but were, as Morris Hillquit put it, "counted out," when the ballot boxes were opened.[2] Furthermore, Simons had made his congressional bid while the party was still disastrously split, and it was not unrealistic to suppose that he could do much better in a campaign that was adequately supported and financed by a strong united organization. Simons' first experiences in socialist politics only whetted his appetite for political discourse and party leadership, and after 1901 he began to take a major role in both.

Politics had always been a rough-and-tumble business in America, but the Socialists promised that they would change all that. Since the end of the Civil War, politics at all levels of government and in both major parties had added the refinements of all manner of corruption.

The outright purchase of votes, which Simons had seen around Packingtown, was only a simple and unsophisticated move in a political
game that was capable of infinite variety. Officeholders and businessmen came together time and again in a great variety of corrupt
bargains. Franker than many was Tammany politician George Washington Plunkitt, who summed up his career by claiming, "I seen my
opportunities and I took 'em."[3]

Good Socialists had what they considered an entirely plausible
explanation for the corruption that marked American political life.
Government was always the tool of the dominant class in society, and
the purpose of government was to perpetuate the control of that class.
Under such circumstances it was absurd to talk about democracy.
America was no more or less than a government of, by, and for the
capitalists. When the Cooperative Commonwealth was finally
achieved, all this would be changed. Majority rule would be a reality
in a nation where government served the interests of working men
and women instead of the selfish desires of a few capitalists.

The Socialist party, however, did not for a moment believe that it
had to wait for that day before it could demonstrate the democratizing effects of socialism. The party itself could serve as a model of
honesty and democratic decisionmaking in its own dealings. Though
there would be party leaders there would be no party bosses; though
decisive action would be taken on matters of importance to the party,
the action would be what the majority of the membership had voted

[1] In addition to the periodicals he edited, he contributed articles frequently
to the *Appeal to Reason, Wilshire's Magazine, Comrade,* and to nonsocialist
magazines such as *The World Today, Independent, The Craftsman,* and the
Progressive Journal of Education.
[2] Hillquit believed, for example, that he had won a congressional seat in
1908 but that the count was tampered with and converted from a plurality of
500 into a shortage of 350; see *Loose Leaves from a Busy Life* (New York:
Macmillan, 1934), 118. Interestingly enough, these evidences of corruption
did not lead the Socialists to abandon their belief that the socialist revolution
could be achieved at the ballot box. Hillquit, for example, after his unsuccessful campaign in 1908, found Socialists "determined to pile up such a huge
majority in the coming election that no corrupt combination of the old parties
would be able to steal it." *Ibid.*
[3] William Riordon, *Plunkitt of Tammany Hall* (New York: Dutton,
1963), 3. First published in 1905.

to have taken. Party conventions would determine who should be the socialist standard bearers in presidential campaigns, but the delegates to those conventions would be chosen by the Socialist party membership in each state, and the size of each delegation should be proportionate to the number of party members within the state. Like the Populists before them, and like the Progressives who were to come, the Socialist party stood foursquare behind the instruments of direct democracy, the initiative and referendum.[4] Where the Socialists differed from the reform parties was in their denial that this kind of tinkering could have the slightest significance in a capitalist society. A choice between thieves was no choice at all.

Certain consequences issued from this determination of the Socialists to be democratic in their party deliberations. Most obvious was the prolixity of discussion that surrounded the consideration of every issue. Free discussion was of obvious importance in a democracy, Socialists claimed, and all viewpoints must be heard before the united action of the party could be taken. Therefore debate was not limited at Socialist party conventions.[5] This was in marked contrast to the procedures of the two major parties. The conventions of Republicans and Democrats, it is true, were never marked with the restraint and decorum implied by those who were amused by the verbal extravagance of the Socialists. Party conventions have traditionally been citadels of overstatement. The major parties, however, usually managed to close ranks in an election year, and the wrangling and trading went on behind closed doors in the not-always-mythical smoke-filled rooms. The public fury was reserved for the opposition party.

The Socialists' affection for free discussion was not the only factor that made for public conflict. At least as important was the fact that socialism as a political movement rested upon the swampy but hallowed ground of ideology. Marxism was subject to a variety of

[4] On the machinery of the Socialist party, see Robert Hoxie, "The Convention of the Socialist Party,"*Journal of Political Economy*, XVI (July 1908), 442–50, and Upton Sinclair, "The Socialist Party," *World's Work*, XI (April 1906), 7431–32.
[5] Charles Edward Russell, *Bare Hands and Stone Walls* (New York: Scribner's, 1933), 198; A. M. Simons, "Publicity in Party Matters," *International Socialist Review*, VI (June 1905), 689.

interpretations.[6] At the same time, it was debated by the kinds of persons who were noted for their verbal pugnacity: by intellectuals, who prided themselves upon their mastery of logic and the sharpness of their discourse; and by men of the working class, who were tough and plain-speaking, accustomed to firm convictions doggedly defended. For all these reasons, everybody knew that a gathering of Socialists was bound to be a good show, a spirited affair, and the thin-skinned among the comrades were ill-advised to enter the lists of socialist politics.

Simons responded to such an atmosphere with gusto, and for as long as political ambition stirred in him he devoted a great amount of effort to the search for a viable constituency—one that believed in him and in his ideas. One possible constituency was agricultural, but though he frequently went on propaganda tours to rural areas and wrote often on the farmer's relationship to socialism[7] he knew that, for the time being at least, his base of power was urban. It was in the city of Chicago that he had first made his mark as a Socialist, and it was there that he would have to look for support. He knew a good deal about municipal problems by now and late in 1901 had been named to the municipal committee of the sp,[8] but he worked con-

---

[6] All the current respected accounts of socialist politics in America dwell tediously upon the quarrels that went on within the Socialist party. None, however, make any comparisons with the standards of political discourse in the major parties at the same time. See, for example, Daniel Bell, "Marxian Socialism in the United States," in *Socialism and American Life*, ed. Donald Drew Egbert and Stow Persons (Princeton: Princeton University Press, 1952), or David Shannon, *The Socialist Party of America* (New York: Macmillan, 1955). Contemporary accounts of Socialist party conventions are more sympathetic and tend to emphasize that the often interminable squabbling among delegates and officials was merely the excess of the party's virtues. See, for example, Charlotte Teller, "The National Socialist Convention," *Arena*, XL (1908), 26–39. Convention politics within the major parties are treated historically in Richard C. Bain, *Convention Decisions and Voting Records* (Washington: Brookings Institution, 1960).

[7] See, for example, "Reply to Farmer's Criticism of the Socialist Party," *International Socialist Review*, II (May 1902), 775–79; "Socialism and the American Farmer," *ibid.*, III (Oct. 1902), 201–202; "The Rural Exodus," *ibid.*, III (June 1903), 737–40; "The Agricultural Army of the Unemployed," *Appeal to Reason*, Sept. 27, 1902, p. 2; "Populism and the Farmer of Today," *ibid.*, Jan. 24, 1903, p. 5.

[8] *Workers' Call*, Nov. 23, 1901.

stantly to learn more and to develop ways in which his party could become a meaningful alternative to the voters of Chicago.

The Chicago Socialist party (SP) was among the strongest in the country. In 1904 Illinois had more card-carrying Socialists than any other state.[9] After 1901 the national party, though nominally unified, was divided into left, center, and right wings,[10] and this division was reflected in the Chicago branch of the party. Simons and Barney Berlyn, an immigrant worker who had led the Socialist Labor party in the city, were both to the left of center and controlled the local organization. The most dominant figure representing the ideological center, and one of Simons' most persistent and vitriolic enemies, was Tommy Morgan. In 1891 Morgan had run for mayor of Chicago on the Socialist Labor ticket, and in 1893 he had, as secretary of the machinists' union, been a leader in the effort to capture the AFL for the Socialists.[11] Though he had once been on the far left, Morgan now considered the ideas of men like Simons and Berlyn to be "anarchistic." On the right wing was the lawyer Seymour Stedman, who represented the old Social Democratic party and still considered Victor Berger to be the soundest of all socialist theorists. At each meeting of the Chicago local, these men and their followers contended on questions of tactics and strategy in the city.[12]

The essence of Simons' position on urban socialism continued to be revolution, American style—speedy triumph at the ballot box and the total overthrow of capitalism. Halfway measures, such as campaigns for public ownership of utilities, were not steps toward municipal socialism at all. The working class could not benefit from government control as long as government was in the hands of the capitalists. Timid steps already taken by the federal government to regulate the

[9] *Socialist Party Bulletin*, I, Jan. 1905, cited in Robert Huston, "Algie Martin Simons and the American Socialist Movement" (unpublished Ph.D. dissertation, University of Wisconsin, 1965), 112.

[10] Ira Kipnis, *The American Socialist Movement, 1897–1912* (New York: Columbia University Press, 1952), 106–36.

[11] Daniel Bell, "Marxian Socialism," 252. On Tommy Morgan see also Louise Wade, *Graham Taylor, 1851–1938* (Chicago: University of Chicago Press, 1964), 74–75.

[12] See Chicago *Daily Socialist*, March 1, Dec. 27, 1902, Feb. 20, 1904, for typical accounts of intraparty conflict.

economy had proved that noble purposes were soon corrupted by capitalist control. There was no reason to suppose that the story would be any different in individual cities.

If the Socialist party captured control of Chicago, Simons contended, drawing upon what he had learned from Belgian socialism, the party would use the opportunity to strengthen the proletariat for the final struggle. They would improve the health and educational facilities of the city, build better homes for the workers, and seek to improve working conditions. Public ownership, however, would have to wait for the day of national victory.[13]

In 1903 the Chicago local found at least one tactic upon which all could agree, and one which exemplified Simons' ideas at this time. The venerable veteran of reform struggle Henry Demarest Lloyd was considering joining the Socialist party; everyone knew that his membership would be a propaganda coup for the organization. Tommy Morgan and Simons, both of whom knew Lloyd, joined in urging him to apply.[14]

The traction issue was then in the forefront of Chicago politics, and Lloyd suggested that the Socialists turn this issue to their own advantage. They could publicize a plan for municipal seizure and improved operation of the transportation system, and then base their election campaign upon this program. Surely, he speculated, this would arouse great public interest in the Socialist party and enhance its chances for early success.[15]

Simons thought it a bad idea. The workingman, he explained to Lloyd, had nothing to gain from a fight on such an issue. Straight socialism was the doctrine preached by the Chicago SP, and it was pointless to turn from this position and go chasing will-o'-the-wisps.[16] Lloyd was astonished, and said so to Morgan: "The limitations of

[13] A. M. Simons, *What the Socialists Would Do If They Won This City* (Chicago: Charles Kerr, 1901).
[14] Lloyd had subsidized Morgan's mayoralty campaign of 1891. Chester Destler, *Henry Demarest Lloyd and the Empire of Reform* (Philadelphia: University of Pennsylvania Press, 1963), 499.
[15] Lloyd to Simons, June 8, 1903, Henry Demarest Lloyd Papers, State Historical Society of Wisconsin—hereafter cited as Lloyd Papers.
[16] Simons to Lloyd, June 13, 1903, *ibid.*

Simons' thought are to me simply incomprehensible. . . . Do you wonder that I, and . . . hundreds of thousands of other citizens ripe for action, cannot see how we are to accomplish anything by joining a party so led?"[17] Morgan replied that socialism was "a great theory" indeed, "to overcome the obstacle of leadership such as Simons'."[18]

Lloyd put away his application for party membership, bewildered and disappointed that what seemed so eminently sensible to himself should be cause for quarrel among the Socialists. Within a few months, Lloyd was dead. Not many arguments among Socialists came to such a conclusive finish.

Once again Simons had staked his position upon his belief that the revolution was near. The congressional elections of 1902 had brought a remarkable increase in the socialist vote: From the 97,000 they had polled in 1900, the Socialists had jumped to a total of 227,000—an increase of 125 percent in but two years.[19] Soon after the election, the party's first national secretary was replaced by William Mailly, whose administrative talents helped turn the party into a more effective political instrument. The membership increased, and the national office paid off its debts; state committees were promised that the national office would help them finance state organizational and propaganda campaigns.[20] At the same time, however, election returns showed occasional Socialists winning local office. The combination of increasing effectiveness at the party's highest level and electoral success in some municipalities set Simons to thinking in new directions. Perhaps local quarrels, which limited the achievement of Socialists in cities like Chicago, could be silenced by directives from above.[21] He urged the National Executive Committee of the party to expand and strengthen the Municipal Committee and to include on it some members who had held public office. In this way it might gain prestige that would earn the respect of party locals and experience that might help

[17] Lloyd to Morgan, June 21, 1903, *ibid.*
[18] Morgan to Lloyd, June 22, 1903, *ibid.*
[19] Kipnis, *The American Socialist Movement*, 145–46.
[20] A. M. Simons, "Socialist Movement in America," *The World Today*, V (July 1903), 939–40.
[21] A. M. Simons, "Suggested Lines of Municipal Activity," *International Socialist Review*, III (Dec. 1902), 329.

other socialist campaigners in formulating platforms and programs.[22] Nothing, however, came of his recommendation.[23]

At the SP's national convention in 1904 Simons pressed his idea once again, and pointed out that socialist parties in Europe had long since formulated guidelines for elected officials and aspirants for local office. What he was asking for was precisely what he had agreed to only reluctantly in 1901—immediate demands.

He was an impossibilist no longer. He had taken the first public steps away from the far left, and he had done so because he was less committed to theory than to the lessons of experience. In France and Belgium he had seen that Socialists could hold local office and still retain their commitment to Marxist revolution, and now, in America, he believed that the same thing was possible. With a strong national party to set the general boundaries for local officeholders, Socialists could press forward in individual communities without sacrificing their desire for ultimate, nationwide success.[24]

This time the party was with him. The SP platform for the elections of 1904 included promises of government jobs for the unemployed, municipal ownership of utilities, a progressive income tax, and protection for organized labor.[25]

All this did not, however, sound so sensible to the Chicago comrades. A rebellion that had erupted shortly before the national convention now broke out anew. The Cook County Central Committee, in the hands of the extreme Left, repudiated the national platform, called it "opportunist," and began to circulate their own platform among socialist groups in other states. They believed that a vote of the rank-and-file membership across the country would, if a referendum were put to them, support the Left.

Simons was determined that no such referendum should ever be held; the struggle must not get out of Cook County. The party membership had already ruled on the 1904 platform, and to reopen

[22] *Worker*, Aug. 30, 1903.
[23] William Mailly to Simons, May 11, 1903, Socialist Party Collection.
[24] *Proceedings, National Convention of the Socialist Party, 1904*, pp. 39–40, 267–68.
[25] *Ibid.*, 315–20.

the issue would rend the party hopelessly in the coming presidential campaign. Therefore, at the next meeting of the county Central Committee, Simons and his temporary allies—Stedman, Berlyn, and Morgan—made certain that all the members of the moderate wing attended. When the time for automatic adjournment occurred, the impossibilists left in disgust. The moderates stayed behind, dissolved the administrative apparatus of their opponents, and called a convention to meet and endorse the national platform.

When the convention was held, a variety of devices familiar to parliamentarians guaranteed that Simons and his cohorts would carry the day. Credentials of doubtful delegates were called into question; the platform committee was carefully selected to exclude all but the moderate wing, which had already expressed its approval of the decisions made at the national level. When disgruntled delegates appealed their rude treatment to national headquarters, they were referred to the Illinois State Committee to have their grievances settled. There they found, on the subcommittee designated to deal with these grievances, the ubiquitous presence of Algie Simons. Their appeals were rejected.[26]

The party was reunited at last, in time for the presidential campaign, and Eugene Debs, the SP candidate, quadrupled his vote of 1900. But struggles like these, during which Simons managed to regain control of his base of political power, could not help but erode the idealism and enthusiasm of winners and losers alike. The party platform of 1904, which Simons had been put in the position of defending before all comers and for which he campaigned vigorously,[27] was unqualified in its praise of American democratic tradition. The party, in fact, claimed to be the true heir of democracy. As the platform committee had reported at the national convention: "The Socialist Party makes its appeal to the American people as the defender and preserver of the idea of liberty and self-government, in

[26] This episode is treated in some detail in Huston, "Algie Martin Simons," 121–24. See also Kipnis, *The American Socialist Movement*, 160–61.
[27] His activities during the campaign were reported in the Chicago *Daily Socialist*, Sept. 10, Oct. 8, 15, 1903. See also Upton Sinclair, "The Socialist Party," *World's Work*, XI (April 1906), 7431, for an account of campaign efforts in Illinois.

which the nation was born; as the only political movement standing
for the program and principles by which the liberty of the individual
may become a fact; as the only political organization that is democratic, and that has for its purpose the democratizing of the whole
society."[28] Men like Simons, in positions of party importance, could
for awhile ignore the apparent contradictions of words and action, and
become as easily fascinated with the power and manipulations of
political life as the most effective Tammany boss. The contradictions,
however, were significant, and they could lead to disenchantment.
Simons was not a moral imbecile; he was a reflective and intelligent
man for whom democracy meant a great deal more than simply
giving everyone a chance to get his hand in the till.

Democracy can function effectively only when its defenders agree
on most fundamentals. This the Socialists had so far been unable to
do. Even the great increase in the vote given to the national ticket in
1904 didn't obscure that fact to Simons. The groups within the
Chicago and Cook County locals, as in Socialist party locals across the
country, were of different social classes, differing in ethnic composition and, of course, in their vision of the Cooperative Commonwealth.
Fracture seemed inevitable in such a political movement, and the
votes and referenda that the party was forever taking in the interests
of democratic decisionmaking were by their very nature divisive.
Each one required the membership to take sides against one another,
in spite of their common purposes.

Still, the major political parties in America had faced similar problems of heterogeneity and had been able to surmount them. Simons
believed that the Socialist party could do the same. After the results
of the 1904 elections were in, the more flamboyant among the comrades claimed that the death knell had been sounded for the Democratic party. Henceforth, one enthusiast claimed, there would be only
Socialists and Republicans competing in national elections, and then
the class struggle would be clear and out in the open.[29]

Simons was not nearly so sanguine. He was pleased with the results

---

[28] Quoted in Kipnis, *The American Socialist Movement*, 159.
[29] Gaylord Wilshire, "The Death of the Democratic Party," *Wilshire's*,
XVI (Dec. 1904), cited in Kipnis, *The American Socialist Movement*, 163.

of the election, but the tempestuous quarrels that had marked the campaign in Chicago made him realize that there were fundamental problems that needed to be solved before socialism could become an effective instrument of social and economic regeneration in America. Furthermore, these problems had to be solved without compromising so much of the party's ideological underpinning that it became just another in a blur of reform parties and sects. The revolt in Cook County had occurred because, personalities aside, part of the membership feared that Simons was tolerating too much ideological compromise. In the years that followed, nearly all disagreements of substance centered around that age-old political dilemma: success with compromise, or failure with unblemished principles.

To increase the harmony and homogeneity of the party, Simons developed several new tactics. One way of preventing membership from straying too far from practical realities was to keep a tight rein upon new party locals and attach them at the outset to established groups. Agitation and recruitment should continue at a fast pace, but all new groups should be linked with a nearby, stronger local so that the control of each would be "in the hands of the older Socialists."[30] Prudent organization and efficient administration could go a long way toward accomplishing desired goals.

In addition to the ideological reason for keeping a tight hold upon the party there was another reason that Simons neglected to mention. Party membership had a curious and disquieting habit of falling away. Memberships once taken out were often dropped within a year as enthusiasm waned. In Cook County, for example, between 1904 and 1908 the party gained between 6,000 and 10,000 converts, but only about 1,000 continued their memberships over that period. One way of combating this kind of apathy was to link all members as closely as possible with the old party faithful, whose zeal had been proved.

A more significant approach, and one to which Simons gave an increasing amount of attention, was what political scientists of a later day would call "socialization." He sought to give the party members functions and activities, not necessarily political, that might foster a

[30] Simons, "After-Election Work," *International Socialist Review*, V (Oct. 1904), 304.

sense of comradeship. Like the leaders of the Grange and settlement-house movements, which had both depended upon social occasions to enhance their solidarity, Simons encouraged a variety of pure and simple social events—picnics, costume balls, and Lake Michigan excursions.[31] It was more difficult to quarrel over party policy with a comrade who had shared beer and a box lunch at the lakeshore than with one who appeared only as a distant antagonist on the other side of a smoky meeting hall.

To further enhance this sense of community, Simons sought to establish a daily party press in Chicago. A socialist newspaper could tell members about one another and about the campaigns, meetings, lectures, and social events that the capitalist press chose to ignore. It could give the faithful their own insider jokes and remind them of the venality of capitalism. In November 1904 Simons began his efforts to convert the Chicago *Socialist*, formerly the *Workers' Call*, into a daily paper.[32] Little came of the project until two years later, when the party decided to publish a daily paper for the last two weeks of the election campaign. In October 1906 Simons was elected to the editorship, and after only a few days the Chicago *Daily Socialist* announced that by popular demand it would try to maintain its daily schedule permanently.

For several years thereafter, the newspaper struggled along, never far from the brink of financial annihilation and always pleading for subscriptions, advertisements, and freewill offerings.[33] Although the paper was supposed to be an instrument of party unity it was attended even at its birth by wrangling among the factions of the Chicago local. Some members believed it would be disastrous to begin such a venture at that time, and that the attention given to the matter was distracting the party from the more important business of campaigning. There was talk that the financial reports of the old Chicago *Socialist* had been juggled to make the paper seem more prosperous than it was, and that the enthusiasm of the rank and file was grossly

[31] The Chicago *Daily Socialist* gave much prominent space to advertisements of socialist activities of this sort.
[32] Chicago *Daily Socialist*, Dec. 3, 1904.
[33] For a sample of the Chicago *Daily Socialist*'s frequent pleas for financial assistance, see the issues of July 6, 8, 9, 10, and Aug. 17, 1907.

exaggerated.[34] No one was certain just what Simons' role was in all this, but the accusations that surrounded him were substantial, and they grew increasingly bitter as the Chicago *Daily Socialist* managed only barely to survive.

By almost any standard, the venture was foolhardy. It was a gamble in futures, dependent for success upon both the unity and party growth that it was designed to engender. When the newspaper failed to do well, its supporters were obliged to continue the evasive tactics they had used at the paper's founding. Promised financial statements did not appear, so the *Daily Socialist*'s actual losses remained a mystery to most until 1910.[35] Circulation figures were equally mysterious. The editor reported on rises and declines, but never divulged exactly how many papers were being sold.

Through it all Simons labored to make the newspaper what he thought the socialist movement in Chicago needed, and he clung to the venture, persuading others to do so as well.[36] Until 1908 he was also editing the *International Socialist Review*, but he gave more and more of his time to the daily newspaper, trying endlessly to prolong its existence until it could take hold and prosper. Like the socialist movement itself, the *Daily Socialist* as Simons knew it never did prosper.

The energy and agility that Simons needed to maintain his position within the party never caused him to lose sight of the fundamental task of winning votes. The sp's most natural constituency was the working class for which socialism promised so much. Organized labor, however, had for many years been successful in resisting socialist efforts to make inroads on its membership. Gompers had defeated the Socialist Labor party's strategy of boring from within; DeLeon's Socialist Trades and Labor Alliance had won few workers away from the AFL. The whole labor movement remained strictly nonpolitical.

Simons deplored the bread-and-butter unionism of Gompers and

[34] The machinations employed to launch the new daily are treated at length in Huston, "Algie Martin Simons," 173–79.
[35] Chicago *Daily Socialist*, Nov. 10, 1910.
[36] "Angels," persuaded through editorial and personal entreaty, rescued the *Daily Socialist* on several occasions. See *ibid.*, March 29, June 23, 1910.

the AFL, but what troubled him even more was that the union did virtually nothing to bring any practical benefits to the workers who needed them most. Great segments of American labor were excluded from the craft unions of the AFL. The most impoverished of the "wage slaves" were not unionized. If they could be organized, their condition could be improved, and their votes could be harvested by the Socialists.

In January 1905, therefore, Simons took part in a conference of labor leaders and radicals to plan the formation of a new, industrial union. The organization was to become the Industrial Workers of the World (IWW). From the January meeting, a manifesto written by Simons was issued, calling for a convention of all those who agreed with the principles contained therein.[37] "Universal economic evils," the manifesto read, "can only be eradicated by a universal working class movement. . . . A movement to meet these conditions must consist of one great industrial union embracing all industries, providing for craft autonomy locally, industrial autonomy internationally, and working class autonomy generally. It should be founded on the class struggle."[38]

The convention was to meet in June, and in the intervening months Simons publicized the aims of the proposed organization and countered the criticisms of the opposition. To some Socialists, the project smacked of dual unionism; to others it seemed ominous that Daniel DeLeon intended to be at the founding convention. Simons brushed aside such arguments. No one needed to fear the "few barnacles on the rotting hulk of DeLeonism."[39] The American labor movement, he insisted, was at a fatal impasse, because the AFL was in league with the capitalists. The union's leadership had engaged in countless corrupt bargains with employers and had sold out the interests of working men and women.[40]

[37] Paul Brissenden, *The I.W.W.: A Study of American Syndicalism* (New York: Columbia University Press, 1919), 66.
[38] "Manifesto of Industrial Unionists," *International Socialist Review*, V (Feb. 1905), 478.
[39] A. M. Simons, "Industrial Unionism," *Appeal to Reason*, June 17, 1905.
[40] A. M. Simons, "Chicago Conference for Industrial Unions," *International Socialist Review*, V (Feb. 1905), 496–99.

When the convention met, Simons, a member of the five-man temporary executive committee, was there, and he read his manifesto to the delegates.[41] When the convention was over and the IWW was an established reality, he exulted in its accomplishments.[42]

Within a year Simons had abandoned the IWW. He had been wrong. DeLeon had struck again; his Socialist Labor party, "almost a corpse," Simons wrote, was "sucking the life out of the I.W.W." The union's second convention had been turned into a "farce," paralyzed by "a bunch of half-crazed fanatics under the leadership of De-Leon."[43]

Cooler heads might have doubted that DeLeon was really the curse of the new union, but it was clear that Simons and the IWW were moving in opposite directions. The Wobblies were drawing back from political activity and turning toward syndicalist ideas of "direct action." Simons was still looking for votes, not violence, from the American proletariat. The votes were not, however, coming from the workingmen of Chicago. In the elections of 1906 the Socialist party vote fell off 50 percent from what it had been in 1904, and the national picture was little better.[44]

In print, Simons attributed the losses to the fact that the Socialists were being "duped" by the major parties. In private, he pondered what was happening in England at the same time, and wondered whether the American Socialist party might not profit from the English example. Twenty-nine candidates of what was shortly to become the British Labour party had been elected to parliament in 1906. H. M. Hyndman's Social Democratic Federation, the nearest English counterpart of DeLeon's Socialist Labor party, had failed to elect a single one of its candidates.

The sequence of events that led to this success had begun in 1901,

[41] *Proceedings of the First Convention of the I.W.W.* (New York, 1905), 99–100.
[42] A. M. Simons, "Industrial Workers of the World," *International Socialist Review*, VI (Aug. 1905), 65–76.
[43] A. M. Simons, "Socialism in the Present Campaign," *International Socialist Review*, VII (Oct. 1906), 243.
[44] A. M. Simons, "Chicago Elections," *International Socialist Review*, VII (April 1907), 623; Kipnis, *The American Socialist Movement*, 170.

when a series of judicial decisions had struck powerfully against organized labor. According to the terms of the Taff Vale ruling, unions were held liable for damages and costs caused by strikes. By subsequent verdicts, unions were denied the right to picket and boycott.

To the British Socialists, these developments had proved to be convincing arguments in favor of Socialists' cooperating with organized labor: not only were the workingmen of England being beaten on the economic front—for the strike that led to Taff Vale was a complete failure—but political reprisals were being taken as well. Political involvement, with the ideological compromises it might entail, appeared to be the only way that British socialism could have a constructive influence upon labor policy.

The results of the socialist and labor alliance were not long in coming. By joining with parliamentary Liberals, the new Labor members of parliament elected in 1906 were able to pass legislation reversing the Taff Vale decision and bans on picketing and boycotting. It was an exhilarating beginning for the nascent Labor party, and though pure Marxism was the loser it was hard to deny, as Karl Kautsky observed, that the class struggle was being waged, and waged effectively, in the British Parliament.[45]

Hitherto Simons had been opposed to any efforts to form a labor party in America. The Socialist party was labor's party, he had claimed, and the only way the political goals of labor could be achieved was for the AFL to cast its lot—and the ballots of its membership—with the Socialists. It had long been clear, however, that Samuel Gompers was about as likely to turn toward socialism as he was to go back to making cigars. Political activity of any kind had been scrupulously avoided by the AFL since its early days, and though there had always been members who disagreed with this position, Gompers had remained adamant.

By 1906 the AFL, like British labor, was facing problems that were

---

[45] Gerald Friedberg, "Marxism in the United States: John Spargo and the Socialist Party in America" (unpublished Ph.D. dissertation, Harvard University, 1964), 83–86; and Chuschichi Tsuzuki, *H. M. Hyndman and British Socialism* (London: Oxford University Press, 1961), 152–61.

essentially political. In February 1906 Gompers took the unprecedented step of presenting a bill of grievances to the Congress and the president. Among other things, the bill protested the perversion of antitrust legislation, the misuse of the injunction in labor disputes, and, above all, the hostility to organized labor of the membership of the House Committee on Labor.

During the election campaign of 1906, the AFL had gone even further than the mere articulation of grievances. It made a great effort to defeat Congressman Littlefield, a powerful enemy of labor, and though the effort was unsuccessful, the incumbent's majority was impressively reduced. In other districts, where antilabor candidates were running, local units of the AFL were encouraged to put up independent labor candidates. A small campaign fund was raised, and the voting records of incumbent congressmen were distributed in various constituencies.

When organized labor looked over the results of the election of 1906, it found much more to be happy about than the Socialists had. Although the Republican party remained in control of the House, its majority had been reduced, and Gompers believed even Republicans would look with more interest upon labor's demands after this initial venture of the AFL into political activity.

Unlike British labor the AFL did not go the next mile and look into the possibilities of labor politics. Most Socialists were not impressed by such timid excursions into the political arena. Most would have agreed with Victor Berger that "all [AFL] proceedings are senile. Sam Gompers . . . has more and more developed into an empty, self-complacent old fool."[46] Simons basically concurred.[47] Still, if the Socialist party was the party of the working class then it had an obligation to seek some means of associating itself with the largest organized body of workingmen in America. And if the Socialists were to be swept into office, they were going to need the vast constituency

[46] Quoted in Philip Taft, *The AFL in the Time of Gompers* (New York: Harper, 1957), 296. The foregoing account of AFL activities in the election campaign of 1906 is based upon Taft's work, 294–97.

[47] See, for example, A. M. Simons, "The Gompers Method of Helping Capitalists," *Appeal to Reason*, March 25, 1905, p. 1.

headed by the much-maligned Gompers. These were the thoughts that came to Simons as he mulled over the discouraging election returns of 1906.

They were not thoughts likely to gain him quick success in Chicago, at least not within the high councils of the local party. Though Simons had managed to hold onto the party machinery, his relations with other Chicago socialist leaders were steadily deteriorating, and ultimately his nonpolitical, paying jobs were affected. In 1906 Charles Kerr, who published the *International Socialist Review* that Simons edited, was beginning to grow dissatisfied with his editor. In 1900 Simons and Kerr had stood together with the revolutionary wing of the party. Kerr was still there, now championing the syndicalist ideas of the Wobblies and eyeing with increasing disfavor the rightward movement of the *Review*'s editor.

At the end of 1907, therefore, Kerr fired Simons and took over the editorship himself. The character of the *Review* quickly changed. Hitherto it had included thoughtful articles on a variety of subjects related to socialist theory. Karl Kautsky, Ramsay MacDonald, Keir Hardie, Jean Longuet, and H. M. Hyndman had all sent articles from abroad, and Simons' own contributions had included, in addition to monthly editorials, hundreds of book reviews and a variety of articles explaining the fine points of Marxist doctrine.[48]

Under Editor Kerr, the *Review* not only became less abstruse and scholarly, but it began to engage directly in local quarrels over theory and tactics. In an obvious slur at Simons, the new editor declared that the *Review* had formerly been shaped by the belief that Socialist party doctrine should be "deliberated in advance by a select few of superior brainpower, who should later diffuse the results of their deliberations among the common man." Kerr claimed that working people knew instinctively what was best for them, and then he proceeded for years to advise their instincts away from "opportunism."[49]

---

[48] For example, "How to Read Capital," *International Socialist Review*, VII (Jan. 1907), 394–97; "Landmarks of Scientific Socialism," *ibid.*, VII (June 1907), 736–39.

[49] Kerr, "Editor's Chair," *International Socialist Review*, IX (Jan. 1909), 535, "Publishers Department," 559.

At the national level of the party, Simons found more sympathy for his ideas. In 1905 he had been elected to the national committee of the SP and in the following year he became a member of the seven-man National Executive Committee (NEC).[50] Among his colleagues on the NEC were Victor Berger, John Spargo, and Morris Hillquit, all more reformist than revolutionary, and all with increasing power over the destiny of the Socialist party.

As originally designed by the convention of 1901, the party had been decentralized. The national committee was supposed only to set party policy between conventions. But despite original intentions the National Executive Committee became increasingly important. For one thing, it was the national headquarters that controlled the states in which Socialist locals were not yet organized. It was the national committee, too, that directed presidential campaigns, held the purse strings of the party, and scheduled and routed the Socialist party speakers who were dispatched about the country. When disputes arose between competing factions of state parties, the NEC acted in judgment, and in most cases it decided in favor of the faction that presented an ideological position most nearly like its own.[51]

It was the national office of the party, too, that maintained official contacts with socialist parties abroad and that sent American delegates to international meetings. In 1907 the national committee chose Simons as a delegate to the Stuttgart Congress of the Second International, and there he came in touch once more with the main currents of European socialism.

All the leaders he had met in 1900 were there—Ramsay MacDonald, H. M. Hyndman, Jaures, and Guesde—as well as some more obscure radicals, Mussolini, Lenin, and Trotsky. Simons was particularly interested in talking about the thorny problem of socialist-labor

---

[50] *Socialist Party Official Bulletin*, II (April 1906).

[51] For an account of some of these disputes and their resolution, see Kipnis, *The American Socialist Movement*, 370–79. The NEC was elected by the party membership and presumably reflected majority opinion. However, regional differences on ideology were always substantial, as David Shannon has pointed out in *The Socialist Party of America*, 1–42, and therefore it was always possible that considerable friction could exist between the national office and one or more regional minorities.

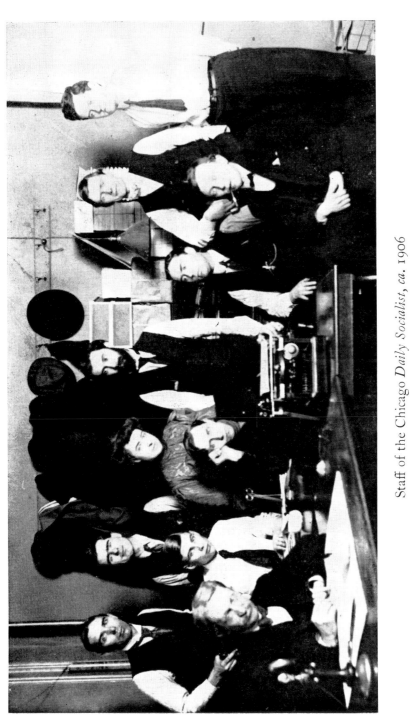

Staff of the Chicago *Daily Socialist, ca.* 1906

(A. M. Simons standing fourth from left)

A. M. Simons on the "Red Special," September 1908

Socialist Luncheon Meeting for the Mission by
the Pro-War Party, August 2, 1918

(*A. M. Simons seated second from left*)

Members of the American Socialist Labor Mission
to Europe, Paris, 1918

(Left to right: *A. M. Simons, Louis Kopelin, Alexander
Kerensky, C. E. Russell, John Spargo*)

movement relations. The Congress did pass a resolution recommending "close cooperation" between socialist-oriented unions and socialist parties, but it offered no suggestions to countries like the United States where the unions were not radical.[52]

The Stuttgart Congress, in fact, seemed only incidentally concerned with matters like these. In 1900 wherever Simons had gone he had heard debates about revisionism and orthodoxy. In America, that was still what the debates were about. By 1907 Europeans were preoccupied with another issue: militarism. The possibility of a general European war had been openly discussed for years. A succession of international crises since the turn of the century had occasioned much rattling of sabers. All the great powers had plenty to rattle; all groaned under an increasing burden of armament; all were prepared on a moment's notice to stiffen the patriotic resolve of their citizens and send their young men marching to battle.

At the very time the Stuttgart Congress was meeting, the Second Hague Conference was also in session. "A thieves' supper," one of the English Socialists called it at Stuttgart.[53] No one at the Hague believed in disarmament and no one believed—despite the fact that this was billed as a peace conference—that war was far away. What was worse, nobody really cared very much.

The delegates to the Congress of the Second International, on the other hand, cared a great deal, and for reasons that were both theoretical and practical. Marx had declared that war was endemic to the capitalist economy and that a period of warfare would occur before the final overturn of that stage of historical development. In practical terms, it was the working classes of Europe who had been customarily thrown into the jaws of war. Confronting both of these circumstances, the Stuttgart Congress tried to devise a viable set of tactics for all Socialists to follow when the call to battle should come again.

Some believed that it was useless to try to stop the war when it came: since this was the terminal stage of capitalism, the sooner over,

[52] Chicago *Daily Socialist*, Sept. 23, 1907.
[53] Chicago *Daily Socialist*, Sept. 7, 1907, James Joll, *The Second International* (New York: Praeger, 1956), 138.

the better. Some were partisans of that will-o'-the-wisp, the general strike, in which workingmen would throw down their tools, troops would desert, and the crowned heads of Europe would find that at last they had called a war to which nobody would come.

It was pleasant, indeed, to contemplate the brotherhood of all workingmen—the assumption upon which the whole notion of the general strike was based. For a while at Stuttgart, it was possible to believe in such a brotherhood. Simons, sending back dispatches to the Chicago *Daily Socialist,* was deeply impressed by what he saw. On the opening day of the Congress, a vast throng of workingmen and their families swept down the road leading from the city to the Volksfestplatz, a field customarily used for military maneuvers.[54] They joined an open-air demonstration that lasted many hours. Twenty-six nations were represented among the nearly 900 delegates. It was the first time that so many nationalities had gathered for a single purpose, and the great crowd of Germans greeted the occasion with nearly limitless enthusiasm. They cheered speech after speech, and when the speeches were ended, they cheered the bands and the choral singing and the dances that followed. They joined in singing Luther's great hymn "Ein feste burg," whose words had been changed for the occasion, to affirm that the mighty fortress was no longer God, but the Second International.[55] "To say that such a sight was inspiring," Simons wrote, ". . . or to attempt in any way to describe the effect is but to show the inability of words to convey the full sweep of the ideas and emotions that sweep through the human mind."[56]

Each delegation at the great rally had sought to present something of its own to add to the gaiety. What could the Americans do? The delegates put their heads together and came to a decision: with gusto they struck up the University of Chicago football cheer—GO, GO, Chica-GO—again and again as the throng urged them on, and soon began itself to repeat the incantation. It was far from the embodiment of revolutionary ardor, but it might have made old John D. Rocke-

[54] Chicago *Daily Socialist,* Aug. 29, 1907; Barbara Tuchman, *The Proud Tower* (New York: Macmillan, 1965), 447.
[55] Joll, *The Second International,* 133.
[56] Chicago *Daily Socialist,* Aug. 29, 1907.

feller tremble to hear the name of his great benefaction fall from
such lips as these.[57]

Brotherhood there was that day, but it was the brotherhood of the
beer garden. August Bebel had a firm grip on underlying realities: if
the German government should declare the nation in danger, he
warned one of the English delegates, every Socialist would "shoulder
his rifle and march to the French frontier."[58]

For five days the Second International debated the duty of the
working class in the face of militarism. The resolution that was finally
adopted did not commit anyone to anything.[59] Ironically, like the
Hague Conference which avoided a commitment to compulsory arbi-
tration of international disputes, the Socialists skirted the matter of a
general strike. If war should threaten, the resolution averred, the
Socialists should try to prevent it; if war broke out, they should try to
stop it. No plans were laid, no course of action outlined, for the
resolution acknowledged the impotence of socialism in the face of a
more powerful ideology, nationalism: the response would surely vary,
said the Stuttgart Resolution on Militarism and International Conflicts, depending upon the nations involved.

Simons clearly saw that this issue was regarded as paramount
among all the delegates to the Congress. As for himself, he believed
in the general strike in time of war, and he hailed the fierce defiance
of Gustav Herve, the French Socialist who shouted that nationalism
was a fatal snare for workingmen. But Simons did not believe that
this issue had much relevance for American radicals. One of his
reports was headlined "Militarism Vital in European Life,"[60] and his
story went on to admit that it was hard for Americans to understand
the importance that was accorded to the question of peace or war.
Because American Socialists were not involved in this Old World
struggle, he said, they could sit back and enjoy it.[61]

[57] Chicago *Daily Socialist*, Sept. 13, 1907.
[58] Quoted by Tuchman, *The Proud Tower*, 449.
[59] The full text of the resolution is in Joll, *The Second International*, 196–98.
[60] Sept. 3, 1907, p. 1.
[61] Simons, "Stuttgart Congress," *International Socialist Review*, VIII (Sept. 1907), 132–35.

Simons also observed that the control of the socialist movement in Europe was coming increasingly into the hands of intellectuals. In this respect, the American SP was following suit. The National Executive Committee was not led by workingmen and, as John Spargo wrote, "It is to the 'intellectuals' that the proletariat owes whatever understanding it has of its position in social evolution, its mission and its opportunity."[62]

Spargo was right. Simons was a perfect case in point. At the very time he took office on the NEC he was editing the Chicago *Daily Socialist* and the *International Socialist Review*, and writing weekly installments of "American History for the Workers." In addition, he was teaching and lecturing. All these were essential activities that could hardly be undertaken by the untutored workingman. Moreover, no wage earner could have taken time off to go junketing to Europe for a Congress of the Second International.

The logic of this was not convincing to everyone in the SP, particularly when the ideas of Simons and his colleagues on the NEC moved steadily to the right. Party leaders had by 1907 abandoned their onetime expectation that socialism was going to be brought to pass suddenly. Even their timid view of revolution had given way to a belief in gradualism.[63] These opinions did not sound particularly representative of a party that had twice nominated Eugene Debs for the presidency. Indeed, by 1908 Simons and some of the other intellectuals who led the party were seriously looking for someone else to be its standard bearer in the presidential election campaign. For the first time since the formation of the Socialist party of America, ideological differences were to break out over the selection of a presidential candidate.

Algie and May Simons were both official delegates to the nominating convention held in Chicago. In spite of the electoral disappointments of the previous two years, Simons maintained his customary

[62] John Spargo, *Sidelights on Contemporary Socialism* (New York: B. W. Huebsch, 1911), 69.
[63] For an account of center-right ideology in these years, see Kipnis, *The American Socialist Movement*, 201–204. For the ideology of specific NEC members at this time, see David Shannon, *The Socialist Party of America*, 10–11, 13, 24–25, 65–66.

optimism in his public pronouncements: socialism was still the most exciting thing that the future held. "There is no power on earth," he wrote as he anticipated the presidential campaign, "that can set metes and bounds to the possible results of [this] campaign. The votes to be gained for Socialism, . . . the onward urge which can be given toward freedom during the coming months may be such as the world has never seen before." "It is going to be a good time in which to be alive," he concluded, "if one is . . . a part of the most vital living thing of today."[64]

The convention itself was far from dull. Although there were fewer working-class delegates than there had been in earlier years— living expenses were no longer provided by the party for the eight days of the gathering—it was a colorful aggregation. Among the 219 delegates were many husbands and wives attending together; ducking in and out among the rows of folding chairs and up across the speakers' platform were many young children, who, like Miriam Simons, had been brought to witness the spectacle. One delegate was intent upon securing for his son's baby book the autographs of all the prominent Socialists who had gathered in Convention Hall.[65]

Under all the local color lay the fabric of conflict. There were the Christian Socialists who were always in danger of colliding with the Marxist atheists; there were the farmers, who had to be continually assured that the Cooperative Commonwealth would not evict them from their land; there were trade union representatives from the AFL who confronted the revolutionary zeal of the IWW delegates; there were the party intellectuals, a favorite target of old veterans of labor struggles. If the Hegelian dialectic were correct, then the clash of so many opposites ought to produce many a new truth.

The big question was who should be the party's presidential candidate. Eugene Debs was still the embodiment of socialism to most Americans. Because of his dislike of party politics and because he rarely attended Socialist party conventions, he had escaped being tarred with the brush of factionalism. In many respects he was the

[64] Chicago *Daily Socialist*, May 12, 1908.
[65] Charlotte Teller, "The National Socialist Convention," *Arena*, XL (July 1908). 35.

Socialist party's war hero candidate; veteran of many desperate campaigns, he had led regiments of workingmen against fearful odds, and this fact alone was enough to make him a strong candidate, whatever his ideological convictions. Unlike some war heroes, though, Debs kept a firm grip on his own limitations. He frankly confessed that when the White House actually came within the reach of the Socialist party, the party would need a different kind of man at its head.

Much of the National Executive Committee believed that the party ought not wait until then. After the convention had placed Debs' name in nomination, Seymour Stedman, declaring that the old warrior was really too ill to carry on a vigorous campaign, nominated Algie Martin Simons. It was not an auspicious moment. As soon as Stedman suggested that Debs' recent throat operation would be a serious limitation in the forthcoming contest, the hall sounded with hisses and cries of "No, No!" To make matters worse, Ben Hanford produced a letter—which he claimed that Stedman had already read —in which Debs explained that his recovery was complete.

Two other nominations were made right on the heels of this uncomfortable disclosure, making it clear to all that the party leadership was concerned with more than the condition of Debs' throat. They were genuinely trying to find a viable alternative. Their failure, however, was decisive. Simons ran last in a field of four, and Debs took the nomination once more, defeating the combined forces of his opposition by about four to one.[66]

Still, the convention had gone a long way in the direction that Simons now believed it should in order to achieve success at the ballot box. Most important, it had been prevented from taking any action that would alienate the potential affections of organized labor—and this, in spite of Debs' longstanding loathing of the AFL and his dedication to industrial unionism.[67] To sanctify what was essentially a marriage of convenience, Simons was named one of Debs' campaign managers, and an arduous, exciting, and ultimately revealing contest

---

[66] *Proceedings of the National Convention of the Socialist Party, 1908*, pp. 145–64.

[67] Debs, like Simons, had been a founder of the IWW but had dropped out within a year.

began. "The present campaign," Simons wrote "will mark a new era in the Socialist movement in America. For the first time, Socialism will become a national force."[68]

As befit such expectations, the Socialist party undertook an unparalleled effort. A train, "The Red Special," was chartered for the campaign, and from the beginning of September until election day, it carried candidates and managers, journalists and local Socialist luminaries, into some 33 states. For Debs the trip became a sentimental journey, for all along the way west he was met by devoted followers, men who had gone into the American Railway Union years before, had suffered firings and blacklistings and worse on account of it, and were proud of what they had endured.[69]

Simons, who accompanied the train as far as San Francisco, was getting his first look at the far west. For the first time in many years he was crossing the agricultural heartland of the nation. It gave him an opportunity to bring his message of an American socialist party to those whom he, like Frederick Jackson Turner, believed most American of all.

It was no pleasure trip. Twenty-six men slept in one car—the same one in which they also cooked and ate and wrote their speeches and press releases. One of the journalists aboard vividly described the method of procedure aboard the Special. "Train pulls up," he wrote. "Band out, plays 'Marseillaise.' Platform swung out, and Simons up and letting the farmers know that he knows something about agriculture that would profit them. Others keep the crowd off the train and away from Debs. Another consults with trainman as to how many seconds are available. Literature men peacefully persuading. . . . Bell goes; Debs speaks five hundred words a minute; gets his leg pulled; platform is yanked back into the baggage car, and most of us have to board the car on the run."[70] For those with a taste for politics, this was heady stuff, and for politicians long immersed in party

---

[68] Chicago *Daily Socialist*, May 16, 1908.
[69] The best secondary account of the "Red Special" is in Ray Ginger, *The Bending Cross* (New Brunswick, N.J.: Rutgers University Press, 1949), 274–89.
[70] Charles Lapworth, Chicago *Daily Socialist*, Sept. 10, 1908.

controversy its refreshment was irresistible. As the Red Special sped across the countryside, the red flag waving wildly from the locomotive, Simons sat at his typewriter, hustling off the dispatches to be sent back to the Chicago *Daily Socialist*. The news of the campaign was all good: a mighty crowd for Debs in Davenport, Iowa; an overflow meeting in Denver, where Simons delivered a "red-hot" speech; 20 percent of the Las Vegas desert settlement population declaring for socialism.[71]

Among these encouraging estimates, Simons included pointed reminders of what the struggle was all about: he described the gold and silver mines in the mountains west of Denver, where human beings spent their lives like moles, searching for riches deep in the earth, and wasted their mental and moral resources in the mining camps and towns that clung to the scarred hillsides. "There is," he wrote, ". . . a sort of hideous artistic perfection in the fact that the production of gold should thus display in condensed form all the horrors of capitalism."[72]

Back east the news was neither so vivid nor so encouraging. Sam Gompers had initiated the AFL's first venture into presidential politics, but he had done so by declaring for the Democratic party candidate, William Jennings Bryan, and claiming that the Red Special was being financed by the Republicans. It was a simple matter to disprove the charge—the party published the names and addresses of the 15,000 persons whose contributions had made the trip possible.[73]

It was not so easy to counter the effects of the AFL's support of Bryan. The effort was made to attack Gompers without alienating organized labor—a neat trick, but one that Simons managed with some skill. He filled the pages of the *Daily Socialist* with illustrations of strikes in which Gompers refused to intervene, bargains between Gompers and groups hated by laboring men, and utterances of Gompers which proved to be lies. At the same time, Simons included articles recalling labor to its glorious traditions—its historic achieve-

[71] Chicago *Daily Socialist*, Sept. 3, 8, 10, 1908.
[72] *Ibid.*, Sept. 10, 1908.
[73] See Kipnis, *The American Socialist Movement*, 212, and Chicago *Daily Socialist*, Aug. 31, 1908.

A typical example of the crude but lurid cartooning
that filled the pages of most Socialist
periodicals and newspapers

(From *The Comrade*, Vol. 1)

No. 11.   Vol. I.

THE COMRADE

The Political Circus.

HOW LONG WILL LABOR REMAIN IN THAT POSITION?

A Ryan Walker cartoon

(From *The Comrade*, Vol. 1)

HELIOS

The Sunrise of Socialism.

An art nouveau reflection of Socialist
expectations in 1902

(From *The Comrade*, Vol. 1)

A typical Marxist cartoon depicting the stages
of history and forecasting the imminent
demise of capitalism

(From *The Comrade*, Vol. I)

ments of universal suffrage, free public schools, and freedom from imprisonment for debt.[74] None of these achievements, he reminded them, had been championed by the schoolbook heroes whose contemporary counterparts were such favorites of Gompers.

As election day drew near, the Socialists grew cautious in their predictions about the vote. The Red Special came back to Chicago on election eve and its weary travelers, after a final rally, went home to await the results of all their efforts. In 65 days Debs and his entourage had addressed an estimated 800,000 people. The venture had cost more than twice what had been originally estimated, and the difference had to be slowly eked out by the membership of the party.

Some optimists in the party claimed that two million votes would go to the Socialists. Victor Berger said they'd surely get a million and a half.[75] Simons was more guarded, but he predicted, in his editorials for the *Daily Socialist,* that the relentless march of socialism would be reflected by significant increases in the vote polled.

They were all sadly mistaken. William Howard Taft was elected with the blessings of Teddy Roosevelt and the American voter. Eugene Debs, loved by many but supported by few, ran little better than he had four years before. With Bryan in the field, Debs had not even been the sentimental favorite.

Betraying no hint of disappointment or discouragement, Simons quickly explained the vote to his readers. It was no surprise to those in the know, he claimed. People were reluctant to throw their vote to a man who had no chance to be elected; Bryan had stolen some of the reform vote; the recent financial panic had caused many men to move, thereby losing their voting eligibility. The election had cleared the air; Bryanism was now dead for sure: "Whether Socialists realize it or not," Simons declared, "the next few months are going to see the most rapid increase in the strength of the Socialist movement the United States has ever known."[76]

To the rank-and-file Socialists, who had been hearing this kind of

[74] Chicago *Daily Socialist*, Sept. 4, 5, 1908.
[75] Robert Hunter, "The Socialist Party in the Present Campaign," *Review of Reviews*, XXXVIII (Sept. 1908), 299.
[76] Chicago *Daily Socialist*, Nov. 6, 1908.

thing for years, the exhortation could not help but have a hollow ring. They paid their dues, contributed to campaign funds, read the interminable pleas to keep struggling publications afloat, and then were asked to believe that this greatest of all electoral disappointments was but a prelude to triumph.

Simons was still full of fight. He intended to see that his latest prophecy, however implausible, should be fulfilled. As he reflected upon the feeble condition of the party, he kept coming back to the fatal defect of socialist politics: it simply did not engage the enthusiasm of American workingmen. He did not believe that the fault lay in the fact that the party was led by intellectuals, for the most successful European socialist movements were so led. He did not think that the alternative lay at all near the revolutionary syndicalism of the Wobblies, for he believed that their methods were totally unacceptable to the great majority of Americans.

With other members of the National Executive Committee, therefore, Simons began to explore the possibility of some kind of working relationship between the Socialist party and the left wing of the AFL. His compatriots on the NEC were sympathetic with such an effort because they felt that however much the impossibilists of the party might squeal, this was the only crucible in which electoral success could be forged. Joining Simons were Robert Hunter, the millionaire New Yorker who was a pioneer in the discussion of poverty in America; John Spargo, the Cornish immigrant who had begun working a 40-hour week in the tin mines when he was ten years old; Morris Hillquit, the lawyer who had long fought the battles of the Lower East Side, and Victor Berger, Socialist "boss" of Milwaukee, and architect of the Socialist-AFL alliance that made the SP so successful in that city.

Still, there was need for caution. The feeling against such an alliance ran so high in some sectors of the party that even to loft the idea as a trial balloon was to court disaster. As the election results in the spring and fall of 1909 showed a continued drop in the socialist vote, and as party membership and receipts also plummeted —this for the first time ever—Simons wrote frankly to his old friend William English Walling about the situation: "There must be a reorganization of the S.P. That is almost unanimously agreed upon. It must be reorganized into a working class party, fighting every battle of the workers, all the time, and using every weapon. I do not like the English policy, but I say frankly it is better than the present S.P. It is doing something." The tone of the letter was far different from the whistling-in-the-dark of Simons' public declarations. It was a hardheaded look at what had to be done. "Unless we are able to so shape our policy and our organization," he continued to Walling, "as to meet the demands and incarnate the position of the workers, we will have failed of our mission." Simons described the changes that he and his colleagues on the NEC wanted to make: simplify the party machinery, appeal directly to union men, and rid the party of demagogues. "There are preparations under way," he concluded, "to bring about an internal revolution, and we will need all the brains at our disposal to steer through the shoals before us."[77]

Alas, Simons had made a poor choice of a confidant. Walling immediately began circulating the personal letter, together with his own interpretation of it, to selected members of the party whom he felt would be most outraged at its contents. As Walling chose to view the letter, it indicated the existence of a conspiracy to establish a labor party and to maintain in power the current membership of the NEC, no matter what the wishes of the party at large. Either one of these charges, if true, would have had an incendiary effect. The mere suggestion of political intrigue was sufficient to set off Socialist tempers, and when the conspiring partners were supposed to be the intellectuals at the head of the party and the despised AFL, holocaust was guaranteed.

Until this time, party disagreements had been modulated by the principle of local autonomy. A serious squabble in one state was not likely to ignite organizations in others. Now, however, the highest councils of the party were implicated in a supposed conspiracy, and locals across the country seethed with the conflict.

Simons was shocked. Though he was by now accustomed to the high pitch at which socialist political warfare was waged, he had

[77] Simons to Walling, Nov. 19, 1909, Socialist Party Collection.

never expected an attack to come from this quarter. Walling had been his friend and associate since Bureau of Charity days on the South Side of Chicago. After Laurence Simons had died, Walling had been one of those who helped make it possible for Algie and May to go abroad. Now he was engaging in the most disreputable sort of character assassination and was betraying the privacy of a personal letter to do so. "The thing that has shocked and pained," Simons wrote bitterly to his erstwhile friend, "as nothing I have had happen to me during my work in the Socialist movement, is the terrible revelation of the character of one in whom I have always had the most complete confidence. There was nothing whatever in the letter that I feared to have published. . . . But the way in which in your circular letter you tore the entire matter from its context, and the false interpretation you put upon my words were disreputable."[78]

The dispute continued as the time for NEC elections drew near. In a letter to the New York *Call*, Simons attempted to explain his position with respect to a labor party.[79] His only interest, he claimed—and the claim was consistent with both his public and his private discussions— was to make the Socialist party genuinely representative of the laboring people of the nation. The other members of the NEC, he continued, shared his desire: "They have endeavored to secure the election of men to the NEC who are active in the labor movement. They seem to have aroused the antagonism of some schemers by refusing to resign in favor of the politicians who have never been connected with the working class movement."

Nothing Simons could write, however, was sufficient to still the conflict, for such a struggle had been brewing for years. It was simply a transfer to the national level of the basic conflict between impossibilism and opportunism, and it was seasoned generously with the traditional socialist mistrust of politics and politicians. The idea that *anything* was going on behind closed doors was sufficient to enrage the party faithful. "Bossism" and machine politics were anathema. Here, in fact, was the nub of the problem. Walling knew that if he could

[78] Simons to Walling, Dec. 1, 1909, Socialist Party Collection.
[79] Dec. 9, 1909.

stir up enough distrust within the party, then perhaps even those who were ideologically in sympathy with the constructive Socialists on the NEC would become suspicious of their leadership and be moved to throw the rascals out. Walling also knew he did not even need a majority of the party to remove Spargo, Simons, Hunter, Berger, and Hillquit, for the voting system was preferential, and the candidates having the lowest number of votes were elected. In a field of many candidates, it was easy for a few voters to dump one or a few by giving them high numbers.

If Walling's hope had been to throw the party into the hands of the revolutionary Socialists, or impossibilists, then his effort was an utter failure. In the balloting for the NEC which was held early in 1910, the party membership clearly indicated their approval of moderation. There was, in fact, only one casualty in the whole affair—Algie Simons. He failed to be reelected to the NEC, and a few months later he lost his seat on the national committee and on the county committee of the party to his old antagonist Tommy Morgan. Simons was also forced from the editorship of the *Daily Socialist.* Privately, Walling wrote Eugene Debs that the election had seen the defeat of "the best of our opponents."[80]

In August 1910 Simons left Chicago and headed for Girard, Kansas, and a new job. His political career was at an end, for he had lost his major locus of power. In the years that he had been an important party figure, he had furnished much of the brains behind socialism's effort to enter the mainstream of American political life. If his abrasive manner and fierce determination had made the enemies that finally proved his political undoing, they were also the principal instruments that had given him the influence and the importance he did attain.

[80] Walling to Debs, Feb. 12, 1910, Socialist Party Collection. David Shannon, in his treatment of this incident (*The Socialist Party of America,* 63–66), assumes that there was a conspiracy among Simons, Berger, and others to take over the party. Extant correspondence in the Socialist Party Collection does contain hints of such a possibility. However, Gerald Friedberg presents evidence from the Spargo Papers to challenge Shannon's assumption ("Marxism in the United States," 87 ff.).

In his first decade as a Socialist, Simons had traversed the ideological ground from the shrill left of DeLeon's Socialist Labor party to the right-center position close to Victor Berger and his Milwaukee Social Democrats. He never discussed changing opinions in print, never chose to explain the circumstances that brought him to new conclusions. He seemed to view his shifts and tackings as simply the natural course of events, evaluated and altered by a steadily maturing judgment. In 1906 he had described "The Evolution of Socialists." Each new party member, he had written, begins as an enthusiastic convert who expects that revolution is imminent, capitalism's swift demise a certainty. The convert starts out as impossibilist and then becomes discouraged when the world moves on as always; if he is an intellectual, he becomes annoyed with the working class, who seem so sluggish in seeking their own liberation. Then as time passes, he discovers that social phenomena are much more complex than he once had thought. With that discovery, he is at a crossroad. "If he has real backbone," Simons concluded, "he will dig deeper and see the forces that are working for Socialism."[81]

Seen in this perspective, Simons, in his years as a party politician of influence, had taken a predictable course. Yet he was not as self-assured and self-approving as he liked to pretend. To the sympathetic outside observer, he had "the look of a man under severe nervous strain."[82] To the careful reader of Simons' editorials in the Chicago *Daily Socialist* and in the *International Socialist Review*, it must have seemed curious that a man so deeply enmeshed in party politics should attribute such base motives to party politicians.[83] To the political enemy it must have been almost irresistible to draw inferences

---

[81] "The Evolution of Socialists," *International Socialist Review*, VI (March 1906), 495.

[82] Charlotte Teller, "The National Socialist Convention," 33.

[83] See, for example, "Socialist Politicians," *International Socialist Review*, VII (April 1906), 625: "Instead of looking on himself as a servant of the party [the party functionary] begins to . . . act like a ruler." James C. Davies in *Human Nature in Politics* (New York: John Wiley, 1963), 45, observes: "It appears necessary for people when they seek to change practices no longer acceptable, as civilization advances by political processes, . . . to shield themselves from guilt by attributing insufferable motives within themselves to the evil ones."

from the shrillness with which Simons attacked the positions he had
lately left.[84]

In truth, the years of political struggle were almost wholly without
any reward but that of experience. They left Simons with a legacy of
broken friendships, vanished opportunities, and ignominious depar-
tures from important jobs. There was more than a little irony in the
fact that his very efforts to enhance the political appeal of the Socialist
party destroyed his own career as a politician. His years of party
prominence, moreover, coincided with the years of his greatest family
responsibilities, and these bore heavily upon him.

[84] See, for example, Simons' editorial, "The Impossibilist," *International
Socialist Review*, VII (June 1907), 809: "It often comes about that those who
constantly and ostentatiously pride themselves upon their 'Revolutionary'
attitude become the greatest obstacles to any forward movement, mere stumbling blocks on the road to progress. Lacking all ability to distinguish between
essentials and non-essentials, they cling fast to old forms of activity."

CHAPTER SIX

Kansas Exile

After the rugged conflicts of Chicago socialism, Girard, Kansas, promised to be a peaceful spot. Simons, though disappointed with his political losses, was enthusiastic about his new job. Julius Wayland, who had long published the *Appeal to Reason,* was beginning a related venture—a literary and artistic supplement to be called the *Coming Nation.* For years the *Appeal* had been filled with breathless stories about greedy and wicked capitalists, simple girls forced into lives of sin, and similar matter. It had been the perfect instrument for the serial publication of Upton Sinclair's *The Jungle.*

Now the management of the *Appeal* decided that it was time to give more attention to the happy aspects of American life. The *Coming Nation* was to be a literary magazine designed especially for socialist families, and in it there was to be nothing to offend the sensibilities of the party's most sheltered daughter. Optimism and uplift were to be the guiding spirits.

These wholesome intentions Simons could endorse wholeheartedly. He believed firmly in the preeminence of marriage and family. Over the years he wrote many articles explaining that the Cooperative Commonwealth, when it arrived, would in no way harm these sacred institutions. Among the Socialists, there were few who were his equal in vitriol, and few in a pugnacious lot who were as pugnacious as he. Like many masters of invective, however, he had quite another side to his temperament. He was always the loving husband and father who brought flowers to his wife and toys to his daughter.[1] He never expected his family to postpone happiness until the socialist millennium, and because he had never quite abandoned the culture of rural America when he repudiated capitalism, he sought through quite conventional means to make them happy.

He had moved his family to the pleasant Chicago suburb of Melrose Park in 1903, when Miriam was three years old. There, in a house with large sunny rooms, surrounded by a grassy lawn and garden, the Simonses had created the kind of life they would have lived if they had been back home in the village of Baraboo. With their neighbors they shared conversation quite different from what had prevailed back in the settlement house near the stockyards. In Melrose Park their neighbors talked not of transforming the economy but of transplanting flowers. Though their socialist friends had visited them at home, the Simonses created an island apart from ideology where they cultivated their garden, watched their daughter play in her sandpile, and now and then invited Grandmother Wood for a visit. It was an island they were to re-create several times during their lives, and it was for this environment that they yearned whenever they were without it.[2]

Simons once explained why he was not a radical with respect to social convention. "Social conventions per se," he wrote, "are neither good nor bad—the presumption is in their favor, especially when they have continued through many social stages, for this shows that they have played some part in social evolution."[3] May Simons felt even more strongly about such matters. She never quite approved of Upton Sinclair, because he had divorced his first wife and written a novel *Love's Pilgrimage,* describing the adulterous circumstances that led to the whole tangle.[4] Now, it seemed, the Simonses would have the chance to direct a publication devoted to the moral and social values they had long held dear.

For people who cherished the atmosphere and values of small-town America, Girard might well have seemed an ideal location and the *Coming Nation* a worthy endeavor. Located in the southeastern part of the state, Girard had a population of about 3,000. Although, like many towns of the American West, it had sought riches and fame

---

[1] May Simons, Diary, 1903–1904, records many such occasions.

[2] The foregoing account of the Simonses in Melrose Park is based upon the diary of May Wood Simons, Jan. 16, 1903–Nov. 11, 1904, Simons Papers.

[3] "After-Election Work," *International Socialist Review,* V (Dec. 1904), 304.

[4] Typescript comments of Miriam Simons Leuck, Simons Papers.

through a variety of small industries, its major source of income was the surrounding farms. Julius Wayland had brought the *Appeal to Reason* to Girard in 1897, but its presence there did little to change the fundamental nature of the town. It was small, conservative, and suspicious of unorthodox opinion. Wayland's children were jeered by their schoolmates and shunned by their neighbors.[5] Mining operations near Girard were begun shortly before Simons' arrival, however, and the immigrant labor they attracted created a socialist constituency where only rural Republicanism had previously existed.

Girard's greatest stir had come in 1908, when Henry Laurens Call, an inventor, presented himself to the editor of the *Appeal* with a plan to build an airplane large enough to fly a delegation from there to the Socialist party convention in Chicago. Some townspeople speculated that Call's real intent was even more radical—that he contemplated kidnapping the Czar of Russia and flying him to Girard, or that the *Appeal* sought to escape its periodic difficulties with the post office authorities by having the paper delivered by air.

The money for the project was raised by the *Appeal*, and thousands of visitors came to Girard for the airship's maiden voyage. Alas, however, the plane never got off the ground and after a short time the Aerial Navigation Company of America, Girard, Kansas, closed its doors forever.[6]

Simons liked Girard. Political speeches delivered in the courthouse square, farmers with their horses and wagons clattering through the dusty streets, and the profound change from the tempests of Chicago —all these awakened in Simons memories of his rural boyhood which, in spite of himself, he was investing with a vague nostalgia. "Tell Miriam we can find a place to put up a swing," he wrote to May, as he looked for a suitable house for the three of them.[7]

Simons was beginning his association with Julius Wayland's publi-

[5] Interview, Harold A. Trout with Walter Wayland, April 18, 1933, cited in Trout, "The History of the *Appeal to Reason*" (unpublished M.A. thesis, Kansas State Teachers College, 1934), 33.

[6] Willis Ernest Lamson, "The Historical Development of Girard, Kansas, and Its Community" (unpublished M.A. thesis, Kansas State Teachers College, 1933), 44–50.

[7] A. M. Simons to May Simons, Aug. 19, 1910, Simons Papers.

cations at a most auspicious time. Fred Warren, an experienced and capable journalist, was editing the *Appeal,* and the vigor of his attacks brought him into frequent collisions with the authorities. The results of these collisions could be measured in the impressively mounting circulation figures of the *Appeal.*

When Simons joined the organization, Warren was subject to a six-month jail sentence and a $1,500 fine. He had been found guilty of inciting to violence through the mails. Through a round of appeals and trials, Warren conducted his own defense, delivering passionate speeches exposing the class-character of the courts and claiming himself a victim of the double standard of justice in America. These legal battles were generously financed by Warren's loyal readers.

After he had been sentenced, the editor paid a visit to Leavenworth penitentiary, was shown what quarters he would occupy and the sort of work he would do while serving his time. Warren returned to Girard and proceeded to publish a series of articles in the *Appeal* exposing prison conditions. This effort was speedily rewarded with a new indictment—for sending obscene matter through the mails.[8] All the while, circulation climbed.

Simons was beginning to feel the onus of having been on the losing side of a number of ventures—the party battles, the *International Socialist Review,* and the always-floundering Chicago *Daily Socialist* —and he welcomed the chance to throw his lot with what appeared to be a winning proposition. He liked both Wayland and Warren at once. "They work on the plan of letting a man show what is in him," he explained to May, "and then if he does not make good get someone else. That is what suits me, and I think I will make good."[9]

Shortly after the *Coming Nation* began publication, Fred Warren presented himself to the jail where he was to serve his six months. He learned that the execution of the sentence had been delayed on orders from Washington. President Taft and Attorney General Wickersham had apparently decided that the publicity value of Warren's prison term would enhance the position of the *Appeal* and those connected

---

[8] Interview, Harold Trout with Fred Warren, in Trout, "The History of the *Appeal to Reason,*" 50–51.
[9] A. M. Simons to May Simons, Aug. 24, 1910, Simons Papers.

with it and would tend to make a martyr of the editor. Therefore a presidential pardon was issued for Warren.

Not to be outdone, Warren managed to have the last word: the pardon was not a union document and so he put a sticker on it which read "Demand the Label on All Your Printing" and sent it back to Washington. Shortly thereafter the subscription list of the *Appeal* passed the 500,000 mark and the first copy of the special issue that marked this event was sent to William Howard Taft.[10]

Simons was delighted with this show of bravado—"What would we do if it were not for our friends the enemy," he asked—and when his own *Coming Nation* hit a snag with the postal authorities he happily predicted rapid growth for the supplement in consequence.[11]

Rapid growth was essential. Julius Wayland, for all his radicalism, was a shrewd businessman who did not run his newspapers out of a spirit of charity. He had made the *Appeal to Reason* the greatest success in socialist publishing by a variety of ingenious promotions, Hearst-like titillations for the masses, and a wise choice of editorial writers. He and Fred Warren had inserted a clause in Simons' contract which declared that Warren could do anything he liked with the *Coming Nation* if it should fail to show a profit in two consecutive months. If Simons, dogged by previous failures in an uncertain business, had needed any additional spur to his ambitions, such a provision was certain to provide it.

He began at once to explore sources of material for the new publication. He wrote Richard Ely at Wisconsin, inquiring whether any students at the university might be interested in writing feature articles—short popular histories of labor unions, perhaps, together with accounts of what the union had accomplished—in order to defray the expenses of their education.[12] May Simons, chosen as a delegate to the Copenhagen Congress of the Second International in 1910, was highly successful in persuading their old friends among the European Socialists to contribute to the *Coming Nation*. Jean Longuet would

[10] Trout, "The History of the *Appeal to Reason*," 48–50, and Ginger, *The Bending Cross*, 304.

[11] A. M. Simons to May Simons, Feb. 2, 1911, Simons Papers.

[12] Simons to Ely, Aug. 25, 1910, Ely Papers.

secure articles from his contacts all over Europe. Hilja Parssinen, a socialist member of the Finnish Parliament would try to do an article each month and Karl Liebknecht, whom May met in Berlin after the congress had closed, offered his suggestions for the success of the paper.[13]

Simons also had access to the talents of Charles Edward Russell, the peripatetic Socialist, muckraker, and sometime political candidate, who did most of the editorials for the new publication. Russell, in addition to his duties on the *Coming Nation*, was a staff writer for Hearst and McClure and did a great deal of freelance work. Every six weeks or so he would come to Girard from New York or Washington and, in the musty atmosphere of the Appeal Building offices, argue about editorial policy with Simons. Despite their quarrels, Simons and Russell became close friends and their friendship endured for three decades. They were both men of wide interests and great ability and Russell had, in addition, a quality that was rare among the earnest spirits of the American Socialist party—a robust sense of humor. This was refreshing indeed, for whatever faults could be ascribed to the American Socialists of Simons' day, taking their mission too lightly was not one. The party had its sentimentalists, like Eugene Debs; it had its theoreticians, like Victor Berger; and it had its debaters, like Simons, but it had few men capable of offering humor.[14]

This, in fact, soon proved to be a problem with the *Coming Nation*. No matter how much its editors aspired to lighten the burdens of life through humorous and optimistic fiction, they found that nobody was writing any. The manuscripts that came to the editors' desks for consideration were more often in the tradition of Upton Sinclair than of anything particularly uplifting, and despite Simons' pleas the situation failed to change.[15] Simons and Fred Warren even had a fling at writing a short story together, perhaps in the hope of demonstrat-

---

[13] May Simons to A. M. Simons, Sept. 1, 4, 1910, Simons Papers.
[14] Simons' friendship with Russell is described by Miriam Simons Leuck in comments accompanying her father's correspondence, Simons Papers.
[15] Simons, "Socialist Writers and Capitalist Horrors," *Coming Nation*, Aug. 19, 1911, p. 3.

ing to their readers just what they had in mind. "We Are Brothers," it was called, and in the tradition of apocalyptic fiction it reached a stunning climax with socialist women on horseback riding between two armies, American and German, and persuading them to lay down their arms.[16] It was no better as prophecy than as literature.

More characteristic of Simons' work were the numerous articles he did on agriculture and the American farmer. Ever since the Unity Convention of 1901 he had been trying to refine an acceptable socialist program for the farmer, and when he took the editorship of the *Coming Nation* he gave the task a great deal of his time. It was no easy job. It is a commonplace that Marxism has never been able satisfactorily to come to grips with the problems raised by the farmer in a socialist society, but it is equally true that capitalist nations have had little better luck. In America secretaries of agriculture have often been the whipping boys of the administrations they served, and that cabinet post has been a political graveyard.

Simons had been grasping this particular nettle since the very beginning of his socialist career. In his early work he had analyzed the defects in Marx's treatment of the farm problem. Simons had been optimistic about the prospects of the small farmer, and had contended that he was not losing his land as Marx had claimed he must. In the *American Farmer*, published by Charles Kerr in 1902, Simons had insisted that the Socialists would not force the small farmer from his land either. Instead, the farmer himself would come to see the advantages of voluntary collectivization and would join willingly in cooperative efforts.

Simons' faith that American farmers would so decide was based in large part upon his almost romantic view of the wisdom and virtue of the sturdy American yeoman. Where other Socialists might become sentimental about the nobility and strength of the industrial proletariat, Simons bestowed his most lavish praise and his most ardent admiration upon the homesteader of the American frontier. "These men were naturally fighters," he had written in 1903, "indeed they were the picked fighters of the nation. They [had struck] once or

[16] *Ibid.*, May 6, 1911, pp. 3–4.

twice against intolerable social conditions in the East, finally gave up
. . . and endured the sufferings of blizzard and isolation in order that
they might form a new society."[17] Men like these would surely fight
for socialism as they had once fought for their homesteads. The
sagacity that had alerted them to the hopelessness of staying in the
East would soon make them see that it was just as hopeless to seek
security under capitalism.

The omissions in all this were considerable. Even if it were true
that the American frontier had produced a special kind of farmer, he
was not the only kind of man on the land in America. In the South
there were tenants and sharecroppers, black and white. In all sections
there were agricultural laborers and migrants. In many areas once
homesteaded, the self-sufficient family farm had given way to highly
specialized operations—bonanza farms in the Dakotas, dairy operations in Wisconsin, cattle-raising on the Great Plains. The needs of
the southern sharecroppers were very different from the needs of a
dairyman, even though both might harbor deeply felt grievances
against the government.

Simons recognized the existence of these differences, and in the
American Farmer he detailed them with some precision. When it
came down to formulating a program that would attract rural Americans to socialism, however, he concentrated upon the midwestern
farmowner—upon the man he thought most characteristically American.

Politically, this was a sound move.[18] Such farmers already possessed
a tradition of political dissent, and they were more likely converts
than disenfranchised Negroes and migrants who were entirely outside
the fabric of American society.

To cast his net in this way laid Simons open to the charge that he
cared nothing for the fate of the little fish and that he was merely
plying the waters of the Populists. In 1908, at the Socialist National
Convention, Simons had reported for the study commission that was

[17] "Populism and the Farmer of Today," *Appeal to Reason*, Jan. 24, 1903.
[18] It was suggested by Karl Kautsky, when he reviewed "The American
Farmer," in *Die Neue Zeit*. Simons reprinted the review in the *International
Socialist Review*, III (Sept. 1902), 156–60.

working on a farm program. The delegates added a plank that called for the collective ownership of all land. They brushed aside Simons' objections that this plank would scare off the farmers who looked to political parties to protect their holdings. A referendum the following year put the matter in Simons' favor again: the party membership agreed that all who used their land in a "useful and bona fide manner" should be allowed to retain it.[19]

The problem was engaged once more at the 1910 party congress, and again Simons was accused of being "populistic," because he advocated government aid, not dispossession, for the farmer. Once more the issue was remanded to the committee for further study, with a report scheduled for the 1912 nominating convention.[20]

All the while, agriculture itself was changing, and in the *Coming Nation* Simons analyzed these modifications and tried to determine how they should shape the farm policy of the Socialist party. He found that his early assumptions about the viability of the small farm were no longer justified. Scientific advances in agricultural chemistry were removing many of the risks that had formerly plagued the farmer, and developments in farm mechanization were replacing muscle with machinery at an ever-increasing rate. Both sets of innovations made agriculture more attractive for the investment of large-scale capital, and the expense and complexity of the new machinery made it unlikely that any but large-scale operators could make use of them. Simons also pointed out that the price of farmland had doubled since 1900. All this made it clear to him that the country boy had about as much chance of becoming a farmowner as the factory worker had of becoming an entrepreneur. Marx had been right after all: concentration would take place in agriculture as it had in all other sectors of the economy. The small farmer was doomed.[21]

It was too bad, but it was inevitable. Simons was no golden age worshiper, despite his admiration for the frontier farmer, and rather than

[19] *Daily Socialist*, June 24, Sept. 15, 1909.
[20] *Proceedings of Socialist Party National Congress, 1910*, pp. 228–46.
[21] Simons, "The Farm That Is Coming," *Coming Nation*, Nov. 4, 1911, pp. 3–4; "The Agricultural Revolution," *ibid.*, July 20, 1912, pp. 5–7, 12; July 27, 1912, pp. 5, 7; Aug. 3, 1912, pp. 5, 6, 12.

wasting time lamenting what was being lost, he turned his attention to the positive aspects of the trends he discovered in American agriculture. One of socialism's great attractions for Simons had always been its promise of rationality—its hatred of waste in human, natural, and industrial resources. It was possible to view the twentieth-century agricultural revolution in America as a major step toward the elimination of waste and the increase of efficiency in this sector of the economy. That noble pioneer family, however heroic its struggles, had never been motivated by large designs. In its westward progress across the continent it had murdered the Indians, destroyed the timber, and exhausted the soil. Now all that could be changed.

Government at all levels, Simons wrote, ought to end the sale of land and begin buying up all acreage that became available. Land so acquired ought to be farmed according to the most advanced methods, and experimental farms ought to be established on which new methods could be tried and perfected. The government ought also to set up processing facilities—creameries, packing plants, grain elevators, and the like—which would pay their workers for the full value of the labor. Consumers would benefit from the efficiencies thus introduced, by paying lower prices for food and other agricultural products.[22]

What this amounted to, as Simons saw it, was government acceleration of a process that was already under way. It was a way of making collectivization look attractive to farmers who still tried to believe they were independent while they groaned under burdens of mortgage debt and high transportation and storage rates. Simons believed that such farmers would ultimately welcome the opportunity to sell their holdings to the government and become part of larger, more efficient, and better-rewarded operations.

In all these articles on agriculture Simons was writing with a twofold purpose. On the one hand, he sought to arouse the farmers who read the *Coming Nation* to an awareness of socialism's promise. At the same time, he sought to convince the eastern wing of the party that such agitation was both necessary and fruitful. Whenever the

---

[22] "The Program for the Farmers," *Coming Nation*, June 1, 1912; "Taking the Little Farmer's Farm," *Coming Nation*, Feb. 15, 1913.

subject had been brought up at party conventions, the Easterners had tended to regard propaganda work among rural people as a deviation from the central purposes of Marxian socialism. Simons knew it was not.

May Simons also wrote regularly for the *Coming Nation*. Like her husband, she tried her hand at a short story. "Ground in the Mill" appeared in the first issue of the new magazine and was anything but the fulfillment of the publication's promise of "optimistic" literary fare. It traced the withering away of a young lady who made button-holes. The villain was capitalism. With this out of her system, May Simons went on to do several good solid articles on education, attempting to familiarize a segment of the lay public with what might be done in the schools if the Socialists could shape educational policy.

The system of public education, she said, was the one existing institution, besides the family, that should be retained after the over-throw of capitalism. As the schools were presently conducted, they encouraged "uniformity [and] mediocrity, not . . . individuality, inventiveness or original thought." As they would be conducted in the Cooperative Commonwealth they would nurture freedom and self-expression. Children would attend meetings of the town council, in order to see democracy at work. The schools themselves would be self-governing, and discipline would be at a minimum. "No one," she claimed "ever saw disorder among those who are interested in a useful piece of work."[23]

Public education administered by Socialists would not seek to make every child identical with every other. On the contrary, it would seek out and encourage the students of talent and genius and guarantee that there should be no more mute inglorious Miltons crushed by the burdens of environment. Socialism would liberate the minds of the young.[24]

[23] May Simons, "Building a New School System," *Coming Nation*, June 10, 1911.
[24] May Simons, book review of Boris Sidis, *Philistine and Genius*, in *Coming Nation*, July 29, 1911, and "The School That Is Coming," *ibid.*, May 4, 1912.

It all sounded a good deal like what John Dewey had been saying, but May Simons knew and admired Maria Montessori's work as well, though the Italian educator was not really discovered in America until a generation later. She quoted with approval Montessori's poignant description of the school pupils of her day, like "butterflies mounted to each desk, spreading the useless wings of barren and meaningless knowledge which they have acquired."[25]

These articles, like her husband's, confirmed the fact that the *Coming Nation* was diverging considerably from its original intentions. However much they might try to concentrate upon describing the society of the socialist future, they always seemed drawn back to detailing the wretchedness of the present. They were following in the familiar path of the muckraking magazines. "Mining Coal and Maiming Men" exposed Kansas' Governor Stubbs' failure to enforce mining regulations.[26] "Pestilence, Flood and Federal Judges" attacked a landgrab that now threatened large areas with river flooding.[27]

As time passed, the careful reader could also detect a growing sophistication in the magazine. The *Coming Nation* had from the beginning claimed to be a literary and artistic periodical, and gradually it was becoming one. Unfortunately, neither of its editors had any particular qualifications for directing a venture of this kind. They had therefore concentrated upon making their magazine "wholesome." There had been a page for children, including games and puzzles along with moral tales about socialist worthies. There had been a women's column and weekly advice on growing vegetables in the home garden.

The fiction published had not been distinguished and sometimes it hadn't even been wholesome. Emanuel Julius turned out a "short short story" for nearly every issue and tried with faint success to master the O. Henry ending. Worse even than Algie and May Simons' respective efforts at fiction and a fair measure of the *Coming Nation*'s early literary standards was Ralph Korngold's story "Good

---

[25] "The School That Is Coming."
[26] May Simons, *Coming Nation*, Nov. 11, 1911.
[27] A. M. Simons, *Coming Nation*, Feb. 3, 1912.

Intentions." Korngold unfolded the tale of a young girl offered a great deal of money to model in the nude for an art class. Realizing that this was the sure road to prostitution, the heroine bravely returned to her job in the laundry instead. There she lost her fingers in the mangle and had to become a prostitute anyway—but one favored only by the lowest patrons.[28] No reader of this sort of fare would believe that the *Coming Nation* would be the rock upon which a great twentieth-century literature would be built.

Yet in the months that followed it was possible to discern a gradual change in the magazine's cultural aspirations. It was evident first in the artwork. The format was changed to give greater prominence to illustrations. Russell's editorials were moved from the cover to the second page, and a full-page illustration was used each week on page one. Sometimes the covers were of dubious distinction, as when the *Coming Nation* presented the first "genuine unretouched" photo of elderly and wizened John D. Rockefeller and implied that his ugly appearance was caused by his lifetime of evil. More often, the covers were first-rate drawings by John Sloan, Ryan Walker, or Art Young, and they were drawings more subtle in conception than the customary socialist staple of obese capitalists and bony child laborers. Early in 1912 J. B. Larric contributed an appreciative article on John Sloan in which the artist was given an opportunity to explain the esthetics of his work and that of other realists.[29]

At the same time, the *Coming Nation* began to eliminate some of its Sunday-supplement aspects and to strengthen its intellectual content. The children's page was the first to go. With it went the perennial "Socialist Scouts" column, which had hitherto reported the successes of little children in signing up new subscribers. The joke department, which had long resembled nothing so much as a page from a Grand Ole Opry script, was much curtailed. The vegetable-growing column ceased.

The articles of serious purpose began to indicate an interest in modern currents of thought. May Simons' articles on education dis-

---

[28] Ralph Korngold, "Good Intentions," *Coming Nation*, Aug. 19, 1911.
[29] J. B. Larric, "John Sloan," *Coming Nation*, Jan. 6, 1912.

played a sound grasp of Dewey's pedagogical theories. The eugenics movement, which was beginning to engage the minds of the progressive generation, was treated both fictionally and analytically in the *Coming Nation*.[30]

The magazine also began to diverge from its sister publication, the *Appeal to Reason*, which, however successful, was never either dignified or sophisticated. The *Appeal*'s juxtaposition of advertisements for get-rich-quick schemes and articles denouncing the profit motive was only its most blatant surrender of virtue. Lacking a financial angel, the *Coming Nation* did spend tiresome amounts of space urging subscribers to keep the faith and promising new literary marvels just over the horizon.

This is not to suggest that the *Coming Nation* would have necessarily been a powerful force for artistic and intellectual innovation if it had not been obliged to pay its own way. Its editors had neither the training nor the instincts of cultural groundbreakers. In Simons' case it was the plea of a journalist who thought he knew what he needed to hold his subscribers. Simons only hoped that the fiction of the *Coming Nation* would provide the sugar coating that would make the serious expository articles more palatable.

In years to come, radical literary magazines were to become something quite different. The most famous of them, the *Masses*, edited by Max Eastman beginning in 1912, distinguished itself as an instrument of the radical intelligentsia. In its pages appeared some of the earliest work of Sherwood Anderson, Vachel Lindsay, William Carlos Williams, Randolph Bourne, and a host of others.[31] The artists of the ashcan school—John Sloan, Art Young, and Stuart Davis among them—found a welcome for their drawings and cartoons at a time when the Gibson girl was the subject most sought after by the mass-circulation magazines. The *Masses* became the extreme Left of what Henry May has called the "innocent rebellion" that seems to

[30] Alice S. Geddes, "The Race in the Running," April 8, 1911, combined social criticism and biological elitism by telling of a wealthy, successful, selfish couple who had defective genes.

[31] Max Eastman lists many more in his autobiography, *Enjoyment of Living* (New York: Harper, 1948), 408*n*.

have taken place in American intellectual life between 1912 and 1917.[32]

Surprisingly enough, several of the significant innovations that both Max Eastman and subsequent historians have attributed to the *Masses* were really made by the *Coming Nation* a year or two earlier.[33] It, not the *Masses*, was the first American magazine to break with the sentimental and genteel traditions of magazine cover art. It, not the *Masses*, was the first to treat illustrations and cartoons as central to the publication's purposes, and not merely as afterthoughts squeezed into the squares and corners left over after the serious matter of the periodical had been set forth. Thanks to the wry wit of Charles Edward Russell, the *Coming Nation* also preceded Eastman's magazine in tempering politics and propaganda with humor. It preceded the *Masses* also in its decision to abstain from all party controversies.[34]

In addition to all this, what can be seen in the *Coming Nation* is the beginning of an important transition in American radicalism. Until around 1912, socialism was tied tightly to politics and economics. Far from being interested in intellectual or artistic innovation, the Socialists did their best to convince Americans that the Cooperative Commonwealth would bring the triumph of the noblest of existing values. True democracy would become a reality. The family would be strengthened and public morality would be improved.

In years to come, literary radicalism was to mean something quite different. Abandoning the effort to give reading matter to a mass public, the radical little magazines were to reverse the stance of Simons, Russell, and the *Coming Nation*. The radical editors of the

---

[32] Henry May, *The End of American Innocence* (New York: Knopf, 1959), 314–17.

[33] Eastman lists the *Masses'* innovations in *Enjoyment of Living*, 411–21, and repeats them in his afterword to William L. O'Neill's anthology of work from the *Masses, Echoes of Revolt* (Chicago: Quadrangle, 1966), 301–303. Among those who have accepted his claims are Willard Thorp, "American Writers on the Left," in *Socialism in American Life*, ed. Donald Drew Egbert and Stow Persons (Princeton: Princeton University Press, 1952), I, 604, and May, *The End of American Innocence*, 314–17.

[34] A paragraph by Eugene Debs on the front page of the first issue announced that the new periodical would not take part in factional conflicts. *Coming Nation*, Sept. 10, 1910.

next generation were to be accused of political and economic naivete along with their literary and artistic avant-gardism. In 1912 and 1913, however, there was little in the experience of Eastman, Russell, or Simons to suggest the possibility of such a reversal. There was, in fact, little to suggest the distinction that the *Masses* would achieve or the oblivion that would swallow the *Coming Nation,* for in those years they were much alike.

Though his magazine was steadily improving in quality and his own competence as an editor was being enlarged, Simons had by 1912 grown discontented in Kansas. The charms of Girard, of which he had once written so warmly, faded quickly. Peace and tranquillity had seemed desirable when the Simonses came fresh from the exhausting conflicts of Chicago. But now Crawford County, Kansas, with its steaming summers, its crabbed and dreary social and cultural life, and its vast distance from the centers of socialist activity made Algie and May feel that Girard was exile, not paradise regained.

For a while it had seemed pleasant to hold down only one job, to go out only occasionally on propaganda missions for the party, and to have time for reflection and research. Simons was able to finish up the American history he had been writing for years; in 1911 *Social Forces in American History* was published. The book was a survey from the age of discovery through the reconstruction period, and the ideas in it were much the same as those in *Class Struggles in American History,* in "American History for the Workers," and in a series of articles he had written for the *Progressive Journal of Education.*[35] His tone, though, was more moderate in *Social Forces.* He admitted that he was writing as a Marxist, and he found capitalist conspiracy to be the engine of American development, but he was so temperate in expressing these assumptions that some reviewers did not even recognize the book as a socialist document.[36]

Even with the book to finish and the *Coming Nation* to edit, Algie

[35] A. M. Simons, "A New Interpretation of American History," *Progressive Journal of Education,* Dec. 1908–June 1910, vols. I and II.

[36] See, for example, *Chicago Inter-Ocean,* Dec. 2, 1911 (clipping in Simons Papers), which called the book an "enlightened interpretation without . . . political partisanship."

and May had time for violin and piano lessons and an occasional movie. But these were the activities of a retired couple. The Simonses were still young and they grew increasingly restive at the realization that the stage of their activity had become so constricted. They began to long even for the sound of socialist voices raised in wrath, and for the company of spirited people who waged pitched battles over more than mailing privileges.[37]

Their eagerness to return to the mainstream of party life was intensified as they watched the surprising success of Socialist party candidates all over the country. After the disappointing showing in the 1908 presidential election and the slight drop in party membership between 1908 and 1909, striking advances appeared in the contests of 1910. Socialist mayors were elected in Milwaukee and Schenectady, and Victor Berger was elected to a seat in Congress—the first time a Socialist had ever attained so high an office in America. By the spring of 1912, the party reported that 1,039 socialists were currently holding elective office, all but twenty of them in municipalities. At the same time, it was reported that party membership had more than doubled since 1910.[38]

Simons still had access to the Socialist National Convention of 1912, though not as a delegate. He was to present the report of the Farmer's Committee. His wife was a delegate from Kansas and a member of the woman's national committee as well, so both made the trip to Indianapolis in May 1912.

Electoral successes had not banked the fires of conflict within the party. On the contrary, they had had an incendiary effect, for each candidate who attained office within the structure of capitalist society implicitly raised anew the question of whether he had been true to the cause. The revolutionary wing of the party was prepared to cry "opportunism" at every turn, and that wing had been gaining in power since 1911, when Big Bill Haywood had been elected to the National Executive Committee.

Six months before the convention opened, an unhappy occurrence

---

[37] Diary of May Wood Simons, Dec. 25, 1912.
[38] *Proceedings of 1912 Socialist Convention, Indianapolis, May 12–18, 1912*, p. 219.

made a collision between the left and right wings of the party virtually inevitable. In October 1910, twenty persons had been killed in an
explosion in the Los Angeles *Times* building. John and James McNamara, two union leaders, were arrested and charged with having
thrown a bomb into the building. Both the Socialist party and the AFL
had raised funds for the defense of the McNamara brothers; Eugene
Debs made a speaking tour protesting their innocence; Algie Simons
wrote crusading articles reminding his readers of other classic miscar-
riages of capitalist justice. Then, late in 1911, the McNamaras confessed to the crime.

It was, to say the least, embarrassing. To the right wing of the
Socialist party, especially those tasting the pleasures of office holding,
the McNamara case seemed a good deal more: it seemed to threaten
all that the Socialists had won. For years the party's soapboxers had
tried desperately to disabuse Americans of the notion that radicals
were necessarily wild-eyed, or that revolution meant going to the
barricades. Simons had frequently explained that ballots not bullets
would usher in the Cooperative Commonwealth, and he had taken
particular pains to show the differences between anarchism, with its
dedication to violence, and socialism, which had essentially peaceable
aims.[39]

It was clear that the McNamara case had damaged the movement.
Job Harriman, the Socialist party candidate for mayor of Los Angeles, had been granted an even chance to win the election, but the
McNamara confession came five days before the balloting, and Harriman was soundly defeated. Therefore the right wing at the Indianapolis convention decided it was time publicly to disavow acts of violence
and to drive from the party all those who supported socialism of "the
deed." After bitter debate an amendment to the party constitution
was passed: "Any member of the party who opposes political action,
or advocates crime, sabotage or other methods of violence as a weapon
of the working class to aid in its emancipation shall be expelled from
membership in the party. Political action shall be construed to mean

[39] See, for example, "Anarchy vs. Socialism," *International Socialist Review*,
II (Oct. 1901), 241–50.

participation in elections for public office and practical legislative and administrative work along the lines of the Socialist party platform."[40] The party had set the stage for its first purge.

Simons was sympathetic with the party's decision.[41] Like everyone else he had been startled by the McNamara confession. In his public declarations he emphasized the environmental circumstances that made the McNamaras desperate enough to turn to violence, and he accused the attorneys of timing the confession so it would do the most harm to the socialist cause. Nevertheless he knew perfectly well that the party would be tarred with the brush of the *Times* bombing.[42] He had spent too much time helping the Socialist party to arrive at its present state of promise to be overly tolerant of misdeeds among the faithful.

Even though he agreed with the majority on this point, his role in the convention was far from that of a peacemaker. His presentation of the farm program precipitated a debate that lasted a day and a half. There were delegates who believed it was a mistake even to waste time developing socialism's appeal to the landowning farmer. "We have so many irons in the fire," Henry Slobodin insisted, "and the getting of the movement to the proletariat is so important that we are not ready to take up this agricultural problem. Let us first approach the wage slave."[43] Slobodin was also disturbed that Simons had left agricultural laborers out of the program.

Simons had his defenders. One after another of the party's rural propagandists rose to urge the program's adoption. They had spoken before weeklong socialist encampments, sold pamphlets and subscriptions, enrolled new members in the party, and heard the grievances of men and women on the land. "We are just as radical as you are," a Texas delegate declared; "we stand for what you people of the north stand for, but you have never had to contend with the Bourbon

[40] *Proceedings, Socialist Party Convention of 1912*, p. 199.
[41] He had attacked the Leftists and Bill Haywood in articles written for the Chicago *Daily Socialist* even before the convention opened. See *Daily Socialist*, Dec. 26, 1911, April 20, 1912.
[42] A. M. Simons, "Los Angeles and Its Lesson," *Coming Nation*, Dec. 16, 1911.
[43] *Proceedings, 1912*, p. 75.

democracy of the South." "Farmers in Minnesota have been told," Delegate Morgan from that state added, "that Socialism will allow them to keep their own little house, lot and patch of land. . . . This has brought them into the movement."[44]

One purge was enough. No one had the heart to turn his back on successes already won among a difficult constituency, and so Simons' program, modified slightly, was finally adopted. It was essentially the same policy that he had been urging in his articles for the *Coming Nation,* and it was to remain socialist doctrine throughout the prolonged agricultural slump of the 1920s and 1930s. It frightened no one among the farmers, because it threatened no one with dispossession. It foresaw quite accurately a continuing process of agricultural concentration and it promised ultimately to turn those forces to the benefit of the very farmers who now suffered under them. To the tenant farmers it promised that "all farm land not cultivated by owners shall be taxed at its full rental value and that eventually actual use and occupancy shall be the only title to land."

Simons' farm program placed a great deal of emphasis upon the efforts that state and national government ought to make to acquire land, and upon the educational functions that socially operated farms could perform. Cooperatives, crop insurance, and government ownership of transportation and storage facilities were also urged, and they had a familiar ring to men and women who had followed the Populists through the campaigns of the 1890s.[45] Finally, still seeking to keep conflict to a minimum, the program concluded with a broad concession to localism: "to each section and to each state must be left the task of working out the further details of a program applicable to the peculiar agricultural conditions in their respective states and districts." It was ample testimony to the distance that American Socialists had traveled since the heyday of Daniel DeLeon.

In other respects, they were still the prisoners of the nineteenth century. Nowhere was this more evident than in the party's testy and reluctant handling of the work of the woman's national committee.

[44] *Ibid.*
[45] The complete text of the farm program appears in Appendix D of *ibid.,* 192.

By 1912 it was evident that women would soon have the vote—they already had it in some states, and it seemed only a matter of time before a constitutional amendment secured a nationwide suffrage. May Simons had long viewed this potential constituency. Just as her husband tried continually to make the party aware of the importance of the farm vote, so she had attempted with comparable determination to convince the Socialists that women, too, had grievances that could be met in the Cooperative Commonwealth.

Her male colleagues found the whole matter a bit distasteful. The very existence of a separate woman's national committee exemplified their desire to provide separate but equal facilities for women in the party. When, at the convention of 1912, May Simons delivered the report of her committee, she included a number of recommendations for vocational education—a subject she had studied extensively. Complaints were heard at once that this constituted "meddling" in matters that should not concern the woman's committee. Comrade Goebel of New Jersey observed that the women might offer recommendations on the conduct of the socialist Sunday schools, but vocational education was quite out of their line.[46]

Such remarks were doubly irritating because May Simons was no militant suffragette parading about in mannish suits or dropping leaflets from balloons. Neither did her report even hint that women ought to look to a larger world than hearth and home for their fulfillment. "The first duty of a housewife," the report declared, "is to her children, husband and home."[47] The aim of socialist propaganda among women was to assure them that socialism would strengthen the family, which had for so long been eroded by capitalism. The most radical aspect of her own behavior in regard to women's rights was her occasional use of the feminist-approved form of her name—May Wood–Simons.

She did have her supporters in the party. She came close to being elected to the National Executive Committee, running ninth in a contest to choose seven members.[48] So discouraged did she become,

[46] *Ibid.*, 28–29.
[47] *Ibid.*, 114.
[48] *Socialist Party Official Bulletin*, VIII, Jan. 1912.

however, at the SP's neglect of the work of the woman's committee, that in 1915 she resigned in protest.[49]

All in all, the 1912 convention was a notable success. Seeing their old comrades of Chicago days made Algie and May even more eager to end their Kansas exile. Their daughter provided them with an additional reason. Miriam finished grade school in 1912, and the quality of secondary education in Girard was not such as to inspire confidence, especially in her mother, who knew all too well that exciting innovations were being made in schools in other places. In Girard, the buildings were dilapidated, the teachers were ill-prepared, and the books and supplies were inadequate. May Simons had put considerable energies behind the effort to make the citizens of Crawford County aware of just how poorly their children were being educated. She ran for county superintendent of schools and lost by only 200 votes. On behalf of the Girard Socialist party local, she wrote a pamphlet, "The Condition of the Girard Schools," in which she tried to stimulate interest in the problem.[50] The physical decay of the schools, she claimed, had gone so far that new construction ought to be begun at once. It wasn't, and in 1916 one of the schools burned down.[51]

In November 1912 Julius Wayland, claiming oddly in this year of Progressive and Socialist promise that the struggle against capitalism had made him too weary to go on singlehandedly, committed suicide. Fred Warren then took over as publisher of the Wayland enterprises, and Simons succeeded in persuading him that the *Coming Nation* would more likely prosper if its headquarters were moved to Chicago. There, Simons contended, the technical resources needed for such a magazine were more readily and more cheaply at hand.[52]

The argument in favor of economy was persuasive because the new venture had by no means approached the success of the *Appeal*. Throughout the year Simons had eyed the circulation figures nervously, and his letters to May, who was away on speaking tours,

[49] M. W. Simons to Winnie Branstetter, chairman, Woman's National Committee, Dec. 21, 1914, *American Socialist*, Jan. 9, 1915.
[50] 1912; a copy is in the Simons Papers.
[51] Lamson, "The Historical Development of Girard," 88.
[52] "On to Bigger Things," *Coming Nation*, Jan. 18, 1913, p. 13.

betrayed his growing concern. "The *Coming Nation* is still not doing very well," he had confessed in March, "but hope to ginger it up soon." "The income on the *Appeal*," he added a few days later, "is very good, but the *Coming Nation* is not doing so very well, because it has not had any pushing since I went to New York. We will give it a boost this week or next at the latest."[53]

The habit of talking of this enterprise as though its success or failure depended solely upon him was both pervasive and ominous. Paradoxically, this man who had so recently argued in his historical writing that the individual could do little that was not determined by forces outside himself, acted quite otherwise in his personal life. He committed himself passionately to each of his undertakings; if it succeeded, he was eager to point out his personal share in it; if it failed, he felt the failure deeply. These were two faces of the same idea—the idea of self-reliant individualism which rested great burdens upon the shoulders of those who accepted it.

By June the *Coming Nation* had still not been "gingered up" enough to improve circulation, and in that month, on the sixteenth anniversary of his marriage, Simons wrote sadly to his wife, "I fear I have not made you happy. But I will promise to do better every day in the future."[54] Compounding his sadness was the realization that the two journalistic ventures that had preceded this one and from which he had been removed—the *International Socialist Review* and the *Daily Socialist*—were now prospering. Both had changed radically in character in order to attain their success, and the prosperity of the *Daily Socialist* was but the prelude to total extinction.[55] In mid-1912, however, these two flourishing periodicals stood in stark contrast to the struggling *Coming Nation* and its editor's frequent appeals for support and subscriptions.

Warren agreed to the move, and the Simonses happily left the

[53] A. M. Simons to May Simons, March 1, 4, 1912, Simons Papers.
[54] *Ibid.*, June 15, 1912.
[55] A newspaper strike closed down all other Chicago papers in 1912 and the *Daily Socialist* added 300 to its staff, put out two editions a day, and borrowed a great deal of money from nonsocialist sources who then assumed control of editorial policy. The expansion was too ambitious, however, and the creditors foreclosed by the end of 1912.

plains of Kansas behind them.[56] The change may have been beneficial to the family, but it did little for the publication. In both April
and May of 1913, the *Coming Nation* lost money, and Fred Warren,
under the terms of the contract with Simons, suspended the magazine
without further ado. The editor was stunned. He could not believe
that Warren would actually exercise this prerogative without at least
making the effort to inform the magazine's readership about its
financial troubles. Socialist journalists were accustomed to the ways of
deathbed rescue: hardly a year went by, even among the old standbys
of the party press, without at least one front-page prediction of
imminent demise unless loyal readers came to the rescue with new
subscriptions, donations, or advertisements. That the *Coming Nation*
should be permitted to go under without such an effort being made on
its behalf was unthinkable to Simons.

Thus it was that he became once more embroiled in a violent
controversy. He sought to prove to the party as a whole that the
Coming Nation had been deliberately destroyed because of the cupid-
ity of its owners. His theory was that Warren and Wayland had
never been interested in the march of socialism but only in lining their
own pockets. They had established the supplement he headed only in
order to increase their profits, and when the *Coming Nation* failed to
match the circulation of its companion publication, Warren and Wayland's heirs decided to waste no more time letting it prove itself. The
whole affair, Simons claimed, was "one of the worst pieces of fraud on
the Socialists I have known of."[57]

Simons at once sent letters to the party National Executive Committee in order to familiarize them with the details of the matter.
"The general integrity of the Socialist movement," he explained,
"requires that you should at least know something of the conditions
that led to the killing of the *Coming Nation*."[58] Among the more
startling revelations of the letter was Simons' claim that Warren had

[56] May Simons, Diary, Jan. 17, 1913.
[57] A. M. Simons to Victor Berger, June 14, 1913, Milwaukee Socialist
Party Papers, Milwaukee County Historical Society, Milwaukee, Wis.—
hereafter cited as Milwaukee SP Papers.
[58] A. M. Simons to National Executive Committee, June 14, 1913, in
Milwaukee SP Papers.

falsified the books in order to hide the fact that the *Coming Nation* had assets in excess of liabilities and that it had made a profit of over $4,000 in its last six months. At the same time, he continued, it had received only $44.81 from the *Appeal* and therefore could hardly be considered a financial drain upon that publication. Simons wrote:

"When I asked that the National Office at least be permitted to consider the possibility of publishing the paper Fred D. Warren telegraphed that the Party could have the paper only upon payment of a sum of between $21,000 and $28,000.

"It seems to me that to have our press in hands that will use it to such ends, and crush it for such reasons is a danger that should at least be recognized by the officials of the Party."[59]

The NEC agreed to hear a confrontation between Simons and Warren, but the national committee overruled it, saying that it was a private matter in which the Socialist party neither could nor should have any voice. Upon hearing this verdict, Simons' fury mounted. He circularized the entire committee, this time charging that the truth was being smothered by "members of the National Committee, who are most closely in touch with Warren, and who are now, or have been, more or less dependent upon him for favors."[60]

This time all the steam in the controversy was furnished by Simons. The party firmly refused to take sides in the matter, and Warren himself, though avowedly willing to confront Simons before official bodies of the party, made his printed reply in a restrained and temperate manner.

Simons was entirely sincere in his belief that he and the *Coming Nation* had been deliberately scuttled. In his letters to May he made the same charges as in his public accusations. "Do not worry about Warren," he told May, "we are on the right side and we cannot lose."[61] "The N.E.C. is a bunch of cowards," he declared, "and dared not offend the *Appeal*."[62] "They are undoubtedly scheming," he

[59] *Ibid.*
[60] Quoted by Patrick S. Nagle to Simons, Aug. 22, 1913, *ibid.* The controversy and Warren's response to Simons are in "Why the *Coming Nation* Suspended," *Appeal to Reason*, June 28, 1913; *Party Builder*, June 28, July 19, 1913.
[61] A. M. Simons to May Simons, July 10, 1913, Simons Papers.
[62] *Ibid.*, July 16, 1913.

wrote of the National Committee, "as is everyone else, but the rest of that force is not to be relied upon for an impartial judgment. They have been laying [*sic*] down on the job too long."[63]

The conspiracies that he had been expounding for years in his propaganda for the party he had now begun to find within the party itself. The evidence for his accusations was skimpy to say the least, and when it came to the suggestion of collusion between the national committee and Warren they were little short of fantasy. A cool-headed member of the national committee wrote Simons some "friendly advice": "If there is no more merit in your case against Warren than in the case you make out against the National Committee, you had better swear off and sober up. Now don't misunderstand me. We, that is you and I—do not get drunk of "red likker"—we get drunk on the exuberance of our own verbosity, and when in this condition we . . . take ourselves too damned seriously."[64]

Sadly enough, the diagnosis was suggestive as far as it went. Simons' problem was not that he was drunk with the sound of his own voice, but he certainly did take himself too seriously. He was a vain man, and though conspiracy-thinking was a common mode of explanation among socialists generally, it was especially marked in Simons, and it was a part of his exaggerated self-esteem. Such thinking implied that his enemies could harm him only by resorting to undercover tactics and dishonest manipulation—in a fair fight, his superior abilities were bound to conquer. His superiority was further demonstrated by his quickness in seeing just what his enemies were up to and if all those with whom he dealt were only as quick-witted as he, the thing would be cleared up in a moment and the blame properly placed.

At the same time, feelings of failure plagued Simons, and these too heightened his inclination to explain things in terms of conspiracy. He accepted nearly all his generation's assumptions about "making good," being a "good provider," and moving steadily upward in his chosen work. The peripatetic course of both his journalistic and his political careers and the three dismissals he had endured within

---

[63] *Ibid.*, July 11, 1913.
[64] Patrick S. Nagle to A. M. Simons, Aug. 22, 1913, Milwaukee SP Papers.

seven years were sources of increasing anguish to him. Even as he claimed to be the victim of foul play, at the age of 43 beginning a new job, he was starting to sign the letters to May, "From your worthless husband" and "From your loving failure."[65] And because she remained in Chicago working without enthusiasm on another periodical, the *Party Builder*, her husband wrote, "I hate to think of you working at anything you do not like for the sake of money."[66]

The strength and significance of these conflicting feelings is made more obvious by looking at the objective reality of the situation. For while Simons had indeed had his share of ups and downs within the party, he had also done a great deal of notable work and managed to earn a decent living under the roof of a difficult, unpredictable, and impoverished master, the Socialist party. Financially, he had done well enough that he and May had been able to buy a small house in Evanston after they had left Girard.[67] Professionally, he had established and maintained a set of valuable contacts with the major figures of European socialism at the same time that he had, through his work on American agriculture, moved the Socialists on this side of the Atlantic in a more characteristically American direction. He had evolved a whole new set of interpretations of American history that were sound enough to earn the admiration of Frederick Jackson Turner and publication by a commercial, not merely a socialist, publisher.

These achievements by no means matched his aspirations any more than they fulfilled the conventional career expectations of the background milieu he had come out of. He had, for the time being at least, fallen between his family's past and his own future successes and into an unpleasant and intolerable present. For awhile, therefore, he responded to it publicly in ways that would distinctly minimize his own responsibility for his plight.

He was, however, far from paralyzed by his misfortune. Even as he sought to "expose" the machinations of his former associates, he began casting about for a new job. Victor Berger, the head of the most

---

[65] A . M. Simons to May Simons, July 21, 28, Aug. 5, 1913, Simons Papers.
[66] *Ibid.*, July 16, 1913.
[67] May Simons, Diary, July 17, 1913, Simons Papers.

successful socialist local in the country, had once offered to make room for Simons on the socialist newspaper the Milwaukee *Leader* if he were ever in need of a position. Simons now took him up on the offer, without enthusiasm, but with the feeling that for the time being at least it was the best he could do.[68] He was distressed because after only a few months in Chicago he was obliged once more to go into the backwaters of party life. He had no way of knowing that he was getting into what would shortly become the most incendiary center of socialist activity. He did not anticipate the events that would completely alter his relations with Berger, the Milwaukee Socialists, and the party as a whole, and that would open the way for a whole series of unforeseen developments.

[68] Simons to Berger, June 5, 14, 28, 1913, Milwaukee SP Papers.

CHAPTER SEVEN

Milwaukee Journalist

On the face of it, Victor Berger had been no more enthusiastic than Simons at the prospect of hiring this explosive new journalist. He had warned Simons that he would have to take a cut in salary and that the *Leader* would have to create an opening for him—something that must have been somewhat painful to one as sensitive as Simons.[1]

In fact, however, Berger needed some new blood for his newspaper. The frantic expansion of the Chicago *Daily Socialist* in 1912 had attracted the leading members of Berger's editorial staff, for the *Leader* was not flourishing, and its employees were understandably attracted to the greener pastures that Chicago seemed to offer.[2] Young Carl Sandburg had worked on the *Leader* until then, and thought it a great paper staffed by devoted men grateful for the chance to write what they believed. But even he could not resist the temptation of real success.[3]

The *Leader* had been founded in December 1911, after a great deal of preliminary fundraising designed to keep it afloat until it could build up a following. Circulation had at first exceeded Berger's expectations, and in March 1912, only a few months before Simons joined the paper, it reached a high of 42,000. The purpose of the *Leader* was to present the news that the other local papers, especially the *Journal*, refused to publish. The Milwaukee Socialists claimed that their own city administration was being inadequately covered by existing papers, and that to present a true account of its achievements the Socialists would have to tell the story themselves.

When it began, the *Leader* was little more than a propaganda paper. It engaged in the customary attacks upon the other local political parties which had, after the socialist victory in 1910, combined to form a united "nonpartisan" front against the Seidel administration. In April 1912 the coalition had been successful in driving the Socialists out of office, and the *Leader*'s circulation began to sag at once.[4]

The paper was running steadily in the red when Simons began working for it. It faced a number of handicaps that its rivals never had to cope with. Street sellers didn't push the *Leader* because it paid lower commissions than the other Milwaukee dailies. In addition, the *Leader* charged that both the *Journal* and the *Sentinel* offered its carriers twenty-five cents for each subscriber it could woo away from the socialist paper. There were even reports that carriers for the *Leader* had been beaten up more than once. Advertising, a staple of any newspaper, was difficult for the *Leader* to obtain. The Milwaukee Railroad, for example, dropped its ads after Dan Hoan, the city attorney in the socialist administration of 1910–1912, began to seek legal means to force the city's railroads to depress their tracks. Berger claimed there was a clear connection between the two events. After Seidel had been succeeded by Mayor Bading, the *Leader* charged that the new mayor had refused its reporters access to city hall and had forbidden other newsmen to pass on to the socialist journalists anything they had learned there.[5]

It was a formidable set of obstacles, but Berger believed they could be overcome. He had every reason to expect that the Socialists' political losses were only temporary and that circulation would rise again with the next turn of political fortunes. Through the years he had built a firm constituency in the city and county. He had begun by winning over the trade unionists and ultimately the great majority of the working class. He had followed his successes there with vote-get-

---

[1] Berger to Simons, June 12, 1913, Milwaukee SP Papers.
[2] Frederick I. Olson, "The Milwaukee Socialists" (unpublished Ph.D. dissertation, Harvard University, 1952), 301.
[3] Karl Detzer, *Carl Sandburg* (New York: Harcourt, Brace, 1941), 86–87. It is unfortunate that Sandburg stopped writing his autobiography after the first volume, *Always the Young Strangers*, and that he did not continue the venture or answer the queries of scholars anxious to learn about his early years. Detzer's book, based on interviews with Sandburg, has, therefore, a value that exceeds its modest pretensions.
[4] Olson, "The Milwaukee Socialists," 234–37, 284.
[5] *Ibid.*, 284–87.

ting appeals to small businessmen. He had a strong organization in every ward—the kind that Simons had been unable to build in Chicago a decade before—and each could be depended upon to mount vigorous propaganda campaigns before every election. Berger had succeeded in changing the image of socialism from one of irresponsible radicalism to that of hard-working honest citizenship.[6] Now he could rely largely upon his organization and his contacts to make up the *Leader*'s deficits.[7]

He relied upon another device, too, as Simons was soon to find out. Berger paid his journalists very little. Once a man had been put on the payroll, he found his duties steadily expanded while his paycheck remained the same. In Simons he had just the kind of editor that such a combination of policies demanded. Simons, accustomed to meager salaries, would never confess that he had too much work to do.

He plunged into his job with spirit and confidence. By now he knew what it took to run such an operation, and he looked forward to the fulfillment of his old dream of a successful socialist daily. He had come a long way from his days on the *Workers' Call* when he had cavalierly disregarded the demands of newsworthiness in favor of pushing socialist doctrine. He was no longer a visionary. "In the arrangement of matter NEWS VALUE should be the test," he wrote shortly before he began his new job, ". . . not the importance to the Socialist organization. There is no use trying to avoid this rule. To attempt it is to court death."[8]

He knew, too, that such a paper should not harangue the faithful. "The rank and file," he observed, "do not want to be continually told that 'every Socialist should' do this or that, or that 'if everyone will take hold this can be accomplished.' But they are tremendously interested in knowing that something has been or is going to be done."[9]

---

[6] The best treatment of the rise of socialism in Milwaukee is Marvin Wachman's *History of the Social-Democratic Party of Milwaukee, 1897–1910* (Urbana: University of Illinois Press, 1945). The foregoing is based upon his analysis, 75–76.

[7] Olson, "The Milwaukee Socialists," 289.

[8] Simons, "Suggestions on Party Builder," Typescript, 1913, Simons Papers.

[9] *Ibid.*

Simons seemed to be a more prudent man now, more interested in being a competent journalist than he had been in years gone by, but he had become by no means languid. He was catapulted at once into the thick of the *Leader*'s activity. For his first two weeks, he took the place of the chief editorial writer, and then he took over the national edition. He wrote editorials, straight news, and headlines, and proofread copy.[10] Writing to his wife about his first days on the *Leader*, he proudly described how his whirlwind efforts impressed his colleagues. "Just as I wrote this," he said, "the managing editor called out, 'How do you do it? No sooner do I send a clipping over there than it comes back all rewritten.' "[11]

Simons still took delight in detecting the scent of scandal on the wind and running the guilty to earth. He was a tireless muckraker, and whenever he described his work to his wife or to close friends, he cast himself in the role of irrepressible irritant. "I have started some more stories that I think will stir things up," he wrote to May only two weeks after he'd started his job. A little later he wrote, "I am enclosing a page from the Miner's Magazine containing a little letter I sent them that I think will help keep things boiling." And not long after that, "I am going to a 'Militia of Christ' meeting tonight, . . . That should be interesting, if they let me in. If they do not, I can only stand outside and whistle."[12]

Now that he was hard at work again, he wasted no more time brooding on the fate of the *Coming Nation*. Both he and May remained convinced that Fred Warren and the NEC were guilty of collusion in a murky conspiracy, but there was nothing that could be done about it anymore. His own ebullience was not matched by his wife, who suffered greatly over her husband's misfortunes. Algie agreed that Milwaukee was "much deader than Chicago,"[13] but compared to Girard it was, after all, teeming with life, and his job soon took his mind off the city he had left. To May, suburban Evanston was home. To see her husband leave it was painful. "Never," she

---

[10] A. M. Simons to May Simons, July 8, 10, 1913, Simons Papers.
[11] *Ibid.*, July 21, 1913.
[12] *Ibid.*, July 21, 29, Aug. 5, 1913.
[13] *Ibid.*, July 11, 1913.

wrote, "in all the years of my life, have there been days as sad and lonely as these. . . . One who goes into a great cause must suffer, but if it could be only I who bear I would be glad."[14] It was melodramatic, perhaps, but her unhappiness was no less real for that. Perhaps the greatest testimony to her spirit was that she still regarded socialism as "a great cause."

In spite of her dedication, she had decided that she could be of greatest help to her husband if she secured a teaching position in the Milwaukee schools.[15] Quite obviously she regarded "help" in financial terms, although in her diary she never even hinted that the family's circumstances were straitened, or even modest. She did, it is true, pride herself upon her thrift. When she had been in Copenhagen in 1910, she had thought it worth mentioning, in a letter to her husband, that though the other delegates were broke, she was still managing quite nicely—even though Miriam was with her.[16]

A teaching job would give the family a measure of security. Miriam, a bright girl, would soon be old enough for college and it was unthinkable that she should be denied the privilege that her parents had so dearly bought for themselves. Thus, in Milwaukee, May Simons became intensely preoccupied with fulfilling her new resolve and with "making good," if she should be given the chance to teach.[17] She read extensively, especially in biology and chemistry, and though she did not obtain a full-time position for the fall semester, she did a good deal of substituting. The prejudice against both married women and Socialists in the schools probably contributed to her initial difficulties, for it is hard to imagine that the Milwaukee School Board had many more earnest and capable applicants than she.[18]

As time passed, she began to find life in Milwaukee more pleasant

[14] May Simons, Diary, July 17, 1913, Simons Papers.
[15] *Ibid.*
[16] May Simons to A. M. Simons, Sept. 4, 1910, Simons Papers.
[17] The references to "making good" are legion in her diary between 1913 and 1915. Each time she did substitute-teaching, she recorded her desire to do well and her anxiety that she might not succeed. She also made note of compliments she received from her superiors and praise that others reported they had heard of her.
[18] May Simons alludes to the handicaps for a prospective teacher, of being married and a Socialist, in her diary, Feb. 4, 1914, and May 29, 1914.

than she had dared to hope. She continued to miss the family's old friends in Chicago and Evanston, but she returned often to visit them, to lecture at Hull House,[19] and to attend meetings of the Socialist party's National Education Committee to which she had been named at the 1912 convention.[20]

More important, both Algie and May Simons were becoming quickly assimilated into the socialist society of America's most socialist city. They took no direct role in political activity, but they soon became good friends of Victor and Meta Berger, and together the two couples attended the theater, lectures, recitals, and the familiar round of socialist rallies.[21] In most respects, the Simonses' responsibilities were about the same as they had been in Girard, with the notable difference that the intellectual and cultural life of Milwaukee had immeasurably more to offer.

Gradually the Simonses began to immerse themselves in activities that had little or no direct connection with socialism or even with social issues. This was especially the case with May, who by the spring of 1914 had even begun to attend the meetings of her old college sorority.[22] Sometimes she regretted that she no longer went off on journeys of recruitment and exhortation for the party. When a violent strike occurred among the miners of Calumet she lamented, "How I wish I could go there but these Germans do not imagine a woman can do anything."[23] For the most part, she was content to expand her knowledge of social issues through reading and listening to other people lecture rather than pursuing the kind of grassroots work she had done in earlier years.

As a young woman, she had been almost exclusively interested in politics and economics and their relationship to the coming socialist victory. Now she was turning to broader intellectual and cultural issues though she was by no means avant-garde in her tastes.

She was, in fact, gradually withdrawing from involvement in radi-

[19] May Simons, Diary, Oct. 18, 1913, Jan. 23, 1914.
[20] *Ibid.*, Sept. 8, 1913.
[21] *Ibid.*, Sept. 8, 1913–May 29, 1914, *passim*.
[22] *Ibid.*, April 30, 1914.
[23] *Ibid.*, Dec. 27, 1913.

calism. Her decision to become a teacher in order to help her husband was perhaps indicative of a larger decision that the course she should seek was the course of stability. Perhaps one agitator in the family was enough. At the end of 1914 she resigned from the national woman's committee of the Socialist party, on the grounds that the committee's work was being ignored by the NEC.[24] Although she remained a member of the Milwaukee local, her resignation severed her final link with the national level of the party. She would let her husband lead the family into the promised land.

The Simonses, taking a vacation in July 1914, went to Baraboo to visit relatives. The Milwaukee Socialists had been defeated again in the spring elections after a spirited campaign, and the future of the *Leader* continued to be in doubt. It was not a carefree summer, but for reasons that went far beyond the electoral fate of the party. Archduke Franz Ferdinand and his wife had been assassinated in June as they rode through the streets of Sarajevo, and throughout the summer, in all the capitals of Europe, the machinery that had long stood ready began to grind irrevocably toward war.

By the beginning of August, when the Simonses ended their vacation and returned to Milwaukee, Germany had declared war on Russia. Within a short time the armies of the Triple Entente and the Triple Alliance were ranged against one another to begin the bloodletting. The wildest rumors flew about amid the welter of mobilization, and the problem of winnowing truth from falsehood became increasingly difficult. Word came that the French Socialist Jaures had been shot dead by a deranged patriot. That was true. Word came that all the Socialist members of the German Reichstag had been shot. That was false. "It does not seem possible," May Simons wrote in her diary, "but it has all been planned to destroy the Socialists. . . . Will the workers be crushed and hopeless when it is over? I can't believe it. They will struggle on, but the day of kings is ended."[25]

In America as elsewhere, Socialists and syndicalists and union lead-

<hr/>

[24] May Simons to Winnie Branstetter, chairman, Woman's National Committee, Dec. 21, 1914, *American Socialist*, Jan. 9, 1915.
[25] May Simons, Diary, Aug. 7, 1914, Simons Papers.

ers waited for the general strike. Surely this war was the death agony of capitalism that had been prophesied so long before. All watched eagerly to see how the German Socialists would respond, for in Germany the movement was more powerful than anywhere else in the world. The Simonses heard that Karl Liebknecht, the vigorous and influential antiwar Socialist in Germany, had been killed. It appeared that socialism was going to have new martyrs around which to rally their opposition to militarism and nationalism. "How well I remember [Liebknecht] at Copenhagen," May Simons wrote sadly. "How little any of us thought then he would be a sacrifice to the movement he thought so much of. . . . How fare others of our friends? If we could only hear from them."[26]

They heard soon enough. Liebknecht was, in fact, in excellent health. He had yielded to the majority of German Socialists and joined the rest of the Reichstag in voting unanimously for war credits.[27] The general strike had been a happy illusion.

Though Simons had been for years preoccupied with the problems of American socialism, he had never lost touch with his colleagues in Europe. Now he was deeply distressed that the international aspects of the movement had been so severely shaken. A special peace conference that had been scheduled to meet on the continent in August had been canceled because of the war, and the actions of Socialist parties all over Europe testified to the frailty of Marxism in the face of national interests.

Simons wrote at once to both Ramsay MacDonald and Keir Hardie, leading members of the British Labour party, to urge that they make every effort to keep the Second International alive. He emphasized the importance of maintaining contacts among the Socialists of all the belligerent nations, and asked their support for some kind of international peace conference. The war had to be stopped, and the International was the only body that could bring representatives of all involved parties together. MacDonald and Hardie both agreed to the desirability of Simons' proposals, but they were powerless. "So-

[26] May Simons, Diary, Aug. 14, 1914.
[27] *Ibid.*, Sept. 3, 1914.

cialism in Europe," MacDonald bluntly and accurately reported, "at the present moment is on the shelf."[28]

At the top level of the American Socialist party, similar proposals were put forth during the last months of 1914, and none of them met with any success. Early in 1915, the NEC voted unanimously to withdraw from the Second International, thus bringing to an end the official efforts of American socialism to achieve a negotiated settlement.[29] Henceforth the party was to concentrate its efforts upon keeping America out of the war, opposing militarism, and maintaining its own neutrality.

Simons was ready to lend his services as a pamphleteer in support of the party's official policy. Since internationalism had failed, America must take the lead in ending the folly. To do this, Simons decided, America must at once place an embargo upon the shipment of food to Europe, or, as he put it, "Starve War, Feed America." This, he believed, would cause the war to grind to a halt, while in America the cost of living would decline. The government could buy up surpluses and make them available to the needy at cost. If unemployment should ensue, the government should mobilize American industry in the same way that European governments had done under pressure of war. In this way, a war in which the American people had absolutely no stake could be turned to their advantage. The NEC ordered a million copies of Simons' pamphlet and distributed it as campaign literature before the elections of November 1914.[30]

Humanitarians in the party could not have helped but be a bit uneasy at this facile solution. To "starve war," one had to starve people. If militarism were truly a rapacious beast, it was not likely to be caged until its legions were too weak from hunger to be able to leap out of the trenches any longer. If war were really the foremost concern of the belligerent governments, then they would certainly let the civilians at home—women, children, the aged, the infirm—go

[28] MacDonald to Simons, Sept. 10, 28, Oct. 7, 1914; Hardie to Simons, Oct. 12, Nov. 13, 1914; Simons Papers.
[29] Socialist party efforts in 1914 to bring about a negotiated peace are treated in some detail in David Shannon, *The Socialist Party of America* (New York: Macmillan, 1955), 85–87.
[30] *American Socialist*, Sept. 19, Oct. 10, 1914.

hungry before they would diminish the fighting efficiency of their armies. The pamphlet's author was clearly interested in America first. Nevertheless, the idea of an embargo was taken up for awhile by Socialists and non-Socialists alike, and it was considered both by President Wilson and by Congress. If enacted, the embargo would have been anything but neutral in its effects, for Britain already had blockaded the Central Powers, and a halt to American exports would have been injurious only to the Allies. In a short time, the peace societies, for a variety of reasons, withdrew their support from the proposal, and the Socialists also ended their agitation for it.[31]

Simons' pamphlet "Starve War, Feed America: How It Can Be Done" had a kind of negative significance, for its appearance marked the last occasion upon which his ideas would be viewed hospitably by the highest councils of the Socialist party. By the end of 1914, Simons had begun to find himself once more in conflict with the NEC, and this time there was to be no reconciliation.

It all began over the issue of militarism, the issue that Simons had found so irrelevant back in 1907. From the first days of the war, Simons had described in his editorials for the *Leader* the Frankenstein of armaments that had finally led the nations of Europe into bloody carnage. The capitalists had built a mighty war machine in order to defend their interests, and now they found that it could not be held in check. Once loosed, Simons predicted, it would ultimately turn upon its creators and destroy the whole social structure that had supported it. "Militarism," he explained, "has not prepared the nations for war. It has plunged them so deeply into debt that at the first hint of war the financial and industrial foundation upon which the military structure is based, and upon which it must move, sinks into the morass of bankruptcy." He recalled the wisdom of August Bebel who, at the Stuttgart Congress back in 1907, had foretold this bitter prospect.[32]

[31] Shannon, *The Socialist Party of America*, 88.
[32] "Frankenstein Is Feasting," Milwaukee *Leader*, Aug. 3, 1914. None of the editorials in the *Leader* were signed, but there are strong reasons for believing that this one, and others cited below, are by Simons. The style is clearly his, and differs markedly from other editorials, probably written by Ernest Untermann, both in style and content. The sentiments are similar to

Bankruptcy did not ensue. The war machine ground on, revolution did not occur, and Simons altered his evaluation of the situation. Militarism was not destroying capitalism; it was destroying socialism. The momentum of the military establishment had swept everything before it, and the moral that Americans ought to draw from all this was, as Simons saw it, that the temptation to arm must be resisted with the utmost determination. The strongest socialist movement in the world had crumbled at the instant it grappled with militarism, and American socialism could expect no better fate if it yielded to the advocates of preparedness.

Reading the situation in this way, Simons was appalled at the tentative peace program that the NEC presented to the party membership in December 1914, for it did not include a strong commitment to disarmament.[33] " 'Not a dollar, not a man,' " he wrote, " 'for purposes of murder,' was once the motto of the Socialists of nearly all the countries involved in war. Because that principle was tampered with the Socialists of the warring countries were drawn over the brink into the bloody ditches. . . . You can trace every step that led to this war and the terrible breakdown of Socialist morale to the day when Socialists first began to find causes for the granting of some consideration to the beast of militarism."[34]

The United States, Simons insisted, was the only great nation that was not in thrall to the armament trust. If it would join with "South American countries, where the grip of militarism is not yet too strong to be easily shaken off, in a proposal to abolish all armaments, and compulsory military service such a proposal can be carried. Here is a magnificent opportunity such as will never come to the world again."[35] This was the unique contribution that American socialism could make: it could give the gift of peace to the world.

---

those he expressed in signed articles he published elsewhere during the same period, and the multitude of historical references, together with references, such as the one above, to events he witnessed, strongly supports the presumption that he did write them.

[33] The text of the proposals appears in William English Walling, *The Socialists and the War* (New York: Holt, 1915), 473.

[34] A. M. Simons, "The Socialist War Policy," Typescript, Jan. 20, 1915, Milwaukee SP Papers, 8.

[35] *Ibid.*, 6.

As always, Simons saw the issue in acutely personal terms. Disagreeing with the NEC, he saw the committee ranged against him as though bent upon a personal vendetta that would destroy his influence in the party. "To me," he wrote Carl Thompson, another of the Milwaukee Socialists, "this is the fight of my life. . . . It is a betrayal of everything I have worked for." In a final burst of anger, he concluded, "I do not enjoy the idea of being driven out of the only place in which I have ever cared to work."[36]

Compounding Simons' irritation was what he saw happening around him in Milwaukee. The city was anything but neutral as one would expect in a community where more than 50 percent of the population had German names. The city boasted several well-established German-language newspapers, a variety of German clubs and schools, and a well-regarded German theater, which, in more tranquil times, Algie and May Simons had attended with pleasure.[37] As soon as the war had broken out, the German-American Alliance, an organization designed to promote the interests of Germans in America, declared its sympathy for the Central Powers. Its Milwaukee branch raised money by selling pictures of Wilhelm II and Franz Josef, and at a rally in December 1914 one of its members defended Germany's invasion of Belgium.[38] The fact that Milwaukee happened also to be a socialist city was about as effective in nurturing neutralist sentiment as the existence of a strong Socialist party in Germany had been in keeping that country out of the war. "Milwaukee Germans," May Simons wrote with irritation, "are showing how little they know of real socialism or internationalism."[39]

Milwaukee's most prominent Socialist, Victor Berger, was defeated in his campaign for Congress in 1914, but his victorious opponent sought the more extreme pro-German vote. Berger was himself sympathetic with the German cause both for ideological and cultural reasons. He felt that a German defeat would bring in its wake the destruction of the Social-Democratic party there, and he could not

[36] Simons to Thompson, Jan. 20, 1915, Milwaukee SP Papers.
[37] Bayrd Still, *Milwaukee: The History of a City* (Madison: State Historical Society, 1948), 455.
[38] *Ibid.*, 456.
[39] May Simons, Diary, Sept. 18, 1914.

accept such a prospect with equanimity. He also held German cultural achievements in high regard, and had several unfavorable stereotypes of the Entente powers. The French, he contended, were syphilized, the British money-hungry. If Germany had not gone to war, a Russian victory was inevitable, and Russia, in her barbarism, stood in bleak contrast to the noble civilization of the German people.[40]

Berger did not at first make the columns of the *Leader* conform to his views. "Let us be fair," one editorial advised late in August 1914; this editorial represented a real effort to counter the cultural pride that accompanied pro-German sympathy in Milwaukee. Written by Ernest Untermann, the editorial reminded its readers, "It is ridiculous to believe that the German civilization is something much grander than the French civilization—or that the German nation is so much better than the English nation."[41] Nevertheless, despite this effort at neutrality, the news columns of the paper consistently gave precedence to the Central Powers' interpretation of events, and nearly every day at the *Leader* offices was a day of struggle between the pro-Germans, Berger and Untermann, and the neutralist and antimilitarist, Algie Simons.[42]

By the early months of 1915, the Milwaukee Socialists were urging a program that included, in addition to an embargo upon all shipments to belligerents, the raising of a "citizens army" in America to repel invasion. Simons, of course, saw this proposal as the first step toward disaster for both the nation and socialism.[43]

Then, on May 1 the Lusitania sailed. "Passengers on Lusitania Are Warned of Plot," the headlines of the *Leader* announced on that day. "Cunard Line officials," the accompanying article related, "laughed at passengers' fears, and said the Lusitania could show her heels to any submarines."[44] Seven days later, the liner was sunk by a German torpedo. The editorial columns of the *Leader* said nothing about the

[40] Frederick I. Olson, "The Milwaukee Socialists" (unpublished Ph.D. dissertation, Harvard University, 1952), 338–39.
[41] "Let Us Be Fair," *Leader*, Aug. 26, 1914; it can be safely assumed that Simons did not write this. The editorial began, "The writer is a German of Germans and most strongly sympathizes with the German people."
[42] Olson, "The Milwaukee Socialists," 334–37.
[43] *Ibid.*, 334.
[44] *Leader*, May 1, 1915.

sinking for more than a week though the subject was front-page news for days. "Milwaukeeans Uphold Ship's Sinking," one news story reported on the day the Lusitania went down; interviews with prominent citizens revealed a widespread willingness to justify what had happened. Many business and professional men, however, declined to say anything at all. The *Leader's* reporter did not speculate upon what this silence might mean.[45]

May Simons was teaching high school in the spring of 1915, and on the day after the Lusitania went down she was appalled to find that her German colleagues there "openly rejoiced over the sinking and destruction of life." "I doubt," she concluded, "whether I ever again could believe in the German having good qualities."[46] This was a rather severe conclusion to draw from what she had heard. In fact, she was by this time prepared to think the worst of the whole German nation. Ever since the early part of 1915, German agents had been attempting sabotage in the United States. Hardly a week had gone by without the disclosure of some new effort to smuggle a bomb on board an American ship or to blow up an American factory. The damage that this sabotage did was minuscule compared to its effect upon American opinion.[47]

Alongside this work of foreign agents was the outspokenness of the German-American community. In Milwaukee, benefits were held to aid the German, Austrian, and Hungarian victims of war, and German-Americans there, as elsewhere in the United States, were frank in their sympathy for their countrymen abroad. Ironically enough, their very frankness was the result of the respect in which they had been held in America. German-Americans had long outgrown the distrust that met new immigrant groups in this country. They had become accustomed to praise from native Americans for their patriotism and their hard-working and law-abiding nature. The confidence that this praise engendered was to be instrumental in their undoing.[48]

[45] "Milwaukeeans Uphold Ship's Sinking," Milwaukee *Leader*, May 8, 1915.
[46] May Simons, Diary, May 30, 1915.
[47] John Higham, *Strangers in the Land* (New Brunswick, N.J.: Rutgers University Press, 1955), 197.
[48] *Ibid.*, 196.

The combination of German sabotage and German-American sympathy with the Central Powers led to an easy conclusion. Surely there must be a connection between the two. German agents were surely profiting from contacts with their countrymen in America. German-Americans must be conspiring against their adopted country.

The virus of conspiracy-theory was one to which both Algie and May Simons were abundantly susceptible. Both had shown time and again the facility with which they greeted personal and party reverses by an ominous leap to assumptions of conspiratorial forces at work. Simons had seen the NEC's war program as an evil designed to drive him from the party; his wife had instantly viewed the war itself as a grand conspiracy against socialism the world over. Now they happened to be in a city where they thought they could actually see conspiracy at work against themselves and the nation. Germans were openly applauding the loss of American lives aboard the Lusitania, and the Milwaukee *Leader,* after a period of discreet silence, came out editorially in justification of the submarine attack.[49]

A new word began to creep into Simons' thinking about the war as he contemplated the acts of sabotage, his own difficulties on the *Leader,* and Milwaukee's defense of the Central Powers. The word was *disloyalty.* American lives were being lost, and German-Americans—naturalized citizens who had proclaimed their allegiance to the United States and all it stood for—were exonerating the murderers. Simons' pacifism was beginning to fade.

How long could America stand by defenseless and see her nationals abused, while within her own borders an outspoken minority applauded the abuse? Disarmament was a noble idea, but perhaps only the defeated nations would be disarmed. In 1915 it had begun to look as though Great Britain and her allies might well become the defeated, and the German military machine might rule the world. "Sometimes," May Simons confided to her diary, "I am almost sick when I think perhaps England will lose after all. I cannot bear to think that anything on that little old island could be destroyed except, of course, poverty and distress. I would like to see all that go, but to

[49] May 17, 1915.

me England is the fairyland of both my childhood and woman-hood."[50]

Still, Simons stuck by his ardent antimilitarism publicly, and by the middle of 1915 the American Socialist party was moving in the direction that he had taken several months before. In 1916, another election year, the party decided to hold no nominating convention but to choose its standard bearers through a nationwide referendum among party members. Debs had declined to run, and the man chosen by the membership was Allan Benson, a journalist who had been comparatively unknown until he had begun writing vigorous antiwar articles for the *Appeal to Reason.*

Benson's campaign was a mere shadow of the bygone days of the Red Special and the stirring oratory of Eugene Debs. The election returns too were shadows of former days. Benson's ticket had polled less than two-thirds of what Debs had received four years before. Something was happening to the Socialist party. The ground that had been gained between 1910 and 1912 was slipping away. The quick victory for socialism that Simons had anticipated in 1900 had yielded to the gradual conquest that he had begun to predict a few years later, and now even that expectation had proved hollow.

Simons had suffered yet another personal defeat in 1916. He had once more campaigned for the National Executive Committee of the party on a platform that included a statement of his views on military preparedness. "The entrance of this nation into armaments competition means that this war will end only in a truce leading to other wars."[51] Once more he had lost. The stage was set for the explosion that had been smoldering since 1914. Simons took to his typewriter as he had after every election since 1900 to explain and interpret the results. This time, however, his postmortem would not be found only in the pages of the party press, and it would not be filled with praise for the noble work of his colleagues. In December 1916 Simons resigned from the Milwaukee *Leader* and began savagely to attack the Socialist party.

[50] May Simons, Diary, June 30, 1915, Simons Papers.
[51] William English Walling and others, eds., *The Socialism of Today* (New York: Holt, 1916), 623.

The first public salvo was fired in the pages of the *New Republic,* and it was directed at both the Milwaukee Socialists and the national level of the party. In an article titled "The Future of the Socialist Party," Simons indicted his erstwhile colleagues. "With the sorrow that comes from the destruction of one's dearest ideal," he wrote, "I say that in many a city the Socialist organization is to-day little more than an organized appetite for office—a Socialist Tammany. . . . In only this, the weakest and worst phase of our movement, are we really in touch with American life."[52] No reader who knew where Simons had been working for the past three years could have failed to guess at least one city he had in mind.

"Intellectually and politically," he continued, "the mind of the party is in Europe. The Socialist Party and press had no criticism of the invasion of Belgium, the sinking of the Lusitania, the Zeppelin outrages, the slave drives in Belgium, or the . . . Armenian massacres." The party had ignored its classic mission by being utterly indifferent to social and economic injustice at home—the profits of monopoly capital, the heightening of class struggle, the relationship between American industry and wartime financial transactions.[53]

Instead, the Socialist party and press had, Simons contended, stifled freedom of discussion, "once our greatest pride," made blatant appeals to race prejudice, expressed rabid hostility to religion, and even ignored the "great pedagogical revolution that is largely led by John Dewey."[54]

What then was the party's future? "I do not believe the Socialist party will die," Simons wrote, but he could not find reasons even for this faint hope. "Perhaps this is because for me to believe this would be to believe that twenty years of my life have been thrown away."[55]

There was much in Simons' indictment that was true. The party's character had been changing in recent years: it had been attracting more and more of the kinds of members it had had in its earliest days when Simons had first begun his crusade to make it more "American."

[52] *New Republic* (Dec. 2, 1916), 118.
[53] *Ibid.*, 119–20.
[54] *Ibid.*, 120.
[55] *Ibid.*

The percentage of foreign-born in the party was growing again: 15 percent in 1912, 35 percent in 1916. Eighty-five percent of the socialist press had been published in English in 1912; in 1916 that percentage had dropped to 70 percent.[56] The mind of the party *was* in Europe, if the election campaign just past was any indication. Benson had based his campaign almost entirely upon opposition to preparedness and had ignored the customary Marxist platform upon which the party stood. So, for that matter, had Simons. As late as August he had opposed military preparedness: he claimed that capitalists sought to build a strong army and navy in America in order to crush the social upheaval that would follow the war's end.[57]

Now he made no reference to his own earlier errors, if, indeed, he considered them such. In his remarks about socialist Tammanies, he said nothing about his own long-term interest in strengthening the party's vote-getting appeal or his pleasure when he saw the rising totals of socialist officeholders. He made no allusions to the fact that he too had concentrated his recent efforts not upon securing social justice in America but upon coping with the problems of international socialism. Instead, he fell again into what was by now a familiar habit: virulently attacking positions that he had just left. He had done it first in Chicago when he left the settlement movement for which he had done yeoman service. He had done it next when he repudiated DeLeon and the Socialist Labor party after taking up the cudgels for DeLeon in a manner very like the master. In personal terms, he had done it most recently when the *Coming Nation* had been scuttled: Fred Warren had almost overnight been transformed in Simons' eyes from noble, crusading Socialist to conniving, money-hungry capitalist.

In one thing was Simons always consistent: once he abandoned an ideological position, he never returned to it. Now that he had become thoroughly convinced that the Socialists had made serious mistakes in recent years, he turned to the task of setting the party right again. Two weeks after his *New Republic* article, he wrote a long letter, published in the New York *Call*, in which he specified the course of

[56] Gerald Friedberg, "Marxism in the United States," 193.
[57] *American Socialist*, Aug. 5, 1916.

action that ought to be taken. He had decided, he said, that the Socialist party had made a mistake in opposing the formation of a labor party under union management. "I think the way out lies . . . along the lines of the . . . English labor movement," he wrote, "with the Socialist Party maintaining its autonomy for educational purposes, but working in close cooperation with a labor party managed and financed by the unions." Such a party might not pursue the policies he thought most wise, but he had "enough faith in the judgment of the working class and in democracy to wish to see something of the kind tried."

The party ought also to "quit our faking on such questions as the embargo." The party leadership, he claimed, had really been trying to help the German-American Alliance and the Kaiser by its talk of starving the war and feeding America. "It is hard to believe that any Socialist is so hopelessly ignorant of economics as not to know that an embargo, by itself, would simply precipitate a panic."

He made a variety of other recommendations. The party must "wake up to the agrarian question"; it must emphasize the need for the socialization of monopoly; it must fight militarism everywhere. The Socialist party needed to organize the young people of the country; the generation that had come into the movement at its founding was growing old. Professional officeseekers, all who might be called politicians, must be driven into the background and the party must not "permit the bending of Socialist principles to make vote traps."[58]

All this was temperate enough, and considerably more constructive than the angry piece in the *New Republic*. It might, however, have been a bit bewildering to the party faithful who had followed Simons through his 1910 denials that he wanted a labor party, or who had read the pamphlet "Starve War, Feed America." But, after all, one should not continue making the same old mistakes simply in order to avoid the charge of inconsistency. The Socialist party must try to recover from the paralysis that the war had inflicted upon Marxism's historic mission, and Simons was prepared to help initiate the cure. Or so he thought.

[58] "What We Must Do," New York *Call*, Dec. 17, 1916.

CHAPTER EIGHT

War and Revolution

In February 1917 Germany resumed unrestricted submarine warfare, and the United States severed diplomatic relations. Hurriedly the Socialist party called an emergency convention to meet in St. Louis to consider the next steps it ought to take. On April 6, a day before the convention opened, Woodrow Wilson went before the Congress to ask for a declaration of war. At St. Louis, 140 of the 200 delegates voted to declare the Socialist party of America unalterably opposed to the war, and in the national referendum that followed, three-fourths of the party membership concurred. The party vowed to oppose conscription, fight military training in the schools, demand the restriction of food exports, and in every way, including mass demonstrations, strengthen public opposition to the war.[1]

Simons was stunned. The party was in the hands of the left-wing syndicalists and the Germans. His two-decade long effort to build an American socialism lay in ruins. No political party that repudiated national loyalty in time of war could hope for any kind of success, Simons knew, forgetting that he had at one time contended that Socialists ought to repudiate national loyalty when compelled to go to war against their worker-brothers in other lands. The Germans were the real militarists, he reasoned, and they must be stopped before they enslaved the world. America must fight fire with fire. "Militarism must be assisted to suicide in its last great sin. . . . Military mobilization at the front and in the shops and on the farms must end in democratic, industrial mobilization for peace."[2]

Equally important, the Germans must be fought at home as well as abroad. Simons had decided that even before the declaration of war. When the pro-Ally anti-Socialist Milwaukee *Journal* asked him to comment upon a peace meeting the Milwaukee Socialists had held in

February, he jumped at the chance. The meeting was, he said, "but one more instance of an effort to use the machinery of the Socialist party in the interests of German imperialism and militarism."[3]

In succeeding months, Simons found the *Journal* a willing vehicle for his attacks upon all things German, and after the St. Louis Convention his spleen knew no bounds. The Germans at the convention had allowed the extreme left wing of the party to triumph in order to produce riots and anarchy in America. I would be a traitor, he wrote, if I were not to reveal "this murderous treason . . . on the part of men whose only excuse must be their mad devotion to German autocracy."[4] He wrote to Senator Husting of Wisconsin, urging that the St. Louis manifesto be suppressed as pernicious propaganda, and when Simons heard a rumor that Victor Berger might be appointed to the forthcoming Root Mission to Russia, he wrote again, giving a list of Berger's "treasonous" activities since 1914.[5]

After the correspondence to Husting had been revealed, the Milwaukee Socialists had had enough. By a vote of 63–3, Simons was expelled from the party.[6] This, he raged, was "formal official warning that anyone who holds a closer allegiance to the United States than to the Hohenzollerns or to Socialism than autocracy is not wanted in the Milwaukee Socialist party."[7]

Many Milwaukeeans felt just as strongly as Simons, though for different reasons. Many chafed at the thought that in the minds of countless Americans, Milwaukee was a German city and that one of Wisconsin's senators, Bob LaFollette, had spoken consistently against taking the road that led to war. The stage was set for reaction:

---

[1] David Shannon, *The Socialist Party of America* (New York: Macmillan, 1955), 93–98, treats the convention in some detail and supplies valuable information on its social, economic, and ethnic composition. He concludes that the delegates represented a good cross section of the party.

[2] Simons, "Pacifism and Revolution," *New Republic*, X (March 24, 1917), 220–21.

[3] *Journal*, March 5, 1917.

[4] *Ibid.*, April 17, 1917.

[5] *Congressional Record*, 65th Cong., 1st Sess., 2087–88. Husting to Simons, May 5, 1917, Simons Papers.

[6] Milwaukee *Leader*, May 2, 24, 1917.

[7] Milwaukee *Journal*, May 24, 1917.

Milwaukee and Wisconsin must prove their patriotism to the nation. In February a group of Milwaukee businessmen and civic leaders had met and formed the Wisconsin Defense League. At first the league's purposes were vague and relatively innocuous: it would help collect statistics for use in calling men to military service; it would help recruiting officers, and it would give whatever help federal and state governments might request.[8] To join, one merely had to give an unconditional pledge of loyalty and 25 cents. Near the end of March 1917 the league hired Algie Simons as a state organizer at a salary of forty dollars a week.[9]

Within a few months, the league had become something more ominous, the Wisconsin Loyalty Legion, and Simons was named head of its literature department. This organization was not merely to aid in the attainment of patriotic ends; it was to serve as an instrument for the repression of the unpatriotic. The definition of "unpatriotic" was broad. The legion urged that the German press of Milwaukee be boycotted; it opposed the teaching of German in the schools; it asked the attorney general to indict those who had framed the platform of the Milwaukee Socialists, because it opposed capitalistic wars. The legion coerced people into buying Liberty bonds, and posted yellow placards on the homes of those who did not comply.[10] And to ensure that America should never again be threatened by foreigners in time of crisis, the legion sought to promote "the disappearance of those distinctively foreign and non-American racial traits which our immigrants have brought from abroad."[11]

The Socialists were particular targets of the legion. In Simons' own Sauk County a mob threatened Oscar Ameringer, socialist candidate for Congress. At Theresa, Wisconsin, 600 Loyalty Legionnaires pre-

---

[8] Lorin Lee Cary, "Wisconsin Patriots Combat Disloyalty: The Wisconsin Loyalty Legion and Politics" (unpublished M.A. thesis, University of Wisconsin, 1964), 45.
[9] "The Wisconsin Defense League," pamphlet, Simons Papers.
[10] G. F. Kull, "Record of the Work of the Wisconsin Loyalty Legion," pamphlet, Simons Papers, and Bayrd Still, *Milwaukee: The History of a City* (Madison: State Historical Society, 1948), 460–61.
[11] "Minutes of State-Wide Non-Partisan Mass Meeting," Wisconsin Loyalty Legion, March 23, 1918, Loyalty Legion Papers, State Historical Society of Wisconsin.

vented Emil Seidel from speaking; at Elroy, a Socialist was arrested for circulating a petition asking that conscription be put to a vote; at Colfax, a party organizer was assaulted.[12]

Through it all, Simons journeyed about the state giving speeches, preaching loyalty, and distributing literature. He found that many of his old friends and associates were doing similar work. Richard T. Ely was head of the Madison branch of the legion. Charles Edward Russell was in London, serving as information officer for the Committee of Public Information (CPI). Guy Stanton Ford was in Washington working for the same organization. His writers and advisers were some of the brightest luminaries of the historical profession: Frederick Jackson Turner and Charles A. Beard were among them. The CPI was intent, as Simons had been years before, upon giving the common people a historical framework that would explain what was happening to the United States and western Europe.[13] This history, of course, did not dwell upon class struggle, greedy capitalists, or exploited workingmen; it concentrated upon less tangible realities—pride of country, loyalty to the democratic faith, and hatred of foreign autocracies. "You," the CPI urged the nation's history teachers, "can help people understand that failure of the past to make the world safe for democracy does not mean that it can not be made safe in the future."[14]

One of Simons' chief responsibilities, as head of the Loyalty Legion's literature bureau, was to see that the CPI's pamphlets of history and exhortation were distributed and read in the state of Wisconsin. A steady flow of such material came from Washington and Simons sent it on to hundreds of towns and villages, under the franking privilege that Ford had secured for the legion.[15] Simons wanted the job done well. Quantities of material, pamphlets explaining "How War Came to America" and "Why We Are at War," were sent to public-school teachers with the urging that they use the material in their history

[12] Olson, "The Milwaukee Socialists" (unpublished Ph.D. dissertation, Harvard University, 1952), 359.
[13] James Mock and Cedric Larson, *Words That Won the War* (Princeton: Princeton University Press, 1939), 158–86.
[14] Announcement in *History Teacher's Magazine*, Sept. 1917, reprinted in Mock and Larson, *Words That Won the War*, 184.
[15] Ford to W. I. Goodland, Sept. 25, 1917, Loyalty Legion Papers.

and English classes and then send them home with their pupils. There was a danger that if the material were simply mailed directly to individual homes it would not be read.[16]

From some of his socialist colleagues Simons received praise for his tireless work on behalf of the war effort. The party intellectuals, men like Russell, John Spargo, Upton Sinclair, and William English Walling, had severed their connection with the Socialist party after the St. Louis Convention, and they too were casting about for ways in which to accomplish the goals of national purpose. Walling wrote admiringly to Simons, "You have been doing so much more than any of the rest of us to set things right in America."[17] Upon hearing that Simons had left the *Leader,* H. M. Hyndman, crotchety patriarch of the British prowar Socialists, wrote, "I am very glad you yourself have cut yourself loose, at any rate for the time, from fugitive journalism. You can do very much better work, as I told you long ago, and as I make bold at seventy-five to tell you again."[18] "His work," May Simons wrote of her husband, "is recognized by all who are worth while."[19]

Once more, May was sharing directly in her husband's activities. She was teaching civics and was firmly convinced of the need to nurture national loyalty in the hearts of the foreign-born. In October 1917 she became chairman of the Americanization Committee of the Milwaukee County Council of Defense and for nearly two years she served with devotion and zeal. "Americanization" was an old goal among a variety of groups in the United States, but until the war came it had aroused little enthusiasm. War had cut off the manpower supply, and many employers saw in Americanization a way of increasing the productivity of the workers they already had. Both the National Association of Manufacturers and the U.S. Chamber of Commerce became boosters for this homefront version of making the world safe for democracy.

All across the country, local Americanization groups embarked

---

[16] Simons to A. H. Naftzer, Nov. 21, 1917, Loyalty Legion Papers.
[17] Walling to Simons, April 16, 1918, Simons Papers.
[18] April 30, 1917, Simons Papers.
[19] May Simons, Diary, Dec. 24, 1917, Simons Papers.

upon their mission. Women's clubs paid "Americanizing visits" to immigrant homes. Fraternal organizations and civic groups sent speakers into immigrant districts to preach the gospel of America. Patriotic leaflets rained upon the ethnic ghettos. The specific goals of all this effort were to urge aliens to become citizens, to give up their native language, and to swear their undying allegiance to all that America stood for—or, at very least, all that the Americanization committee stood for.[20]

In Milwaukee, May Simons' group professed two goals: a common language and "a united intelligent citizenship." Within each ethnic group of the city, a committee was set up to acquaint other members of that group with the opportunities for Americanization that were available. Night schools and the public schools were already fitted to help in this work. The committee also sent several hundred letters to local employers, requesting information as to which men needed such instruction; when the response indicated that much work was to be done, the Americanization Committee went before the Milwaukee School Board and got an appropriation of funds to pay teachers of factory classes. "Many employers," May Simons wrote in an article describing the work of her committee, "have shown a keen interest in this matter."[21] In some cases, teachers met classes in the homes, boardinghouses, and churches of immigrants, teaching English to the newcomers and preparing them to meet the requirements for citizenship.

The public climax of May Simons' efforts came after the armistice, when a pageant of Americanization was held in the Milwaukee Auditorium. "It is a remarkable thing," the Milwaukee *Journal* purred, "that Milwaukee which has been slurred at as Prussian, is the only city in the United States which has been able to produce the pageant which was written . . . in 1915 and given its first public presentation here." It featured the presentation of 613 new citizens before the "altar of liberty," where, "after being accepted as of the United States, [they] turned and were met by the Colonial Dames and Sons

[20] John Higham, *Strangers in the Land* (New Brunswick, N.J.: Rutgers University Press, 1955), 242–50.
[21] Milwaukee *Journal*, Nov. 10, 1918.

of the American Revolution, who gave them . . . welcome . . . while the Battle Hymn of the Republic was sung."[22] It was a solemn moment indeed. Perhaps somewhere in the audience there was someone who was struck with the contrast between this outpouring of pride and the one in Stuttgart in 1907, when the songs of revolution had filled the air. There was nothing revolutionary about the work of either the Loyalty Legion or the Americanization Committee. The assumption that underlay both was that the America of the Constitution and free enterprise must be unquestioningly embraced by all. America was a finished work.

Within a few months after the loyal forces of Milwaukee had been marshaled, an editor of the Milwaukee *Journal* proudly announced, "There is . . . a tireless and determined effort here inimical to America, . . . but it has been curbed. It has been fought, it has been exposed to public gaze, and for the time at least it stands baffled and defeated."[23] The loyalty enthusiasts could claim a number of concrete achievements in Milwaukee. The German theater stopped giving German-language performances in 1918. The Deutscher Club became the Wisconsin Club, and the German-English Academy became the Milwaukee Academy. The statue of Germania was removed from the Germania Building, and the structure was renamed. When the public schools opened in the fall of 1918, its students were no longer required to take instruction in a foreign language. On the menus of Milwaukee restaurants Bismarcks were transformed into American beauties, and sauerkraut into liberty cabbage. Milwaukee families once known as Koenig became King, and Baums were reborn as Trees.[24]

Federal legislation soon came to the aid of those who feared that even such accomplishments were not enough. The Milwaukee *Leader* ran afoul of Postmaster Burleson, and was muzzled. Victor Berger was convicted under the Espionage Act. Outside Wisconsin, hundreds of Socialists were indicted for speaking against conscription. In Chicago the national office of the party was raided and the party leaders

---

[22] Milwaukee *Journal*, May 19, 1919.
[23] June 15, 1917, quoted in Still, *Milwaukee*, 460–61n.
[24] *Ibid.*, 461–62.

were indicted under the Espionage Act. At Canton, Ohio, Eugene Debs delivered a two-hour speech in which he accused those who had left the party of lacking "the fiber to endure the revolutionary test." He also mentioned the war and was promptly arrested for using "profane, scurrilous and abusive language." He was convicted of violating the Espionage Act and sent to the federal prison at Atlanta under a ten-year sentence.[25]

Back in Milwaukee, the man who had ridden the Red Special across America with Debs, worked with Berger on the *Leader*, and served for years at the executive level of the party continued to look for new ways to achieve the fulfillment of America's historic mission of democracy. To the casual observer, Algie Simons' ardent nationalism was startling. Here was a Socialist who for twenty years had declared that the nation-state was only a tool of capitalistic oppression, suddenly throwing himself unreservedly into the conflict. If only he were younger, he lamented, he would shoulder a rifle and defend his homeland against its enemies. When the chance came in 1918 to tour the frontlines, Simons was fierce in his determination to be where he could see the shells bursting and the troops pouring out of the trenches on the attack.

In certain respects, Simons had always been a nationalist. For years he had written and spoken about the desperate necessity of making socialism into an *American* political faith. For years he had spoken in the nativist shorthand that made the term *Anglo-Saxon* equivalent to man's noblest virtues and that endowed the characteristic American, the pioneer, with the best in human nature. This kind of nationalism, however, had not been exclusionist or isolationist. Simons had always been deeply interested in European contributions to socialist theory, and had translated many foreign Marxist classics into English.

With the American declaration of war, Simons grew ardent in his determination to protect the nation from all enemies foreign and domestic, and from all ideas that might carry the taint of evil foreign designs. The phenomenon is a familiar one. War, the ultimate threat

---

[25] David Shannon presents a brief, well-documented account of repressive actions taken by the government against Debs and others during the war, in *The Socialist Party of America*, 108–17.

to individual and nation alike, has traditionally served as social ce-ment. It has also served to annihilate dissent, as President Wilson himself acknowledged even as he wrote his war message.

In spite of that, not all loyal citizens seek with such determination as Simons to find outlets for their patriotic zeal. In part, his actions were the consequence of a deep sense of unfulfilled responsibilities. For years he had been troubled that his socialist activities were keep-ing his family from comfort and respectability, and though his wife shared his radical convictions he worried constantly—probably with good reason—about money and about the environment in which his daughter was being reared. No man can be expected to be indifferent to the succession of political and journalistic failures that had dogged Simons' heels. To be dismissed from job after job was not a sequence of events easily borne by one who wanted to do well by those he loved. To be attacked virulently for years by one's political enemies became difficult to tolerate when its effects ceased to be relaxed by political success.

Therefore, when war came—a war that was promptly translated at all levels of society and politics into a struggle for all that Americans held dear—Simons was predisposed not to be found wanting again. He had always been the staunchest defender of American democracy. Now he had the chance to defend it in a time of utmost crisis. His transformation from neutralist to nationalist was made easier still when Russia left the war. Once "Tsarism" was out of the contest, it was no longer merely a conflict between rival autocracies. It was a conflict between democracy and "Kaiserism."

As political observers of the nonwestern world have found in recent years, popular loyalties are easily transferred from socialism to na-tionalism. Wars of *popular* liberation easily become wars of *national* liberation. In societies that are in transition, when old values can no longer be depended upon, both socialism and nationalism serve some of the same functions. Both cut across established patterns of loyalty; both slice through the layers of social hierarchy.[26] The individual

[26] James C. Davies, *Human Nature in Politics* (New York: John Wiley, 1963), 354.

capable of applying himself devotedly on behalf of one could be expected to apply himself with equal devotion to the other, if the right combination of circumstances arose.[27]

For Simons, that combination of circumstances presented itself in 1917. The party for which he had worked so long seemed to have sold its American soul for a mess of pro-German, antidemocratic, militaristic pottage. Familiar with an environment whose institutions and values were shifting decisively, Simons had first looked to socialist politics as the tool that would build a new society upon the rock of science. By 1917 it had clearly failed to make even a convincing start. It seemed to Simons that the Socialists had made their most disastrous mistake, one that he couldn't explain away.

Yet even as he set upon the Kaiser's minions in Milwaukee and found himself in league with the very kinds of capitalists he had once excoriated, he struggled to create a new socialism. Ever since 1914, Simons had foreseen that the conflict would precipitate vast changes in the societies it involved. At first he merely reiterated the customary Marxist assumptions about the causes of war and the death throes of capitalism. Then he came to focus upon militarism and autocracy, instead of purely economic factors. "There is but one great consolation in this hideous horror," Simons had written in the *Leader* in August 1914, "When Europe rises out of this bath it will rise cleansed from the foulness of militarism and class rule . . . a Prussian Yunker [*sic*] will no longer be squatted upon German culture . . . a French bayonet will no longer be driven through the delicate artist life of France."[28]

Gradually, Simons came to believe that the war was having a great constructive influence upon society. Never an advocate of violent revolution, he now chose to believe that the revolution he had foreseen taking place at the ballot box would instead be accomplished

---

[27] In these times of antiheroes and skepticism about the quality of human action it is perhaps necessary to make it perfectly clear that the foregoing is not intended as a description of fanaticism or the fanatic. Simons and the other notable Socialists who left the party and applied themselves to the war effort were not wild-eyed neurotics looking for a new cause in which to become involved.

[28] *Leader*, Aug. 7, 1914.

more subtly. "Certainly things have not moved as planned," he admitted in March 1917. "Democracy . . . which was to work the popular will in all things, has, for the moment been shoved aside by sterner methods of measuring strength. . . . It is time for radicals, reformers, revolutionists and progressives to . . . awake to the fact that unless those who possess special knowledge and ideals of social progress act quickly and wisely in connection with the war-created forces, they will have passed the supreme opportunity of social service."[29]

He described some of the social achievements the war had brought about in Europe and Great Britain, and pointed the direction that men like himself ought to move: "The place that has been won for labor in the parliaments of the world must be strengthened. . . . The war need for woman's services must lead to her complete political and social emancipation. The care of peoples in war must show the way to the abolition of poverty in peace."[30] After America entered the war, Simons found increasing evidence of radical social and economic changes wrought neither by the voter nor by the revolutionary. At the federal level, he saw wartime measures that placed more severe restrictions upon the rights of private property than any of the old-line Socialists had ever imagined a capitalist government could achieve. The War Industries Board was given vast powers over industrial output. The Lever Act granted the executive branch comparable powers over the production and distribution of food. In December 1917 Wilson put the nation's railroads under government control.

The time had come for the American radical to work in concert with measures like these and to extend them when the pressures of war were past. Aiding him in these goals, Simons believed, were the idealism and devotion to democracy that were also the fruit of the war. No longer was the radical to hunt for the materialistic motives that lay back of every action of a capitalist government. Instead, he must draw from the reservoir of solidarity and good will which the

[29] "Pacifism and Revolution," 220–21.
[30] Ibid., 221.

exigencies of war had created. And what of Marxism? Simons considered himself a radical still, but he had put his Marxism in a drawer, as William James once said of his own religious faith, and when he came back it was gone.

Simons immediately began to seek an organizational vehicle for his new opinions, and he looked first to the labor movement. In September 1917 he attended an organizational meeting of the new American Alliance for Labor and Democracy. Headed by Samuel Gompers, the Alliance was designed to attract working class loyalty to the war effort, but it was also stern in its insistence that war profits be limited and that labor's hard-won rights be protected. Simons was optimistic about both the personnel and the potential of the new Alliance. "It is like one of the first Socialist conventions," he wrote of that September meeting. "All the best brains of the movement are here. There is nothing left in the S.P. worth taking."[31]

What the Alliance really proved to be was an arm of Creel's Committee of Public Information, designed to keep labor on the job. Within six months it had set up 150 branches, distributed nearly two million pamphlets, and sponsored 200 mass meetings. The Alliance saw to it that "Pay-Envelope Stories"—tiny pamphlets written to inspire either efficiency or patriotism—got into the pay envelopes of a million workers. It tacked up posters on a hundred factory bulletin boards: "When we win the war," a typical sentiment explained, "we can settle our other disputes. If we shouldn't win the war, the Kaiser would settle them for us."[32]

The Alliance saw things just as Simons did. Strive for national victory now, and the struggle for social justice would be more easily achieved later. "When this battle is won," the Alliance announced in a letter to all the local unions in the country, "and the world, chastened and rejuvenated, will sit down to the task of readjusting social conditions on principles of universal right and justice, we have every reason to expect Labor to be an important factor, probably *the* important factor in its deliberations."[33]

[31] A. M. Simons to May Simons, Sept. 5, 1917, Simons Papers.
[32] Mock and Larson, *Words That Won the War*, 189–92.
[33] Quoted in *ibid.*, 198.

The Alliance refused to become involved in political activity. Therefore Simons turned to his socialist colleagues who had left the party after the St. Louis Convention, and sought to establish some viable political entity that would express their common goals. The result was the Social Democratic League, and it included, in addition to Simons, men like Russell, Walling, John Spargo, and Upton Sinclair. In October 1917, in a convention at Chicago, it managed to form a series of fragile alliances that would unite the forces of reform in America. An amalgam of prohibitionists, Socialists, single-taxers, and old Progressives proclaimed themselves the National party. "We scarcely look for any revolutionary achievements by this new party," Simons admitted with candor. "For better or worse, the American people seem to be wedded to the two . . . party system. Third parties have their part to play as educational institutions and political gadflies, but as instruments to execute the popular will the American people will apparently have none of them."[34] The National party was not to achieve even those modest goals. It dissolved after its next convention in 1918.

Still Simons pressed on with his conception of the new society that was to be created from war's holocaust. As always, his expectations were both personal and public. On his way to Philadelphia to meet with the League to Enforce the Peace he wrote his wife, "Our best years are before us, and I think we will be able to do many of the things we planned yet."[35] The members of the Social Democratic League (SDL) were at Philadelphia too, and they urged Simons' program of social reconstruction upon the League to Enforce the Peace. The controls that the government had put on the American economy must be continued after peace had come and must be the foundation for further controls that would democratize industry. The old Second International could never be restored. Instead there must be a world organization and economic internationalism. The domestic program of the SDL was radical enough, but its international aspects were for the most part respectful echoes of the Fourteen Points that

[34] "The National Party," *Independent*, XCII (Dec. 29, 1917), 578.
[35] A. M. Simons to May Simons, May 15, 1918, Simons Papers.

President Woodrow Wilson had announced to a joint session of Congress in January.[36]

All these plans and programs were, of course, predicated upon an Allied victory. In the spring of 1918, however, victory was anything but assured. The German army had launched a series of offensives on the western front, and by June two German salients threatened Paris. American troops had not yet arrived in great numbers, and the German high command was eager to capitalize upon their own numerical superiority which they knew would be temporary.

What was particularly troubling to Allied supporters was the war-weariness that was sweeping the continent. For four years the nations of Europe had been sending their young men into the trenches. For four years Europe had been laid waste, and thousands of lives had been sacrificed for the gain of a few yards. One major power had already been forced to leave the war, her will to fight destroyed, her social fabric in tatters. Troop mutinies among the French and Italian armies were spreading, and each gave fresh hope to the Kaiser's armies, freed as they were from the constrictions of a two-front war. There was little talk in Europe about the great new society that could be erected upon the war's foundations. People wanted only to be done with the fighting, and in each country there was a remnant of antiwar Socialists whose preachments were now beginning to sound increasingly sensible.

Simons believed that the loyal American Socialists could do something about this. With the hopes of both the SDL and the League to Enforce the Peace in the forefront of his thoughts, he went to Washington to see Louis Post. Post was an old single-taxer who had long edited a weekly journal in Chicago, *The Public*, which he had begun about the time Simons came to the city.[37] Now assistant secretary of labor, Post had recognized that he and Simons had become kindred spirits in their attitudes toward socialism and postwar recon-

---

[36] Social Democratic League of America, *A Program of Social Reconstruction After the War* (New York, 1918).
[37] Frank Luther Mott, *History of American Magazines*, IV (Cambridge: Harvard University Press, 1938), 62, 304.

struction[38] and together the two men worked out a plan for communicating with European socialist and labor periodicals. "My idea," Simons wrote to Ernest Poole, who was to edit and distribute material abroad, "is to divide the line of campaign in two directions. One, to show that labor is solidly behind this war and is gaining great victories for democracy and for itself during the war, and second, to show the many drifts among people who have supported the socialist ticket toward support of the war. . . . These are the two points where pro-German propaganda is making its best hit upon the labor and socialist circle."[39] The Committee on Public Information, for which Poole worked, had since its very inception expended a great deal of effort and money disseminating its propaganda abroad, and it put its resources behind this new effort.[40]

Simons was covering labor news for the Milwaukee *Journal* now, and his articles were suitable for distribution by the CPI abroad. Reporting on the AFL convention held in St. Paul in June, Simons announced that "whatever differences there may be in the labor movement of this country . . . there is a united determination to fight this war to a finish."[41] He declared that labor leaders were discovering that great gains were being made for workingmen by the tactics which war had made necessary. Labor no longer had to wait for the tedious legislative process to ameliorate its condition. Instead, administrative commissions were doing the work, and doing it quickly. "On all those dealing with the conditions of labor and the relations between employers and employees," Simons wrote, "labor is receiving representation, generally upon an equality with employers." Because decisions were the result of joint agreement, they went into effect at once. "Moreover," he concluded, "the union, the instrument through which this is accomplished, and the results insured, grows steadily in power and remains completely in the hands of its members."[42]

---

[38] Post to Simons, Dec. 15, 1917, Simons Papers.
[39] Simons to Poole, May 31, 1918, Simons Papers.
[40] Mock and Larson deal extensively with this lesser-known aspect of the CPI's work in *Words That Won the War*, 235–334.
[41] *Journal*, June 13, 1918.
[42] A. M. Simons, "Union Men Will Not Tie Up with Any Party," *Journal*, June 14, 1918. This aspect of Simons' work for the CPI is dealt with

In spite of these efforts, pacifist propaganda was making headway abroad. Its burden was that the workers of America were opposed to Wilson's war aims and to continued U.S. participation in the conflict. As evidence that such sentiments were strongly held, pacifists cited the impressive vote that both Berger and Hillquit, vigorously antiwar Socialists, had received in recent elections.[43]

The Social Democratic League, therefore, conceived of a mission to Europe, consisting of prominent American prowar Socialists who would attempt to rekindle the enthusiasm of their European comrades. A similar mission had been sent to Europe in February under the leadership of Samuel Gompers, but its contacts had been largely with trade union groups. Moreover, Gompers' longtime hostility to radicalism diminished his effectiveness as an emissary of hope to workingmen abroad. The members of the Social Democratic League, on the other hand, represented a middle way between the Bolshevism that frightened the governments of western Europe and the AFL's bread-and-butter unionism that offended radical leaders abroad.

As the league explained its proposed mission to Secretary of State Lansing, it would attempt to win European Socialists to the support of Wilson's war aims; it would confer with men like Ramsay Mac-Donald and Jean Longuet who led the antiwar Socialists in Britain and France and would seek to persuade them to abandon their opposition to the conflict; it would also seek to quash any efforts to rebuild the Second International along its prewar lines, for to do so meant to yield control of international socialism to the Germans.[44]

---

in correspondence in the Loyalty Legion Papers, State Historical Society of Wisconsin. Simons to Louis Post, May 20, 21, 22, 1918; Will Irwin to Simons, May 27, 1918; and Simons to Ernest Poole, May 31, June 1, 6, 10, 1918. Will Irwin was director of the foreign section of the CPI at this time.

[43] Miriam Simons Leuck, "The American Socialist and Labor Mission to Europe, 1918, Background, Activities and Significance: An Experiment in Democratic Diplomacy" (unpublished Ph.D. dissertation, Northwestern University, 1941), 227–28. This dissertation, by Simons' daughter, is a thorough account of the mission that Simons headed in 1918. It relies almost exclusively, however, upon material subsequently deposited in the Simons Papers at the State Historical Society of Wisconsin and is extremely generous in its evaluation of the mission's significance.

[44] William E. Walling, Henry L. Slobodin, and J. I. Sheppard to Lansing, June 12, 1918, Social Democratic League, *One Year's Activity*, 3.

Lansing granted his approval. At his request the members of what was to be known as the American Socialist and Labor Mission to Europe assembled in New York at once. On June 14 Simons received word that he was to go with the group, and the next day he was on his way,[45] still not clear just what plans had been laid for the mission, but grateful for the chance to serve his country.

Simons was chosen chairman of the group. With him went Louis Kopelin, a socialist journalist; John Spargo, long a leader of the eastern intellectuals of the party; and Alexander Howatt, an official of the United Mine Workers. Charles Edward Russell and George Herron were to join them abroad. Once in New York, Simons' familiar enthusiasm began to grow. "I have learned a little more about the mission," he wrote May before he sailed. "It is a bigger thing than I thought. Lansing and President Wilson have both said they consider it the most important mission that has yet gone across. There will be ample funds for any work to be done."[46] That promise alone was a welcome change from most of the ventures with which Simons had been associated. It looked like there would even be a place for May in the months ahead: "This thing gets bigger every moment," Simons wrote again on the same day. "They now want you to come over a little later and have us open up a headquarters in Paris for Socialists during the war." He repeated the encouraging words about the project's support: "There will be ample funds behind us, and the full backing of the government."[47]

It was a heady experience for the longtime radical to find himself this close to the hub of power. When red tape threatened to hold up the mission's departure, "it took a telephone message direct from Lansing to straighten things out," Simons reported.[48] When his ship docked at Liverpool on July 2, he debarked to find the streets lined with American flags[49]—so many of them, he confided to his wife, that he was made almost homesick at the sight.[50] It was even a bit titillat-

[45] May Simons to A. M. Simons, Aug. 3, 1918.
[46] A. M. Simons to May Simons, June 18, 1918, Simons Papers.
[47] *Ibid.*, Second Letter.
[48] A. M. Simons to May Simons, June 19, 1918, Simons Papers.
[49] A. M. Simons, Diary, July 2, 1918, Simons Papers.
[50] A. M. Simons to May Simons, July 5, 1918, Simons Papers.

ing to discover that his hotel room had been searched and his papers ransacked shortly after his arrival.[51] It was a kind of perverse acknowledgment of the mission's importance.

What Simons found around him in England was further proof that much work needed to be done. "There is a strange 'tactic of despair' that seems to have seized everyone," he wrote sadly, "—a lack of faith in their government, in democracy, in victory, in the ability to use victory—in everything. It is not at all the spirit I expected to find."[52] It was a vivid contrast to the spirit of idealism he had seen in America, where people talked of making the world safe for democracy and fighting a war to end war, and where Simons himself had been captured by a vision of a new world about to be born. It was a vivid contrast, too, to the Turnerian image of the indefatigable Anglo-Saxon, who pressed on for justice and security no matter what the hardships, even into the unbroken frontiers of a new world.

As he met his old friends in London, he found that they were filled with pessimism about the war and about the future. H. M. Hyndman, though a longtime supporter of the war effort, now could not see an end to it in sight. The leaders of the warring nations, he claimed, did not want to win, for they feared the downfall of aristocracy and the onset of social revolution.[53] Ramsay MacDonald declared that victory was impossible, and spoke admiringly of Trotsky's work.[54] Most sobering of all, however, was a long and quiet chat that Simons had with English socialist leader John Burns about the meaning of the war.

The war would last another two years, Burns declared, and it would be won not by the nation that could stand the longest, but by the one that would be the last to fall. There would be military stalemate, and the people at home would revolt. The resources of all nations would be exhausted, and once the artificial prosperity of the war was gone, there would be economic collapse. Perhaps some kind of social reconstruction could be undertaken, but much more likely

[51] A. M. Simons to May Simons, July 8, 1918, Simons Papers.
[52] A. M. Simons to May Simons, July 6, 1918, Simons Papers.
[53] A. M. Simons, Diary, July 2, 1918, Simons Papers.
[54] *Ibid.*, July 3, 1918.

consequences of the war were callousness, brutality, and the triumph of autocracy all over Europe.

As for himself, Burns said, he would continue to support his government. There was nothing else he could do. "The call of the horde has come," he told Simons, "and reaches deeper than class or any other social division." His own son was at the front, the lad's room at home "his mother's shrine." "There are," he said in measured tones, "six million such rooms in England."[55]

What Burns said did nothing to deter Simons from the main purposes of his mission or to soften his resolve that the war must be prosecuted with vigor to a successful conclusion. Quite the contrary. The conversation did, however, mark the beginning of his awareness of the war's cost. In the weeks to come he was to be less certain that every bit of opposition to the war was somehow the work of German propagandists. There were abundant reasons for western Europe to be sick to death of the whole struggle. There was no need to find foreign agents at the heart of their weakening of nerve. As he traveled through England, France, and Italy, he came upon scenes that constantly reminded him of the hardships that he and his family had been spared, and that convinced him anew of the importance of what he was doing. "I am sure we are helping to win the war," he wrote to his wife and daughter. "I only hope I can help to keep from you the terrible sacrifices that have fallen upon the women of Belgium, France and England."[56] "If only I can help to make the world a little safer for you and Miriam," he wrote again, ". . . I care for nothing else."[57]

Throughout the first half of July, the mission remained in England, meeting with all the major figures of the socialist and labor movements, trying to win their endorsement of Wilson's war aims and seeking to build the foundations of a new socialist international. G. D. H. Cole wished for an Allied victory, but he was certain that

---

[55] *Ibid.*, July 4, 1918. The quoted portions are in quotation marks in the diary.

[56] A. M. Simons to May Simons and Miriam Simons, July 22, 1918, Simons Papers.

[57] A. M. Simons to May Simons, Aug. 23, 1918, Simons Papers.

democracy would be a casualty, permanently disabled by the conflict and its aftermath.[58] George Lansbury believed that Wilson would never be able to persuade a peace conference to accept the Fourteen Points—European diplomats, said Lansbury, were too skillful for the innocent Americans.[59] Camille Huysmans sneered at the notion of expecting great things from the Allied democracies or from democratic institutions per se.[60] George Bernard Shaw declared that war destroyed the moral fiber of statesmen.[61]

There were a few who found some cause for hope. Sidney and Beatrice Webb assured Simons that Ramsay MacDonald's antiwar stand was not endorsed by a single union, and that some of the pessimists, at least, had only an insignificant following.[62] John Hodge, the minister of pensions, agreed, and even suggested that great things might be accomplished in the period of reconstruction that would follow the war.[63] H. G. Wells expressed enthusiasm at Wilson's idea of a League of Nations, and found time, in his conversation with Simons at the Reform Club, to digress a bit and talk about his own methods of writing.[64]

Two public meetings were held by the mission while it was in England, one in West Ham, the other in Trafalgar Square, and Simons spoke at both. The crowds were good and, as Simons wrote, "All agree that I succeeded in getting my story across, and it certainly received a big ovation."[65]

It was impossible to measure the impact the mission had upon morale in England. Aside from guesses about minds being changed, two concrete achievements could be counted. First of all, Simons had had a chance to reply publicly to charges that the civil rights of Germans in America had been consistently violated and that the violations had been condoned by the American government. It was an

[58] A. M. Simons, Diary, July 6, 1918.
[59] *Ibid.*
[60] *Ibid.*, July 10, 1918.
[61] *Ibid.*
[62] *Ibid.*, July 7, 1918.
[63] *Ibid.*, July 11, 1918.
[64] *Ibid.*, July 12, 1918.
[65] A. M. Simons to May Simons, July 14, 1918, Simons Papers.

issue dear to his heart, and when the British *Labour Leader* asked him to comment on the matter he gladly responded. Naturally, he said, neither he nor his government approved of "certain outrages against pro-Germans in the United States. . . . In the one lynching case . . . special federal and state prosecutors were sent to assist the local states attorney in prosecuting the supposed members of the mob." But, he continued, "There are nearly 30,000 enemy aliens from Germany alone in America. Fully nine-tenths of these are still virulently pro-Kaiser. Yet . . . most of them are going about their work undisturbed. It seems to me that if we have erred in this matter it has been upon the side of laxity and good nature."[66]

The other accomplishment the mission could count as it went to France was a manifesto, drafted by a committee of British and American Socialists, that was to be the first step in the formation of a new international. It was to be submitted to the workers in the Allied countries only, for as long as the war continued the new body was to be "international" in a restricted sense. It was a bit disappointing, too, to discover that the old socialist conflicts had arisen even over this sketchy and tentative project. Though the conferees agreed upon the general aims of the new organization, they began to quarrel at once over the phrasing of those aims and over the matter of who could be trusted to carry on the work.[67] Nevertheless, Simons reported to his wife that their "plans for a general cooperation of the pro-war Socialists of all the allied nations is going through, and I honestly believe that will be worth a division on the Western front."[68]

The mission arrived in Paris on July 20, and there they found the tactics of despair even more widespread than in England. Among the Socialists, the pacifist minority that urged a negotiated peace had been gaining ground over the prowar majority. The far Left had become Bolshevik, urging an immediate end to the war and the beginning of revolution to create the dictatorship of the proletariat. For this reason and because of longtime distrust of Britain, even the prowar Socialists

[66] A. M. Simons, letter published in *Labour Leader*, July 17, 1918, clipping in Simons Papers.
[67] Leuck, "The American Socialist," 259.
[68] A. M. Simons to May Simons, July 20, 1918.

were hesitant about the formation of a new international. They feared the further subdivision of the socialist movement, and they feared British domination. Apparently the Gompers mission in February had only made matters worse among French workingmen, for it had proudly asserted to an exhausted people that America was ready to keep the war going indefinitely to achieve victory.

What needed to be done was to convince the French working class not only that America was wholeheartedly behind the war effort but also that Wilson was sincere in his Fourteen Points and in his determination to see them realized. Therefore, publicity was of the utmost importance to the mission in France. The CPI set its wheels in motion, and soon every meeting, conference, and luncheon were amply reported in the French press. "We have received fully 100 columns of notice," Simons wrote early in August, ". . . and have been quite the sensation of the day. The worst trouble is that we are now so much in the lime light that it is harder to do some of our work."[69]

Simons refused to think of himself as merely a public relations man, spreading propaganda across allied Europe. In one sense, he liked all the attention that he and his mission received; he reported to his wife how many times a day his picture had been taken, and he urged May to write the CPI for copies of the photographs.[70] At the same time, he wanted his mission to deal with matters of substance— to get down to the hard work of forming meaningful alliances among the Socialists of western Europe and of hammering out a program to which all could subscribe. He grew impatient with the endless round of pleasantries and picture-taking, and enthusiastic when he felt he had at last broken through the crust of social custom. "For the first time [we] really got down to business," he wrote of a meeting with Socialist Deputies. "Not that I doubt but what we had accomplished much before but most conferences had consisted in listening to our statements, then telling us how much they loved us and America, and then 'Try this wine.' There had been no real clash of opinions. But this time I insisted that they tell us on what fronts they disagreed."[71]

[69] A. M. Simons to May Simons, Aug. 4, 1918.
[70] *Ibid.*, Aug. 8, 1918.
[71] *Ibid.*, Aug. 1, 1918.

The task of the mission grew easier near the end of July, because the promises of American aid were being impressively redeemed. Marshall Foch had begun a counteroffensive against the German salients, and 270,000 American troops were engaged in this effort. By early August the Second Battle of the Marne was over, the German armies driven back. All the advances of Ludendorff's spring offensive had been canceled out. Among the people that Simons talked with in France, no one was predicting a quick end to the war, even after the Marne offensive, but they were heartened by what was going on. "Military events seem to be making our work easier," Simons reported only a few days after the counteroffensive had got under way, "although there is still much to do and a great need of our work."[72]

Simons found in France, as he had in England, that thoughtful people, Socialists and non-Socialists alike were skeptical about the future of democratic institutions in Europe.[73] This was partly because of the obvious failure of the parliaments of Europe to control the events that had led to war in 1914. The alliances that had given the march to war a momentum of its own had only the faintest connection with the popular will of the nations involved. The skepticism about democracy was pronounced among Socialists not so much because it had failed, but because something else had worked so much better. The parliamentary Socialists had seen a tiny and obscure clique take control of a whole empire and work a revolution almost overnight. In a few months, Lenin and the Bolsheviks had made more social and economic changes than a whole generation of Marxists had eked out through parliamentary processes. In addition, Europeans saw, as Simons had, that the war was initiating changes that were made administratively and that cut through many a Gordian knot of theory and controversy.

To some extent, all these factors militated against the success of Simons' mission, expecially the part that was concerned with setting up the framework of a new Socialist International. The international, as described by the members of the American Socialist and Labor Mission, sounded a bit old-fashioned. It was a faint socialist echo of

[72] *Ibid.*, July 22, 1918.
[73] A. M. Simons, Diary, Aug. 2, 6, 1918.

Wilsonian war aims and far from able to capture the imagination of European radicals the way the Third International would a year later. Jean Longuet, grandson of Karl Marx and one of Simons' closest friends in the French socialist movement, was content to call the mission's proposed international, "a flag, a symbol, a Sorel myth if you wish."[74] Jules Guesde, another longtime colleague, believed that the present was "a time for fighting, not for conferences."[75]

Gradually, Simons' own interest was taken up more and more with matters that were only incidentally concerned with the mission's official aims. Perhaps it was because the military situation was improving so rapidly that an end to the war seemed in sight. Perhaps it was because the multitude of impressions and experiences to which Simons was subjected reinforced his initial ideas about the war's significance. In any case, he became increasingly convinced that once more he was riding the wave of the future, and if he could but comprehend its dynamics and anticipate its motion, he might yet be one of the first to enter the promised land.

All around him, he saw the ruins of the past and the wreckage of the present. There was Alexander Kerensky in Paris, a "striking personality," Simons thought, a man who had held Russia in his grasp for a brief instant, and let it slip away, clinging to the hope that the allied intervention could drive the Bolsheviks from power.[76] There were people like M. and Mme. Le Roux, not nearly as unique as the exiled Kerensky, but the more significant for the familiarity of their plight: all their male heirs had been lost in the war. It seemed to the Le Rouxs that French civilization itself was doomed, for unless a new infusion of blood came from somewhere, population in France would decline severely, and the nation that had always been the last stand of Europe against invasion would crumble.[77]

---

[74] Longuet is quoted by Simons in his diary, July 29, 1918.

[75] *Ibid.*, Aug. 5, 1918.

[76] According to diary and letters, Simons and the other members of the mission saw Kerensky three times: July 17, 27, and 29, 1918. Simons termed Kerensky a "striking personality" in his letter to May, July 19, 1918. The other two meetings are referred to in diary entries for the above dates.

[77] A. M. Simons, Diary, July 30, 1918.

There were the battlefields of the western front, where devastation could be seen at firsthand. Simons and the other members of the mission spent a day near Château Thierry, an area that had just been retaken by Marshal Foch's army. They ate their dinners on the battlefield and passed through Vaux, which had been totally destroyed by the artillery barrage that preceded every Allied advance. And on their way back to Paris, the American Socialists saw a few peasants on the road, beginning to return to their lands and to harvest whatever might be left.[78] Simons and his colleagues visited the Neuilly Hospital in France, where they saw the skillful work of surgeons who managed to repair the damage that bullets and shells did to the human beings who survived at all.[79]

As Simons rode on to Italy he tried to describe what he thought was happening to the Europe he had known. "The world is completely torn to pieces," he wrote, with a haste that made him ignore his own mixed metaphors, "and I am watching the wheels go round. It is like sitting at the side of the French Revolution, multiplied a thousand times in a civilization infinitely more complex than that of France in the eighteenth century."[80] "We are . . . sitting on a volcano," he wrote later from England, "playing with the most powerful social forces ever unchained, and the end is not yet."[81] "You and I," he said to May, "have had a part in the biggest thing that ever happened. Your Americanization work is something of transcendent importance—only do not work too hard," he advised with an eye to the future. "The biggest work will come after the war, and America must lead."[82]

By the time the socialist mission reached Italy, where opposition to the war was pronounced among the working classes, and where the government openly stated its disagreements with Wilson's war aims, Simons was doing at least two jobs at once. He was participating in the endless round of luncheons, dinners, official meetings, and private

[78] *Ibid.*, Aug. 3, 1918.
[79] *Ibid.*, Aug. 1, 1918.
[80] A. M. Simons to May Simons, Aug. 10, 1918.
[81] *Ibid.*, Sept. 7, 1918.
[82] *Ibid.*, Aug. 30, 1918.

conferences that were the essence of the mission's work, and he was gathering material for the book that he had been writing for almost a year now, "The Vision for Which We Fight." He was jotting down notes about the war's constructive effects: agricultural cooperatives had grown in Italy during the war, he was told, and so had the unions.[83] Impressive hospitals had been built by co-ops; the docks of Genoa were run completely by co-ops; shipbuilding co-ops were returning damaged craft to service in quick order.[84] At the ministry of education, Simons learned that educational reform had been pushed hard throughout the war.[85] At the Fiat works he discovered what a considerable role women were occupying on the assembly lines. Everywhere he went he asked questions, collected printed matter that he sent home, and steadily began to piece together the evidence in support of his optimistic view of the postwar world. "I have been behind the scenes as no one else has been," he wrote of his experiences, "and if I am able to use my knowledge it should be worth while."[86]

All the while, an unmistakable counterpoint to the mission's activities began to be heard in Italy. Because the Italians had been such an unsteady ally, vast propaganda offensives had been launched from Washington, both by the Committee on Public Information and by State Department agencies, and all designed to stiffen the nation's will to fight. Secretary of State Lansing, however, had never trusted the CPI's head, George Creel.[87] The secretary considered Creel too radical, and since Creel had Wilson's confidence nothing could be done to remove him from the CPI. Lansing displayed his mistrust in a variety of ways, including efforts to quiet the CPI's voices abroad in favor of his own.

One clash came in Italy. Captain Charles Merriam, political scientist from the University of Chicago, was the head of the CPI staff in Rome, and he labored tirelessly to counteract the pacifist and anti-

---

[83] A. M. Simons, Diary, Aug. 9, 11, 1918.

[84] *Ibid.*, *passim*, Aug. 10–13.

[85] *Ibid.*, Aug. 14.

[86] A. M. Simons to May Simons, Sept. 7, 1918. See also Aug. 10, 1918.

[87] In his memoir Creel quotes a number of Lansing's derogatory evaluations of him, *Rebel at Large* (New York: Putnam's, 1947), 158–60.

Ally sentiment that abounded.[88] He received little cooperation from officials of the American diplomatic corps serving in Italy, and when the American Socialist and Labor Mission arrived, he received none. No paths were smoothed, no channels of communication opened.

In terms of the mission's accomplishment, it mattered little. They were able to establish their own contacts, even though neither Simons nor any of his companions had the kinds of association among the Italian Socialists that they had with the French and English. Merriam himself was both cooperative and full of praise for what the group had done: in his report to the CPI Merriam declared, "This Commission . . . [has] done excellent work in Italy. The work of the Commission should be followed up. It is quite possible that a well-directed campaign would result in weakening the war opposition which is largely based on ignorance of facts, on pro-German sentiment, and on the activities of a number of anarchistic leaders."[89] Simons claimed that "some ridiculously overenthusiastic Socialists in Italy tell us we have turned the tide and saved the day and perhaps the Allied cause in Italy."[90]

In a more subtle way, the intramural conflict served for Simons as an unpleasant echo of less happy days. On the side of the establishment for the first time in his life, Simons found that conflicts were similar to those in the old radical environment from which he had come. That was no bother. He was still no man to shrink from a fight. What was significant was that the CPI–State Department infighting seemed to confirm what so many of Simons' contacts had been saying about the ineffectiveness of government in getting things done. For the time being Simons was too preoccupied with his notion of a vision for which the people of the world were fighting to ponder very long the implications of what had happened in Italy. Before many more months had passed, however, he would begin to draw new conclusions from the set of data he was gathering abroad.

On September 13, Simons sailed from Liverpool. His ship, the *Caronia*, was convoyed the first two days out and darkened for the

[88] Mock and Larson, *Words That Won the War*, 286–91.
[89] Quoted in Leuck, "The American Socialist," 293.
[90] A. M. Simons to May Simons, Aug. 21, 1918.

entire journey. The mission could be called a success. The crowds that
had attended the rallies in England, France, and Italy had been large
and friendly. The private conferences, which provided an exchange of
views, had been frank enough to enable Simons and his colleagues to
correct mistaken impressions of America's aims and to hearten spirits
that had been paralyzed between the threats of Bolshevism and
militarism.

A later generation, less optimistic than they about the power of
propaganda and high ideals, would find all this uncomfortably intan-
gible. The new international had not been established. No organizational framework had been set up to continue the contacts between
European and American Socialists. The end of the war seemed in
sight at last, and it no longer seemed so important that such a
framework be maintained after the cessation of hostilities, despite the
widespread fear of reaction abroad.

For Simons it had been a gratifying experience. He had wanted
desperately to contribute to the war effort, and he had been given the
opportunity to do so. It was all very well to travel about Wisconsin
urging faith and loyalty, but the work of the Loyalty Legion paled
beside the chance to be an emissary of the federal government to the
very spots where the shells were falling and where the social fabric of
western civilization was being rent in a dozen places.

It was not an easy journey, and it was not a remunerative one.
Simons declared, without complaint, that it was the hardest work he
had ever done,[91] and took his customary pride in his own inexhausti-
bility. "During the first few weeks," he had reported to May, "we
nearly walked Kopelin and Howat to death, and they have never
been able to work all night as Spargo and I have almost done."[92] He
worried that his wife and daughter might be short of money in his
absence,[93] but when his $40 weekly salary began to arrive in Milwau-
kee he declared it was too much: "If possible send part of it back," he
wrote to May, "but don't strap yourself."[94]

[91] A. M. Simons to May Simons, Aug. 18, 1918.
[92] *Ibid.*, Aug. 4, 1918.
[93] *Ibid.*, July 3, 20, 1918.
[94] A. M. Simons to May Simons, Aug. 5, 1918. J. G. Phelps Stokes to
May Simons, July 30, 1918, makes it clear that this was the salary previously

Back in the United States, Simons met with the administrative committee of the Social Democratic League and presented the report of the mission, which was endorsed at once. He went on to Washington to present the report to Secretary of State Lansing. "You have done a great service," Simons remembered Lansing as saying, "not only to the Allied cause, but to humanity."[95] The next day, Simons talked with Woodrow Wilson. It was heartening, indeed, to hear his own sentiments echoed by the president. "This war was started by statesmen," he told Simons, ". . . but peace will be made by peoples." "Such power as I have," Wilson continued, "[is] due to the fact that I have sought to know the mind and heart of the peoples of the world. Statesmen are still talking in terms of an age that is gone—of 100 years ago—of boundaries and dynasties and spheres of influence."[96]

Soon, Wilson thought, that would all be over. American troops by the thousands were pouring onto the western front in hot pursuit of the exhausted armies of imperial Germany. A peace conference was not far off, and just beyond that lay the challenging work of reconstruction. Simons left Washington with a headful of ideas about the years that lay ahead, refreshed and encouraged by the knowledge that the Cooperative Commonwealth, though called now by other names, was still attainable.

---

agreed upon, and regrets that it is such a small fragment of "Mr. Simons' earning power."

[95] A. M. Simons, Diary, Sept. 25, 1918.

[96] Recorded by Simons in his diary, Sept. 26, 1918.

CHAPTER NINE

The New World

Simons was glad to be back home after his two-month absence.[1] Apart from his reluctance to remain away from his family, he had too many irons in the fire to leave them untended so long. He was eager to finish his new book, *The Vision for Which We Fight,* and he wanted to shape a postwar program for the Wisconsin Loyalty Legion, a program that would, he hoped, "make some headway against the reaction that seems impending."[2]

Then there was the matter of the Social Democratic League and his own relation to the socialist movement in general. By the time the armistice finally came, the Socialist party was shattered. Its old centers of power in the west were gone; the Green Corn Rebellion had killed the party completely in Oklahoma; the party press had been crushed and its leaders sent to jail. Where the Espionage Act was not invoked, local citizens did their part to heap disgrace upon any Socialists who spoke out against the war.

The Bolshevik Revolution had added further complications to a situation that had been already complicated enough. At first, most American Socialists had welcomed the Bolshevik coup; then, when Lenin began talking about the dictatorship of the proletariat and other entirely proper Marxist dogmas, many of his erstwhile American sympathizers fell away. What was happening in Russia no longer seemed the fulfillment of democracy and freedom.

Nevertheless, after the severe treaty of Brest–Litovsk, the attitude of many American Socialists began to change in favor of supporting the Allies, and after Wilson had declared his Fourteen Points as America's war aims, these same Socialists tried to persuade the party to change its official antiwar position. The National Executive Committee had met in August 1918 to consider this possibility, but it accomplished nothing. The meeting had quickly degenerated into a conflict between the left and right wings of the party.[3]

Actual party membership had gone down only a little during the war, and within a year it was to increase about 65 percent. The new center of power was in the Northeast, and the new members were largely eastern intellectuals and immigrant groups who had been impressed both by the Bolsheviks and by the revolutions in eastern Europe.[4]

Everything that had happened to the party between 1917 and 1919 was almost the precise opposite of what Algie Simons had wished for in his twenty years of socialist activity. As he saw it, the Social Democratic League was America's last hope for a socialist movement built upon American realities and aspirations. He knew it was a slim hope, and he was too old to believe that therein lay the challenge. "Somehow," Simons confided to his old friend Russell, "my enthusiasm for starting Socialist parties . . . seems to be somewhat dulled by long experience. Perhaps it should not be. Perhaps I should start in on the umpty-umpth with the same energy and wild enthusiasm and great expectations that I did on the first. But I just can't do it."[5]

Russell was the head of the league now, and he wanted Simons to work as an organizer for it.[6] Simons refused. There were other things he wanted to do, and he feared that the SDL was already falling prey to the ills that had proved fatal to the Socialist party. "It [the SDL] is falling into the same ghetto psychology that damned the s.p. Its headquarters should be outside N.Y. or at least it should not have its governing body where they do not even consult with anyone outside."[7] When Russell pressed him for further suggestions about advancing the league, Simons tried to be helpful: "It looks to me as if the biggest thing for the League to do would be to try to hitch up with

---

[1] A. M. Simons to May Simons, Aug. 18, 23, 1918, Simons Papers.
[2] Simons to Russell, Nov. 21, 1918, Simons Papers.
[3] David Shannon, *The Socialist Party of America* (New York: Macmillan, 1955), 118–19.
[4] *Ibid.*, 121.
[5] Simons to Russell, Nov. 26, 1918, Simons Papers.
[6] Russell to Simons, Nov. 21, 1918, Simons Papers.
[7] Simons to Russell, Nov. 21, 1918, Simons Papers.

the new Labor Party. Is it not possible to form some sort of combination of the various language federations that have offered to join the League, and the new Labor Party and the League? Something along the plan of the English Labour Party? Excuse the comparison."[8] His heart was not in the task, however, no matter how much Russell urged him to keep faith with the new organization.[9] Simons wryly observed, "Sometimes . . . I have a longing to quit reforming the world and go to earning a living. I never will. The habit is too fixed. But the desire will arise."[10]

Simons drifted out of the SDL almost at once, and the organization itself faded away within a year. On the international scene, the hopes held by the American Socialist and Labor Mission for a new Allied International also faded. In place of what Simons, Spargo, Russell, and the others had wanted there was now the Third International, directed from Moscow and embraced by what Simons called the "boudoir Bolsheviks" in America. As far as Simons was concerned, the remnant of the Socialist party that had not been pro-German during the war was now pro-Bolshevik, and he cared for neither.

His objections to Lenin and the Bolsheviks were thoughtful, even though in predicting their imminent collapse he was as wrong as he had been about the collapse of capitalism in America.[11] Both in the articles he was writing and in letters to close friends he expressed the same kinds of criticisms. Lenin and his party had turned Russia upside down, and it was folly to believe that incredible hardship and suffering would not follow this utter disruption of both government and economy. Bolshevism, Simons contended, did not represent a forward movement for the Russian proletariat: "It is catastrophic," he wrote. "This differentiates it sharply from the genuine labor movement which grows only as it slowly gains power and schools its members to use that power."[12] The point was, as Simons put it to Russell, "You can seize a state and run the old machinery with almost

[8] *Ibid.*, Dec. 16, 1918.
[9] Russell to Simons, Dec. 6, 1918, Simons Papers.
[10] Simons to Russell, Nov. 26, 1918, Simons Papers.
[11] *Ibid.*, July 20, 1919.
[12] Simons, "Bolshevism and Shop Stewardism," *The National Civic Federation Review*, March 5, 1919.

anyone. But seizing a factory is much more apt to shut it down than make it pay a profit."[13]

For the American radicals who had been attracted to the new order in Russia, Simons had only ridicule: "They think a man having a fit is moving faster than the one who walks quietly toward his object."[14] He found it hard even to take them seriously, especially the young Greenwich Village intellectuals who seemed a very parody of revolutionary ardor. "Did you ever see the comedy," he asked Russell, "in that crowd of nice, bright professional men and women shouting for a proletariat revolution (to make the aforesaid nice bright etc. dictators for the proletariat) while at the same time they swing a spiked club upon all the organized proletarians . . . to drive them away."[15]

The kind of amusement he expressed over the American Bolsheviks he was also beginning to use on himself. In his years of party prominence he had been deadly serious about his mission. Now, for the first time, he was able to have mild fun at his own expense: "while you and I agree," he wrote to Russell, "the world is still safe."[16] But there was one matter he could not take lightly. He stood adamant against any efforts to pardon or reprieve Socialists who had been accused of pro-German activities during the war. When the *New Appeal*, the latest incarnation of the *Appeal to Reason*, launched a crusade for the release of all who had been convicted under the Espionage Act, Simons refused to be associated with it. "There are those who did all they could to prolong the war, save the Kaiser, and kill democracy," he insisted. "Why kiss and make up? Not for me."[17] When Louis Slobodin, secretary of the Social Democratic League, tried to get Simons to sign a petition for a general amnesty, he refused, until it was amended to exempt those who spoke in favor of a German victory.[18] He agreed completely that there were Socialists

[13] Simons to Russell, July 20, 1919. See also Simons, "Bolshevism, Famine Road for Workers," Milwaukee *Journal*, April 27, 1919, and Simons, "Constitution of Bolsheviki Sets Up an Autocracy," *Journal*, May 11, 1919.
[14] Simons, "Bolshevism, Famine Road for Workers."
[15] Simons to Russell, July 27, 1919, Simons Papers.
[16] *Ibid.*
[17] *Ibid.*, Nov. 26, 1918.
[18] Slobodin to executive committee of SDL, March 15, 1919; Simons to Slobodin, March 19, 1919; Telegram, Slobodin to Simons, March 21, 1919.

who had been wrongfully imprisoned—Debs was one of them, and he deeply regretted the fact that the Supreme Court had turned down Debs' appeal.[19]

To deny that any of those imprisoned had spoken in favor of the Central Powers was simply not true. If it were, he said, "then the Appeal and all of us were liars during the war. . . . We know that for many, though by no means all, their attitude toward the war was part of the German propaganda. . . . They distorted news, misled labor, wrecked the Socialist Party, . . . prolonged the war and caused the death of men in the ranks."[20] As Simons saw it, they owed a debt to American society, and they ought to pay it.

Perhaps he would have felt differently if the European situation had seemed to hold more promise. He saw nothing to suggest that Germany was prepared to turn swords into plowshares, and he found that German-Americans were no more contrite. Victor Berger had campaigned successfully for the Congress in 1918, and his campaign had been based upon frank appeals for the German vote in Milwaukee and upon praises for the work of his countrymen abroad. "Of course the Germans are unreconstructed," said Simons. "They are worse now than during the war."[21]

The heart of Simons' quarrel with socialism was not so much its alleged pro-German orientation during the war or its flirtation with Bolshevism afterwards. Those were only outward manifestations of a disease that ran much deeper—the disease he had always warned against, and one whose symptoms he had perceived during the time he was on the National Executive Committee. It was the mortal illness of estrangement from the masses of working people in the

---

[19] In a letter to Upton Sinclair, Dec. 6, 1919, Simons Papers, Simons claimed that he had been in Washington a few weeks before and had gone "to see what could be done about getting Debs out. I was told that I presented the first really new evidence in the case and that it would go to President Wilson."

In 1921 Simons wrote to Guy Goff, assistant to the attorney general, asking for an amnesty for Debs (Simons to Goff, March 28, 1921, Simons Papers). Goff replied that he would give Simons' appeal "serious consideration" (Goff to Simons, March 30, 1921, Simons Papers).

[20] Simons to Slobodin, March 19, 1919, Simons Papers.

[21] Simons to Russell, Nov. 21, 1918, Simons Papers.

United States. Simons had come to realize by 1918 that the treat-ment he had most often prescribed was for the symptoms, not for the disease. His constant pleas for Americanizing the party and his search for ways in which the party could gain political power were, as he saw them now, only therapeutic, not curative.

When Socialists had gained political power they had done nothing to change the fundamental class structure. Simons wrote, of the socialist city he knew best, "Labor has gained less in Milwaukee since its policies have been directed by the 'Socialist officials union' than in any comparable city in America."[22] He claimed that Victor Berger had "often boasted of the fact that, owing to his direction of Socialist tactics, there are fewer labor disturbances in Milwaukee than in any other industrial city in the country."[23] The boast, Simons insisted, was not made because the worker's lot was so much better in that city. He produced statistics that showed Milwaukee to have the lowest union scale in more trades than any city but Buffalo. At the very time when wages were rising most rapidly elsewhere, they remained "below the point of healthful physical existence" in Milwaukee.[24]

All Simons' war experiences reinforced his disenchantment with politics. Nationalism had destroyed the strongest party of parliamen-tary socialism in Europe, and nationalism had wiped out all the political gains the American Socialist party had made between 1912 and 1917. At the same time, the exigencies of war had done more to fulfill socialist goals than all the propaganda efforts, election cam-paigns, and socialist officeholders had done in twenty years. The friends and colleagues he had talked to abroad felt much as he did, and for the same reasons. Over and over he had heard their skepticism about political processes and their admiration for the governmental measures that exercised some control over economic life. In Europe

[22] A. M. Simons, "Socialism in Milwaukee and the Wage Scale," *Milwau-kee Journal*, July 22, 1918.

[23] *Ibid.*

[24] *Ibid.* Two articles by John Laslett, though not about Milwaukee, tend to support Simons' assertion that socialism did not benefit labor as much as AFL unionism did. See Laslett, "Reflections on the Failure of Socialism in the American Federation of Labor," *Mississippi Valley Historical Review*, L (March 1964), 634–51; and "Socialism and the American Labor Move-ment: Some New Reflections," *Labor History*, VIII (Spring 1967), 136–55.

the emphasis had been upon skepticism, and it was to increase after the peace conference. Parliaments were impotent, it seemed to many, democratic processes obsolete and ineffectual.

Simons was not pessimistic. His new expectations were revealed in his book *The Vision for Which We Fought* and in the lecturing he did in Wisconsin for the League to Enforce the Peace and the Wisconsin Loyalty Legion. Wherever he spoke, he found tremendous interest among his audience in the period of reconstruction. "There is an enthusiasm in these gatherings," he wrote, "that I have never seen . . . in almost thirty years of propaganda talking. . . . Everywhere the question is, where can we learn more of the changes that are upon us?"[25]

His book was to fulfill that desire to learn more, and he had worked feverishly on it in order to finish the manuscript by the time the armistice was signed. It was not intended as a scholarly treatment of the consequences of the war; it was to be only suggestive. It did not put forward a program; it only postulated problems.[26] The book proceeded to show the gains each group in society had made during the war. "When the war opened," Simons wrote, "trade-unionism . . . was making almost no headway against the great trusts, and these were usurping a constantly increasing percentage of the industrial field. . . . The war has gained this victory without bloodshed or open conflict."[27] Before the war, industry had been "based upon the idea that conflict of forces produced the highest efficiency." The war, however, had "given industry unity; has made industrial progress a scientific social problem and developed some of the machinery for solution; it has temporarily partially removed the element of private gain as the dominant incentive and replaced it with the motive of common good. On these foundations," Simons concluded, "a new society can be built."[28]

War had also changed the nature of the state. Administration was growing at the expense of legislation. "Such an evolution," Simons

---

[25] Simons to Richard T. Ely, Nov. 23, 1918, Ely Papers.
[26] A. M. Simons, *The Vision for Which We Fought* (New York: Macmillan, 1919), preface.
[27] *Ibid.*, 53.
[28] *Ibid.*, 18.

explained, "leaves behind many vestigal [*sic*] organs in the body politic. For the moment, Congress appears as one of these."[29] Some people complained that democracy was injured in this development, that popular discussion and decisionmaking had been thwarted, and that democracy was being increasingly removed from decisionmaking. This, said Simons, was like complaining that one could not stop a conflagration with a mass meeting in the space needed for the fire engines.[30]

The book was not published until February 1919, despite Simons' pleas to his publisher for haste.[31] By then the eagerness and interest that he had found in November and December was gone. The book sold only eight hundred copies.[32] He took it as simple testimony to the fact that people were tired of thinking about the war and wanted to get back to the old ways of doing things. The vision for which they had fought had evaporated. The ground swell of reform which Simons had worked so long to initiate and which he thought the war had finally set in motion was gone.

A lifetime of radical activity had made Simons resilient. As each dream died, another grew in its place, nourished by the experience of what had gone before. In a final valedictory on radical politics, "The Uselessness of Protest Parties," Simons announced that the Socialist party had accomplished nothing in its twenty years of work. Because of the form of American government, he said, "No protest party starts with any hope of success in electing its presidential candidate. It is therefore quick to degenerate into a cesspool, drawing off . . . the very elements that in the main stream might have been extremely helpful." He congratulated his old adversary, the AFL, for its wisdom "in deciding to follow the road that leads to success, instead of the one that is marked only by glorious sacrifices and inglorious failures, by great expectations and no realizations."[33] So saying, Simons returned

---

[29] *Ibid.*, 65.
[30] *Ibid.*, 78.
[31] Simons to Macmillan's, Nov. 23, 1918, Simons Papers.
[32] J. P. R. Budlong, Macmillan's, to Robert Huston, Oct. 29, 1958, cited in Huston, "Algie Martin Simons and the American Socialist Movement" (unpublished Ph.D. dissertation, University of Wisconsin, 1965), 332.
[33] "Uselessness of Protest Parties," *American Federationist*, XXVII.

to the work of preparing himself for yet another career, a career in scientific management.

Frederick Winslow Taylor, the father of scientific management in America, had no radical skeletons in his closet. He was a firm believer in capitalism and devoted his life to making American industry more efficient and hence more productive. He drove himself hard, and, as he held his ever-present stopwatch over groups of workingmen, he worked to develop ways in which he could drive them just as hard. There is, Taylor frequently explained, no substitute for "the real monotonous grind which trains character."[34]

Taylor believed that if one studied every step in a manufacturing process, one could set up scientifically determined criteria of productivity for both men and machines. There was no place for unions, strikes, or collective bargaining in this scheme of things. Wages, hours, and working conditions were matters to be determined "scientifically" by experts. The man who did factory work couldn't possibly understand the complexities of what he was doing, and therefore he had no right to interfere with the deliberations of those who did understand.[35]

Such ideas might seem at opposite poles from the ideas of the thoughtful generation of progressives and radicals who had worked since 1900 to humanize capitalism. Taylorism seemed antithetical to the beliefs of Simons, who had for years attacked the greed of employers and sought to improve the lot of the American proletariat and urge them to prepare for leadership in the forthcoming Cooperative Commonwealth. Yet there was much in the thought of Taylor that the social reformers found attractive, and much that Simons came to admire.

Before World War I, the good news of efficiency had swept America. It had begun with the Eastern Rate Case of 1910–1911, in which Louis Brandeis argued before the Supreme Court that the railroads could meet their deficits without a rate increase, if they but introduced

[34] Samuel Haber, *Efficiency and Uplift* (Chicago: University of Chicago Press, 1964), 7.
[35] *Ibid.*, 23–24.

the new science of management into railroading. He produced a swarm of witnesses who testified to the savings that had come to a variety of industries that had taken on the techniques of scientific management. He concluded that such techniques could save the railroads $1 million a day.[36]

To the Socialists, this began to sound like what they had been saying for years. True, they were deeply concerned about moral values and about the quality of human life, but they also rested their arguments upon a foundation of rationality and an abhorrence of waste. In 1912 Simons had written *Wasting Human Life*, a Socialist party pamphlet that was first serialized in the *Coming Nation*, and in it he declared, "Socialism rests its indictment upon the proudest boast of the capitalist class—that class makes its plea for existence on ground of its efficiency in management of industry. So once in feudal times did kings and nobles plead as a reason for their existence that they protected those whom they plundered."[37]

In the same pamphlet, Simons had enumerated all the wasteful practices that were inevitable under the capitalist organization of economic life. Unemployment, industrial accidents, the advertising industry, undermechanized farms, modern fashion, and shoddy goods were all listed in his indictment. He had a word to say, in 1912, about scientific management too: "We hear much, in these days, of 'efficiency engineers.' . . . The text from which all these sermons are preached is that the workers of today are producing less than half what they might produce. . . . But because this movement comes from the side of the employers the workers have quickly learned that it is but a mask for increased exploitation, and instead of welcoming it they revolt against it. If the increased product flowed into the hands of those who produced it, the 'efficiency engineer' would be welcomed in every shop."[38]

The Milwaukee socialist administration had employed both John R. Commons and Harrington Emerson as consultants on scientific

---

[36] *Ibid.*, 52–55.
[37] A. M. Simons, *Wasting Human Life* (Chicago: Socialist Party, 1912), 1–2.
[38] *Ibid.*, 88.

management; during World War I and shortly thereafter Henry Gantt, one of Taylor's outstanding disciples, had pushed his attack on inefficiency to include an attack on the profit system itself. Taylor's work seemed to have implications that went far beyond the factory.[39]

The Socialists were not attracted only to promises of efficiency. Taylorism had another beguiling aspect that commended itself to the weary veterans of radical struggles: its emphasis upon leadership by experts. Year after year Socialist party intellectuals had gone before audiences of workingmen to persuade them of the logic of socialism. Avalanches of propaganda—in newspapers, pamphlets, from street-corner orators and candidates for office—had poured over America. Election after election had come and gone, without registering any indication that the working class had been roused to wisdom and action. It all seemed to prove what many radical intellectuals had always suspected: that the conditions of the working class were not going to improve unless wiser heads directed the task. Now, perhaps, the experts could step behind the scenes in factories and offices and, if they were experts of the right sort, accomplish many of the goals of socialism. The example of Herbert Hoover's war work was persuasive. As "food dictator," his skillful administrative efforts had done much to save untold thousands of Europeans from starvation, and his admirers, which included progressives and radicals alike, believed that the methods of engineer Hoover could be put to good use in transforming industries.[40]

By 1919 another possibility made Taylorism attractive to many who had been Socialists before the war. The virus of Bolshevism might begin to infect America unless steps were taken to prevent it. Scientific management, with is promise of social control and class harmony, might immunize the American working class against the foreign threat. To the onetime radical who could accept neither Bolshevism nor middle-class hostility to labor, the ideas of Frederick

---

[39] Samuel Haber, *Efficiency and Uplift*, 47.
[40] *Ibid.*, 48. Hoover's right-hand man at this time was Edward Eyre Hunt, a founder of the Harvard Socialist Club and director of the Madison Square Garden pageant that had been held on behalf of the iww strike at Paterson, New Jersey; see *ibid.*, 156.

Winslow Taylor, refined by men of genuine social concern, might offer significant alternatives.

Simons began to familiarize himself in 1919 with the literature of scientific management, and by September he was, as he reported to Louis Post, "putting all my time, aside from what is always a negligible thing to a fool reformer like myself, the work of earning a living, upon employment management, with especial reference to the shop committee system. To my mind, this joint management, in some form or another, while no solution, is the only next step that will save us from a social explosion."[41] Simons was well aware that his new interest was far less grand than his dreams of old, but he thought it no less important for that. His approach to Taylorism did not emphasize the autocratic, stopwatch methods of the master, but stressed instead the role of the management expert as a kind of scientific mediator between the interests of employers and employees. "I feel," Simons wrote, "that unless labor does understand the management of industry and begins to share and cooperate in it that any attempt at a labor ruled society will certainly bring a collapse of all society."[42]

His radical colleagues responded to his new enthusiasm in various ways. George Herron was full of praise: "You hold the cue to a true entrance upon labor evolution and solution. . . . This much is certain: there is no solution through socialist politics—no more in Europe than in America. . . . The solution lies through the actual transmutation of labor and production from within."[43] Upton Sinclair was appalled. "When you get tired of waiting," he predicted, "you will become a rebel again."[44] "I feel a great pity for you," he wrote. "You must be wretchedly unhappy, and the course of history will be a series of blows in the face to you."[45]

Simons replied jauntily, "Save your tears—All my friends agree I am looking better than for years. I am working night and day and having the time of my life. . . . just believe I am happy without a

---

[41] Simons to Post, Sept. 18, 1919, Simons Papers.
[42] Simons to George Herron, Dec. 10, 1919, Simons Papers.
[43] Herron to Simons, Sept. 17, 1921, Simons Papers.
[44] Sinclair to Simons, March 23, 1920, Simons Papers.
[45] Sinclair to Simons, March 28, 1920, Simons Papers.

hard thought against anyone on earth, a condition I could never be in the S.P."[46]

A more thoughtful commentator was Henri DeMan, Belgian-born socialist intellectual who had tried his hand at scientific management and then had given up the venture. Gently he tried to make Simons aware of the problems that might lie before him. "Is it wise," he asked, "for a man who has thus far been associated with the labor movement, and owes whatever influence he has to his association with that movement, to go in for . . . work where he will find himself at the mercy of interests that are antagonistic to that movement?"[47]

Simons was not to be dissuaded. In January 1920 he began teaching a course in industrial management in the extension division of the University of Wisconsin, and took a position as personnel management expert for the Leffingwell-Ream Company, Management Engineers. His new career was off to a flying start.[48] "Am very glad you are going to take that University job," Louis Post wrote when he heard of Simons' appointment. "You can fill the bill, and the discipline of reserving your fighting disposition won't hurt you."[49]

Simons' teaching was a great success. His students, who were mostly personnel managers and corporate executives, gave him an ovation after the last class.[50] The applause was doubtless soothing to the abrasions Simons had collected in years past. But of greater consequence was the material he had gathered and the ideas he had developed for presentation to his class. He reworked his lectures, added some material, and in 1921 published his first book based on his new interests, *Personnel Relations in Industry*.

His approach, as revealed in the book, used the ideas of Frederick Winslow Taylor as a takeoff point and tried to apply them, together with what he had read of industrial psychology, to problems of human relations and worker-satisfaction in industry. "Because scien-

[46] Simons to Sinclair, March 30, 1920, Simons Papers.
[47] DeMan to Simons, March 19, 1920. See also DeMan to Simons, March 13, 1920.
[48] May Simons, Diary, Nov. 28, 1919; Wisconsin Board of Regents to Simons, Jan 22, and March 1, 1920, Simons Papers.
[49] Post to Simons, Dec. 28, 1919, Simons Papers.
[50] May Simons, Diary, May 22, 1920.

tific management came into industry through the engineering department," Simons explained, "it inevitably suffered in the beginning
from neglect and misunderstanding of the human element."[51] In his
work, he intended to correct that misemphasis. His primary assumption, nonetheless, was based upon production, not upon the human
element: "The fundamental function of industry is, to produce the
goods needed by society, and to this everything else must be secondary. Whatever interferes with production threatens industry and the
society built upon it. Whatever increases production strengthens, im-
proves, and develops industry and makes possible a higher social
evolution."[52] Simons did not argue, as he surely would have in 1912,
that some kinds of production were more useful or beneficial than
others, and in subsequent books on vocational guidance he offered
advice impartially on how to succeed in advertising, social settlement
work, and banking.[53]

To ensure high productivity, the wise factory manager or personnel
expert would keep in mind the host of variables that contributed to
the zeal and satisfaction of the industry's employees. A keen knowledge of human nature was required. "By far the most important
elements in man's original nature," wrote Simons, "are the instincts.
. . . Civilization . . . consists largely in bending these instincts to
social purposes, and their resistance to change constitutes one of the
reasons for the slowness of progress."[54] Simons cited a whole handful
of psychologists who had illuminated the nature of man's instincts—
William McDougal, E. L. Thorndike, Jacques Loeb, and John B.
Watson among them. The principal source of wisdom for Simons,
however, was Thorstein Veblen, whose concept of the instinct of
workmanship informed all of the onetime Socialist's writings on scientific management. All the industrial ills that Simons now sought to
cure stemmed, he thought, from an ignorance of this fundamental
fact of human nature: "The suppression of the instinct of craftsman-

---

[51] *Personnel Relations in Industry* (New York: Ronald Press, 1921), 13.
[52] *Ibid.*, 3.
[53] A. M. Simons and James McKinney, *Success Through Vocational Guidance* (Chicago: American Technical Society, 1922), 127–34; 175–82;
255–58.
[54] *Personnel Relations in Industry*, 36.

ship through monotonous work, lack of participation in planning, irregularity of employment, arbitrary management, poor adjustment of workers to work, indifference to character of output, and many other features of modern industry, has produced exactly the standard reactions that are always found in such instinct suppression."[55]

Efficiency, the byword of Frederick Winslow Taylor, was honored by Simons, not only because it directly increased production but also because "the one best way" meant less fatigue for the worker and hence greater possibility of the fulfillment of his instinct for workmanship.[56] Joint management, through shop committees, would further enhance the worker's interest in what he was doing. Unlike Taylor, Simons would not place all responsibility for industrial planning and management in the hands of the expert, for this would decrease the worker's sense of involvement and heighten his antagonism toward his employer. "The attempt to put all the 'heads' together in the planning department," Simons explained, "leaving nothing but 'hands' in the shop, led to a righteous revolt of labor, and upon this rock scientific management was almost wrecked."[57]

There was still a major role for the "expert" in Simons' scheme of industrial democracy. The personnel manager would, through job analysis and psychological testing, fit the worker to the job. He would help determine the eligibility of employees for raises and promotions. He would run classes to familiarize employees with the history of his particular industry and with its role in American economic life. He would help prepare employees to take responsibility on shop committees.

To employers who feared that conflicts would inevitably occur when factory planning was done by management and labor together, Simons had a reassuring reply. The scientific method would be the solvent of discord. "Have a means of determining, testing, and standardizing facts, and both sides will accept the decisions based on such a method. People do not quarrel about the multiplication table."[58] The

[55] *Ibid.*, 44.
[56] *Ibid.*, 208–209.
[57] *Ibid.*, 127.
[58] *Ibid.*, 295.

science of socialism had been faulty; social science could now take its place.

Before World War I Simons' ideas would probably have been as unwelcome to industrialists as to radicals. Now they made more sense because some of them had previously been tested. Henry Ford's $5.00 day, granted in January 1914 and followed by the establishment of a "sociological department" to determine a worker's fitness for such a wage, had first alerted the business and industrial community to the virtues of considering the human element in scientific management. Ford had reduced both turnover and absenteeism in his factories. When labor became increasingly militant through the war years and in the postwar period, the lessons of Ford were increasingly instructive. With the accompanying rise of the psychological testing movement, which foretold the possibility of perfecting the human machinery in the factory, many once-hostile eyes began to look approvingly upon the new "science" of personnel management.[59]

Once more, therefore, Simons was a pioneer of sorts. He took the raw material of psychology and scientific management and tied them into a package that could, he thought, benefit employers and employees alike. He was, however, an innovator without disciples. As industrial psychology grew and prospered in the 1920s, it developed along lines that were considerably more sophisticated than the simplistic faith in scientific method that he had exalted. Much more experimentation and testing needed to be done, and it was carried on by professional social scientists who decided early that the instinct of workmanship was a frail reed upon which to base the control of an advanced industrial society.

The firm of Leffingwell-Ream dissolved in 1920 upon the death of one of the partners,[60] and Simons took a position at the American School in Chicago. For nearly ten years he served as secretary and supervisor of foreman training for the school, which provided correspondence courses for those who wished to complete work for a high school diploma. He wrote several more books on personnel manage-

---

[59] Loren Baritz, *Servants of Power* (New York: John Wiley, 1965), 32–35.
[60] Note by Miriam Simons Leuck in May Simons Diary, April 6, 1920.

ment,[61] and developed curricula and programs in personnel management for the school. He contributed many articles on vocational guidance to the Milwaukee *Journal* and for awhile contributed a daily column on the same subject to the H. H. and Elizabeth Allen Syndicate.[62]

For Simons these were years of tranquillity and comparative financial security. Once more he and his family were living in Evanston. His daughter graduated from the University of Chicago in 1921 and enrolled at Northwestern University for graduate work in history.[63] His wife had resigned from the Milwaukee Americanization Committee in 1919, because it was, she said, being taken over by a group of "extreme reactionaries."[64] With the ratification of the women's suffrage amendment, May turned her attention to the work of preparing new voters to use their right wisely. She became a member of the League of Women Voters while the Simonses were still living in Milwaukee, and she lectured widely before schools of citizenship that were set up under the league's auspices.[65]

After moving to Evanston, she continued these activities, became state chairman for citizenship training in the Illinois league in 1922, and eventually became president of the state organization. All the while, she continued graduate study and in 1930 earned her Ph.D. in economics.

The decade of the 1920s was a discouraging one for radicals in America. The reaction that Algie and May Simons had seen sweep through the Wisconsin Loyalty Legion and the Americanization Committee was prevalent everywhere. Simons, who felt by 1918 that there was no longer any place for him in radical politics, now began to find it hard even to decide on a presidential candidate he would be willing to vote for. The progressives of the 1920s—LaFollette, John-

[61] *Production Management* (Chicago: American Technical Society, 1922), 2 vols.; with James McKinney, *Success Through Vocational Guidance.*
[62] Clippings, Simons Papers.
[63] May Simons, Diary, April 6, 1921, Simons Papers.
[64] *Ibid.*, Nov. 28, 1919.
[65] See, for example, Milwaukee *Sentinel*, April 1, 1920, Milwaukee *Journal*, April 27, 1920, and miscellaneous clippings, 1920–1923, Simons Papers.

son, and Borah—were unacceptable in Simons' eyes. "They belong to the 19th century in their liberalism," Simons wrote, "and to the 18th, at least, in their foreign policy."[66] Simons came to favor the idea of Henry Ford for president. "He is on the square," he wrote of Ford, "he is an organizer; he has the engineer's point of view, which is what we need now more than anything else. He has a good labor record, and he gets things done."[67]

Simons' old friend Charles Edward Russell was depressed by what he saw happening in America, but Simons still did not allow himself the luxury of disillusionment. "Of course it was not easy," he confided to Russell, "to watch all that you had worked for and bet your life on go into the discard, but I have always felt that the dead-rot had entered the body of the S.P. by 1912. . . . At the same time I can see [that] its 'spirit still goes marching on' in most of the things that mark growth."[68] As he described the work that he and his wife were doing, he expressed his continuing optimism: "We think we see some tremendous movements carrying society along toward democratic, working-class control, that are operating with little regard to politics. Not that I believe in disregarding politics, but at this moment the political world seems to be in the zodiacal sign of the ram—that is it is backing up to get some space for another bump ahead."[69]

The 1920s had their satisfactions for Simons, though. He was doing work that he enjoyed. He had brought his family back to Evanston where they were able to live comfortably if not lavishly. He still worried about money, especially now that he was in his fifties and thinking about his and May's years of retirement, but his wife constantly assured him that they were doing just fine.[70] In the summer of 1923, May went to New York City on business for the League of Women Voters, and while she was there she visited some of their old comrades who were still in the socialist movement. "Oh, Lord," she wrote her husband, "I am more thankful than ever for our new life.

[66] Simons to Russell, Nov. 23, 1922, Simons Papers.
[67] *Ibid.*
[68] Simons to Russell, Nov. 23, 1922.
[69] Simons to Russell, Jan. 19, 1925, Simons Papers.
[70] A. M. Simons to May Simons, July 19, 1923; May Simons to A. M. Simons, July 22, 1923, Simons Papers.

Algie, it was awful. While I was there the [New York] *Call* office kept calling up having spasms about a threat to stop if it could not get some money tomorrow."[71]

Simons also received an occasional indication that the work he had done as a Socialist had had some lasting effect. "I was sitting with five or six radical members of the House of Commons," Russell wrote from England, ". . . when one of them remarked that the writings of the American Socialists had done more to stir and encourage the radical movement in England than all other causes together. . . . He then said . . . that particularly your writings had been powerful and effective, and he deemed that the radical cause owed an inestimable debt to A. M. Simons."[72] It was kind of Russell to report this message to his old friend. It was pleasant for Simons to feel, at least now and then, that his work was not forgotten.

His radical friends abroad were not forgotten either. In 1925, Miriam Simons went to Paris to be married. The bride was given away by Jean Longuet, the grandson of Karl Marx.[73]

Tranquillity for Simons, which seemed so sure in the 1920s, was to pass with the decade. The crash of 1929 and the depression that followed struck the American School hard. Potential students soon found that they had little money to spend on such frills as correspondence courses, and little reason to expect a job when they finished. In 1930 Simons began looking for another position. Personnel management, too, lost its value. Employers were not interested in harmony and high productivity in the shop when they could no longer sell their products and when workingmen became grateful for the chance to toil even for Dickensian industrialists. Long ago Simons had thought that a financial crash would sound the death knell of capitalism and the summons to power for Socialists like himself. Now he found that capitalism still lived, but his own new world was destroyed. He was sixty years old, and he had no dreams left.

What he felt about this latest defeat can only be surmised from what came after. If he confided his feelings in letters to friends, the

---

[71] May Simons to A. M. Simons, July 20, 1923, Simons Papers.
[72] Russell to Simons, July 23, 1922, Simons Papers.
[73] May Simons, Diary, Feb. 4, 6, March 16, 1925, Simons Papers.

letters have not survived. He destroyed many of his papers when he left Evanston in 1944, though he saved much of his correspondence from the period after he obtained a new position. He kept no diary of these years, or if he did, he destroyed that too. May's diary, usually an anxious record of her husband's disappointments, was silent after noting in December 1929, "Business is not good."[74] He had no vision of himself heading some popular movement, or through personal expertise guiding America to a prosperous utopia. He only wanted work, and in this desire he was very like the rest of the American people who had been stunned by the crash.

Simons was more fortunate than many. His old friend Herbert Phillips arranged for him to work as a researcher for the American Dental Association, compiling data on the financing of medical care through various forms of insurance. It sounded like dreary work indeed for a man who had once taken all society as the province of his investigations, but Simons gave no hint that he thought it such.

Phillips was increasingly troubled by the existence of great numbers of Americans who sought neither medical nor dental care. The coming of the depression had squeezed such expenditures out of many family budgets. Perhaps new ways of financing medical care could be found—ways that would benefit both the sagging income of doctors and dentists and the deteriorating health of men and women of modest means.

In 1927 the American Medical Association (AMA) had set up a Committee on the Costs of Medical Care (CCMC) that was allied with Phillips' interests, and in 1930 the American College of Dentists decided to finance a study of dental economics. The AMA's committee included representatives from all fields allied to health, and the dental study would presumably contribute to the general conclusions of the CCMC.[75] It was this study of dental economics that Simons was

---

[74] May Simons, Diary, Dec. 24, 1929. Miriam Simons Leuck notes that her mother kept no more diaries after the death of her granddaughter in Oct. 1930, and implies that May's profound bereavement caused her to leave off keeping her diary. The last entry, however, was made nearly ten months before her granddaughter died.

[75] Interview, Robert Huston with Herbert Phillips, cited in Huston, "Algie Martin Simons," 346; A. M. Simons and Nathan Sinai, *The Way of*

to undertake in cooperation with Dr. Nathan Sinai, who was to provide the medical background that Simons lacked.

For nearly a year Simons and Sinai studied programs of health insurance in the United States, and in 1931 they went to Europe to investigate similar problems and programs there. As Simons watched the scenery slide by on the way to New York, he saw much to remind him of that long-ago trip from Madison to Cincinnati. In 1895 depression had held the country tight, and now he could see the strings of empty freight cars that testified to yet another economic crisis.[76] On shipboard, the newspapers he read to help pass the time were filled with reports of ever-declining stocks.[77] He read the reports with a different interest than in earlier years. His wife wrote to Miriam and Gerald, "We watch the stocks and bonds in the states. Any more of ours gone up? I mean have they gone into any more receiverships?"[78] Apparently the Simonses had acquired some stake in capitalist enterprise in the 1920s and now, it seemed, capitalism had failed them too. The insecurity that had dogged them through their years in the Socialist party was still on their heels. Their capacity for anger, however, had dwindled along with their ability to believe that they could help direct the course of history.

Simons was pleased with what he learned of health insurance during the trip. He found once more that, "Unfortunately for the facts they do not fit into our carefully worked out theories."[79] He wrote at length about the kinds of problems that government insurance programs had encountered abroad, and he sounded every bit as interested in them as he had been in conflicts over Marxist orthodoxy and revisionism three decades before. But his first concern this time was definitely for the welfare of his new employers, not for the health of those they benefited. He revealed a curious ability to talk about dentists and doctors as he had once talked about industrial workers.

Health Insurance (Chicago: University of Chicago Press, 1932), vii–viii; A. M. Simons to May Simons, March 22, 1930, Simons Papers.

[76] May Simons to Miriam Leuck, June 13, 1931, Simons Papers.

[77] A. M. Simons to Miriam and Gerald Leuck, undated (between letters of June 15 and June 22), Simons Papers.

[78] July 7, 1931, Simons Papers.

[79] Simons to Miriam and Gerald Leuck, July 2, 1931.

He believed, for example, that industrial and government clinics ought to remain under the control of the medical personnel "so as to prevent 'sweating.' "[80]

When the trip was over, Simons and Sinai published *The Way of Health Insurance*, which presented the findings of their research. It was as judicious a performance as Simons' long-ago article on railroads for the *Wisconsin Transactions*. "He who says, without qualification, 'I am against health insurance' or 'I am for health insurance,' " the authors declared, "is speaking out of great depths of ignorance or great heights of prejudice."[81] Simons and Sinai listed several conclusions based upon their research: there was no important opposition to the principle of health insurance in any country where it already existed; all agreed that the insured received better care than they had before they were insured; doctors' and dentists' incomes were at least as high, and in some cases higher; medical indifference or hostility to insurance programs produced public hostility to doctors and dentists, and a greater tendency for people to seek medical aid from quacks and unqualified practitioners.[82]

The book constituted a moderate approval of medical and dental insurance for low-income groups. It warned the professions that they must keep the control and administration of such programs in their own hands insofar as possible, so that the programs could be pegged to the medical realities of each situation. It warned against unlimited benefits, and it never suggested that health care was a right which government owed to all its citizens. Yet even this temperate approval of health insurance was anathema to the medical and dental fraternity. When Phillips presented Simons' and Sinai's conclusions and recommendations to the AMA's Committee on the Costs of Medical Care, they were rejected.[83] When Simons' and Sinai's original grant had been expended, the Dental Association did not renew it.[84]

Simons was hired at once to work for the Bureau of Medical

---

[80] A. M. Simons to Miriam Leuck, July 27, 1931.
[81] Simons and Sinai, *The Way of Health Insurance*, 204.
[82] *Ibid.*, 204–209.
[83] "Final Report of the Committee on the Costs of Medical Care," *Journal of the AMA*, XCIX (June 4, 1932), 1224–25.
[84] Huston, "Algie Martin Simons," 349.

Economics of the American Medical Association, and for twelve years he prepared pamphlets, bulletins, and journal articles for the bureau. All had a single theme: health insurance of any kind, under any form of direction save that of private insurance companies who protected individual subscribers, must be fought tirelessly. When Simons wrote his last public article on the subject, he had even outstripped the zeal of the AMA in his opposition. By 1941 the AMA was coming around to the view that group hospitalization and medical society plans might meet a genuine public need and, at the same time, halt the threat of compulsory health insurance.[85] But in 1947, when he wrote of insurance programs in operation in other countries, Simons declared, "No unprejudiced visitor returns from any of these systems with praise for its operations or vital statistics of its accomplishments in improving the health of the people insured."[86] In fact, he himself had returned with praise for such programs in 1931.

What had happened this time? What had brought Simons from a position of cautious approval of schemes designed to protect the health of people of humble means, to his adamant stance against such programs? The evidence to answer such questions is scanty and confusing. The whole decade was confusing to Simons. This is clear from all his remarks on the New Deal, which itself provided so satisfying a home to so many reformers. It gave no comfort to Simons. He did not see it as a manifestation of that onward-moving spirit he had described so consolingly in his letters to Russell in the 1920s. Simons had voted for Hoover in 1932[87]—at last he had a candidate with "the engineer's point of view"—and when FDR took office, Simons was not impressed. "There is no doubt," Simons wrote in March 1933, "that capitalism must 'fish or cut bait' or be drowned within the next six months, and I don't see much that looks very hopeful."[88] Hopeful? This was not the talk of a man who looked forward to the birth of a new "social stage." What troubled him most of all was that he could

[85] James G. Burrow, *AMA: Voice of American Medicine* (Baltimore: Johns Hopkins University Press, 1963), 251.
[86] "Hiatus in Sickness Insurance," *Christian Science Monitor Magazine,* Jan. 4, 1947, p. 6.
[87] May Simons to Miriam and Gerald Leuck, Nov. 8, 1932.
[88] A. M. Simons to Miriam and Gerald Leuck, March 5, 1933.

see no clear direction in which the New Deal was moving. FDR talked in generalities; no one knew what he intended, or what the future might hold.[89] As for Simons, he was as puzzled as anyone: one day capitalism seemed doomed, the next day, it seemed to have one kick left in it. He was tired of trying to read the portents.

Instead, he devoted himself to protecting a group of professionals whom he described as sturdy individualists, trying to guard themselves against the incursions of politicians, bureaucrats, and businessmen. His disillusionment with officeholders grew, and he came to comment with increasing cynicism upon them. Of Roosevelt he wrote, "he may not be any worse than Hitler. The world seems to be short of dictatorial timber of a high grade, so I suppose we will have to put up with culls."[90] When his son-in-law became engaged in chemical research that involved the measuring of infinitely small spaces and distances, Simons remarked wryly, that it would "come in handy. . . . I want someone to give me the exact dimensions of the average congressman's intelligence."[91] What Simons referred to as "the welfare bunch" was "becoming the tool of as fine a lot of highbinders as ever ran a utility combine."[92]

The men of the medical profession must be protected against control by such fools as these, and health insurance must be fought in order for doctors to retain their age-old right to minister to the sick, regardless of the dictates of petty bureaucrats. Doctors were guided by a different definition of value than shaped the thought of politicians and businessmen: doctors went where they were needed, not where they could obtain the most money; doctors needed to be free to practice as they saw fit. Equally important, their patients needed, as an aid to their recovery, the sense of personal responsibility they gained from knowing they must pay their own bills.

In these years that Simons spent with the AMA, new characters were filling old roles. He described doctors and dentists as he had once described the pioneer farmers of the middle western frontier: rugged

[89] *Ibid.*
[90] *Ibid.*, Feb. 12, 1933.
[91] *Ibid.*, Jan. 15, 1933.
[92] *Ibid.*, Feb. 9, 1933.

individualists, facing all the hardships of an unfriendly environment, in order to fulfill their destiny. It was an equation that left out a good deal.

Simons' world had been shaken up once too often. Confronted with forces that seemed beyond his understanding, he took refuge in the certainties that remained. He was left with a small world, but a comfortable one. His work was not difficult for a man who had spent his life hunting down information that would serve a cause. Essentially a propagandist, he knew well how to marshal the facts he needed. He had time to read what he liked, to visit old friends, and to tend his garden. He was more than ready for such a life.

Neither his letters nor anything he published ever related his new activities to his old ones. Identifying paragraphs for articles he wrote for public journals described him not as a former Socialist, but as author of *Social Forces in American History* and of books on personnel management or, more simply, as assistant director of the AMA's Bureau of Medical Economics.[93]

This was in marked contrast to the assiduous efforts he made in the 1920s to relate his work for management to his previous radicalism. An observer with a deeper sense of ideology than Simons had would probably have seen his anti-New Deal conservatism as merely the culmination of more than thirty years of drift toward the right. Now, by the middle of the 1930s Simons had come back, after a long but steady journey, to the Republicanism of his elders.

[93] See, for example, Simons and R. G. Leland, "Do We Need Compulsory Public Health Insurance? No," *Annals of the American Academy of Political and Social Science*, CLXX (Nov. 1933), 121–27, and Simons, "Mistaken Claims for Socialized Medicine," *Christian Science Monitor Magazine*, Sept. 22, 1945, p. 9.

CHAPTER TEN

Reminiscence

In 1944, at the age of 74, Simons retired from the Bureau of Medical Economics and, with his wife, moved to Brooklyn, New York, to live with his daughter and son-in-law. He had hoped to write history after his retirement, but the ill health that compelled him to give up his job with the AMA continued to plague him. Though he occasionally jotted down an idea or an outline for an article, he never got anything more substantial on paper. Some of his old colleagues were writing their memoirs now, but Simons never tried, or, if he did, never thought the product worth saving.

Perhaps he did not wish to relive so many unhappy endings. The Socialist party, as he had known it, was dead. Personnel management had taken new directions, and even the fight against health insurance was beginning to turn against the AMA. His most substantial scholarly effort, *Social Forces in American History,* seemed forgotten. Economic interpretation had had a considerable vogue in the historical profession, but the historians who followed him had begun from different assumptions than he. Charles A. Beard, the most influential of the school of economic interpretation, had gone to the works of the founding fathers, not to Karl Marx for his inspiration.

Though Simons chose not to publish any reflections upon his long and troubled career, he heard now and then from scholars who were interested in what he might have to say about his historical writing, about his colleagues, or about the fate of radical politics in America— and he was a willing respondent.[1] In 1946 a young Princeton student, John Harmon, came to Brooklyn to interview Algie and May Simons, and found them eager to talk about the old days. Simons was most voluble about the years that were most distant. He was proud of his frontier origins, that was clear. He did not mention the possibility that he had been something less than an eager hand as a farm boy, nor that the farm itself had been lost. Instead, he talked about self-sufficiency; his family had never been really poor, he said, but his grandmother had woven the cloth for the clothes her grandchildren wore, and he himself had been given a rifle when he was twelve, so that he might help provide game for the family table.

Sauk County was not untouched wilderness when Simons was a boy. There were small iron-mining operations near North Freedom, and the railroad ran through the village, which itself boasted a variety of shops, businesses, schools, and churches. Nevertheless, Simons remembered his boyhood as the boyhood of a pioneer, digging out a farm from the woods of Wisconsin.

Of his own tribulations within the Socialist party Simons said little, and about his lifetime of ideological meandering he seemed unusually inarticulate. He did not repudiate his radicalism, never called himself mistaken for having given so much of his life to the socialist movement, and in some ways considered himself a critic of the establishment still. He was distressed to learn that young Harmon planned a career in advertising when he finished Princeton.[2]

Musing about his own past, Simons seemed somewhat mystified: "You never know," he said "what forces are pushing you around."

The forces that pushed A. M. Simons around were many. Some were of his own making; some were made by his family and by his heritage; some were inherent in the American environment of his generation. He was unsuited, both physically and temperamentally, for a life on the land, but he never entirely repudiated the values of rural America. He was sober, industrious, and fond of hearth and home, and he retained a distrust of "the East" that erupted at Socialist party conventions as it had among the Wisconsin farmers who cursed the evil bankers of Wall Street.

When as a young man Simons found that he had abilities that could provide him with another way of life, he worked hard to develop them. This was especially true of the first gift he discovered,

<hr/>

[1] See, for example, Sigmund Diamond to Simons, Nov. 14, 1939; and Simons to Diamond, Nov. 18, 1939, Simons Papers.
[2] Harmon to Simons, Oct. 26, 1948, Simons Papers.

his capacity for debate. He was capable of unmitigated wrath, and he delighted in the clash of opinion. He grew extraordinarily angry with nearly everyone who disagreed with him. He was never able to write as well as he spoke, and his writing nearly always displayed the heat and hyperbole so effective on the public platform, but so often inappropriate and offensive when engraved on the printed page. Simons went through life as a debater, always able to switch over, prepare new arguments, and plead the opposite side of the same question.

Why his zeal for argument should have led him into radicalism instead of into business, law, or even major-party politics, it is nearly impossible to say. His teachers at the University of Wisconsin were undoubtedly influential in directing his interest toward social issues, but neither Turner nor Ely, the two men who did the most to shape Simons' thinking, turned away from the respectability of professorships in a major university.

Having decided upon social work, Simons was also clearly influenced by the sheer shock-value of what he saw in South Chicago in the 1890s. He was appalled by the conditions in which laboring men lived and worked, but not all social workers reacted as he did. He might, conceivably, have resolved to put as much distance as possible between these unhappy victims and himself.

Instead, he made a fatal mistake that he was to repeat time and time again: he mistook the meaning of his own experience. He assumed that because the workers of Packingtown were wretched, all American workers everywhere were wretched. He assumed that because the radicals he met in Chicago were so persuasive in their predictions of social collapse, social collapse must be imminent. Perhaps he even believed that because his family had lost their land, farmers everywhere must lose theirs.

When World War I came, Simons' conclusions were based upon just such a misreading of what he had seen and heard. When the German community in Milwaukee championed the cause of their brethren in the fatherland, he assumed that a great web of pro-German sentiment threatened to ensnare America and destroy all that he and his forebears had worked to build. When he went abroad to hearten the spirits of workers in France, Italy, and England, he believed that he had gained indispensable information that was accessible to no one else.

His unshakable conviction that his own experience—whether based on research, observation, or interview—was a certain guide to action, led him to press his arguments relentlessly. It also led him time and again to modify his expectations and arguments on the basis of new, personally accumulated data. In a country that was changing rapidly in almost every way, this meant that his own ideas must be modified often.

One of Simons' most accurate perceptions was that socialism, to attain success in America, had to be tied to traditions and institutions that were characteristically American. Socialism was a fragment torn from the culture of another continent, and to live successfully in a new environment it had to unite itself with indigenous forms of life that were already thriving. Simons tried desperately to put such traditions as America had to the use of radicalism, and to develop that sense of community spirit and common endeavor that the Marxists called solidarity. All his historical writing, his struggling newspapers, and his insistence upon including farmers in the embrace of the Socialist party were designed with that end in mind. In his desire to unite the hopes of socialism with the institutions of America, he jettisoned the idea of violent revolution in favor of the ballot box.

Yet he underestimated the vigor of the life to which he sought to attach this foreign graft. It was socialism that was choked out. The very individualism that was Simons' pride turned each new move toward solidarity into a quarrel. The very freedom of choice that he exalted produced blizzards of newsprint and a politician's nightmare of factions. Simons seems never to have expected that Socialists would be marked so strongly with the characteristic features of the culture they attacked. Certainly he did not understand that no one was more strongly marked than he.

Simons' abhorrence of violent revolution was real, and it was lifelong. It was one of the most powerful forces pushing a verbally incautious man toward caution. He wanted class struggle without bloodshed, and when it began to look as though he could not have one without the other, he left off trying to foment the struggle.

If Simons had a single flaw of character that drove him toward errors and bad judgments, it was his vanity. Just as he believed in the universal validity of his own experience, so too he believed that he should be more respected than he was and always thought his work more substantial than his colleagues and his public were willing to grant. He was, in short, a bad loser. The ignobility with which he took defeat denied him the comfort of many admirers in a nation where losing is bad enough, but losing without grace is nearly unforgivable.

In only one significant controversy, and that very late in his life, did he refuse to become involved or try to claim more notice for himself than he might have deserved. As historians discovered *Social Forces in American History*, they were intrigued with the possibility that, antedating Beard's work, it might have influenced him. To one such suggestion, Simons replied, "Several scholars have . . . tried to build up the idea that Beard had copied my work without credit. . . . I have always refused to become involved in any such petty personalities, considering them as being wholly beneath any real question of historical discussion."[3]

It was his history for which Simons was remembered. Most works on American historiography show a passing acquaintance with *Social Forces;* analyses of economic determinism in American thought include at least a footnote of credit to the irascible Socialist who anticipated ideas that others were to treat with less haste.

In truth, Simons' history should be regarded not so much as a curiosity, but as an important part of a much larger body of thought that made up a middle western attack upon the genteel tradition in America. Literary critics were to call this rebellion against the genteel

[3] Simons to Howard K. Beale, undated, Simons Papers. William A. Glaser made the most thorough comparative study of Beard's and Simons' economic determinism in "A Critique of Two Economic Interpretations of Politics, Charles A. Beard and A. M. Simons" (unpublished Ph.D. dissertation, Harvard University, 1952). Glaser was not, however, interested in determining any possible influence of one man's work upon the other's.

It is conceivable, though unlikely, that Beard saw Simons' lectures on American history before his own work on the Constitution was completed. Beard was teaching at the Rand School when Simons' school for worker education folded, and Simons offered his course material to Rand.

the "vernacular tradition," and in Mark Twain they were to find its most distinguished practitioner.[4] The writers of the vernacular tradition, like Simons in his historical writing, protested against an optimism that did away with everything disturbing or unpleasant by declaring it contrary to God's will and therefore not truly real. Such writers questioned the merits of institutions that proclaimed such a viewpoint, especially the church and the school, and they often identified these attitudes with New England in particular and the East in general. Out of this literary revolt against gentility grew a new kind of hero. Uncontrolled, unpretentious, and unlettered, the vernacular hero was a man incapable of drawing the veil of respectability over the testimony of his senses.

Simons' history provided an accompaniment to the themes of the vernacular tradition. He tried to show that American democracy was the product of the vernacular rather than of the high culture, and that it was produced by the masses of workingmen and farmers—his own version of the vernacular hero—in response to their needs. The true democrats of the American past were unlettered and unpretentious men and women who moved instinctively toward the fulfillment of goals to which other classes in society gave only lip service.

Henry Nash Smith, commenting upon the significance of the vernacular tradition, has observed, "During the two or three decades following the First World War, the attitudes Santayana taught us to call genteel virtually disappeared from serious literature."[5] In the same decades genteel attitudes also disappeared from American historical writing. Even the kinds of schoolbooks that A. M. Simons had once attacked so vigorously began to find more than high ideals as the shaping forces of American civilization. Perhaps Simons sometimes wondered whether the parents or grandparents of the schoolboys of this new generation ever remembered the Chatauqua lectures or the

---

[4] The term *vernacular tradition* gets its name from the particular kind of speech of low-life characters that authors used to make their most telling points. Kenneth S. Lynn, *Mark Twain and Southwestern Humor* (Boston: Little, Brown, 1959), and Henry Nash Smith, *Mark Twain: The Development of a Writer* (Cambridge: Harvard University Press, 1962), present excellent studies of the vernacular tradition.

[5] Smith, *Mark Twain*, 3.

articles published in the *Appeal to Reason,* or the pamphlets in the Pocket Library of Socialism where he had expressed similar ideas so long before.[6]

He never publicly claimed such influence for his work, but he was always aware of his kinship with middle western ways of thinking. He always considered that he owed more to Frederick Jackson Turner than to Karl Marx, and in his old age he came intellectually and emotionally to cherish the culture and the values of his youth more deeply than any of the other gods he had followed.

In 1949 Simons made his last visit to Wisconsin. He traveled alone, for his wife, who had accompanied him on so many journeys, had died the year before. He went to see old friends, and at Lake Delton he was received by his former colleagues at the AMA. "They almost laid down the red carpet for me," he wrote to Miriam with obvious pleasure. There was "a host of relatives I never knew—some of whom traveled miles to see me." But the trip was not easy. Simons was suffering from arthritis and from increasingly severe attacks of angina.[7] But he was a proud old man, and his hand was as steady as ever as he wrote fondly to his daughter. When the reunions were over and he was preparing for his return trip, he wrote to Miriam, "I think I have seen everybody I ever intended to, and done all I planned."[8]

On March 11, 1950, after a period of hospitalization following an automobile accident, Simons died.[9] He was interred in the family plot at Baraboo, a few miles from his birthplace in North Freedom. Only a simple stone marks his grave, for the Socialist party of America gave immortality to no one. In its years of promise it attracted wise men and fools, and some who were a mixture of both.

[6] The relationship between Simons' history and the vernacular tradition is treated more fully in Kent and Gretchen Kreuter, "The Vernacular History of A. M. Simons," *Journal of American Studies,* II (April 1968), 65–81. Portions reprinted here by permission.

[7] Typescript comments of Miriam Simons Leuck, Simons Papers.

[8] Simons to Miriam Leuck, June 2, 1949, Simons Papers.

[9] He died in New Martinsville, W. Va. Gerald Leuck was transferred to New Martinsville shortly before May Simons' death, and both the Simonses joined their daughter and son-in-law there (note by Miriam Simons Leuck, Simons Papers).

BIBLIOGRAPHICAL ESSAY

There is an abundance of materials upon which the biographer of A. M. Simons can draw. The basic collection is the Algie M. and May Simons Papers at the State Historical Society of Wisconsin. The value of the collection is enhanced by the excellent notes of explanation and amplification provided by their daughter, Miriam Simons Leuck. Other collections at the Society contain important Simons letters. The papers included are those of Daniel DeLeon, Richard T. Ely, Morris Hillquit, Henry Demarest Lloyd, and the Loyalty Legion. Elsewhere, the Milwaukee Socialist Party papers at the Milwaukee County Historical Society and the Socialist Party Collection at the Duke University Library contain relevant material.

In addition, Simons wrote prolifically for several newspapers and periodicals: the *Worker's Call*, Chicago *Daily Socialist*, Milwaukee *Leader*, *International Socialist Review*, and *Coming Nation* are the principal ones, and he wrote occasionally for at least a dozen others. The State Historical Society of Wisconsin has a vast collection of socialist and labor magazines and newspapers. It is often difficult to determine which newspaper articles have been written by whom. We have assumed, in the case of periodicals that Simons edited, that the editorials were either written by Simons or that he was sympathetic with the ideas in them.

Simons also wrote a number of books and pamphlets on a variety of subjects. He was not a distinguished stylist. He did his best writing in the years immediately after his conversion to socialism, when his indignation against capitalist society ran high, and the sincerity of his protest made his literary shortcomings more forgivable. It is, therefore, unfortunate that *Social Forces in American History* is the book for which he is best known. *Social Forces* was a reworking of ideas that Simons had developed years earlier in *Class Struggles in American History* and in his series "American History for the Workers." *Social Forces* was no better documented than those other efforts, but it is more easily accessible than the earlier and more original material that appeared in pamphlets, newspapers, and periodicals. It is definitely not representative of Simons at his best.

In his published writing and in his public speaking, Simons communicated an air of shrill confidence, infallibility, and often arrogance. His personal papers, particularly his correspondence with his wife and daughter and, in later years, with Charles Edward Russell, reveal a much more sympathetic individual. From these letters one gets the sense of what it was like to be a Socialist in America early in this century, always hoping that the next election would bring about the Cooperative Commonwealth, but realizing increasingly that these goals were drawing no closer and were ultimately unattainable. Simons brooded about such things, as all professional Socialists must have done from time to time, and he revealed his misgivings and apprehensions, as well as his family and nonprofessional interests, in his correspondence.

This is not true of the only diary he kept—or at least the only one that survives—the record of his experiences abroad with the Socialist and Labor Mission in 1918. This diary was clearly intended to provide preliminary data for an official report on the mission. May Simons' diary, kept intermittently for a period of many years, is a personal record of a woman who was obviously intelligent, ambitious, and devoted to her husband and daughter. Mrs. Leuck prepared the typescript of the diary for inclusion in her parents' papers, and she deleted parts which, she says, were personal references to herself.

It is well to keep in mind that, according to Mrs. Leuck, the Simonses destroyed many of their letters and papers before they left Evanston in 1944. One can only speculate upon what was lost in this way. Family correspondence may have been among the papers discarded, for there are no extant letters to or from any of Algie or May Simons' relatives. Other evidence makes it clear that family ties were always maintained, although there seems to have been more contact with May's family than with her husband's.

Several unpublished dissertations and theses have proved particularly helpful on Simons and the socialist milieu he worked in. The A.B. thesis by John Harmon, "Algie Martin Simons, 1870–   " (Princeton, 1946), is of special interest because Harmon interviewed both Algie and May Simons several times and recorded considerable information on their early years in Wisconsin and Chicago. These are, of course, recollections made in old age, and they are subject to the limitations inherent in such recollections. However, when one compares A. M. Simons' memories of family and boyhood recorded in 1946 with his account of his early years made when he had just entered the socialist movement, there are no contradictions—only differences in emphasis and vocabulary. In 1946, for example, Simons no longer referred to his origins as "proletarian," and he chose to speak approvingly of values like self-reliance and individualism.

Robert Huston's dissertation, "Algie Martin Simons and the American Socialist Movement" (University of Wisconsin, 1965), concentrates upon Simons' socialist career, with which Huston is not sympathetic, and it too provides valuable information gained from interviews and correspondence with members of Simons' family. Most useful is the data Huston gained through several interviews with Simons' daughter. Mrs. Leuck is presently in ill health and unavailable for interview or correspondence.

Miriam Simons Leuck's dissertation, "The American Socialist and Labor Mission to Europe, 1918, Background, Activities and Significance: An Experiment in Democratic Diplomacy" (Northwestern University, 1941) is interesting but of limited value to the scholar. Historians interested in the mission would do better to go to Simons' diary and letters directly, and to the files of the Committee on Public Information at the National Archives. A new book on the CPI is currently in preparation by Jackson Giddens of the Massachusetts Institute of Technology.

William A. Glaser's dissertation, "A Critique of Two Economic Interpretations of Politics, Charles A. Beard and A. M. Simons" (Harvard University, 1952), is a detailed comparative analysis of Beard's *An Economic Interpretation of the Constitution* and Simons' *Social Forces in American History*. Glaser's article, "Algie Martin Simons and Marxism in America," *Mississippi Valley Historical Review*, XLI (Dec. 1954), 419–34, views Simons as a characteristically American Marxist but gives insufficient attention to the changes that Simons' ideas underwent through the years.

Gerald Friedberg's dissertation, "Marxism in the United States: John Spargo and the Socialist Party in America" (Harvard University, 1964), is well researched and well written. Spargo followed almost the same ideological course as Simons. He lived until 1966 and in 1964 supported Barry Goldwater for the presidency.

The M.A. thesis by Lorin Lee Cary, "Wisconsin Patriots Combat Disloyalty: The Wisconsin Loyalty Legion and Politics" (University of Wisconsin, 1964), concentrates not upon the League's propaganda functions with which Simons was chiefly identified, but with its political campaign to elect one of its own to the U.S. Senate.

Frederick I. Olson's dissertation, "The Milwaukee Socialists" (Harvard University, 1952), is extremely useful in detailing the course of socialism in America's most socialist city. A long letter from Simons to Olson which is in the Simons correspondence, attempts to answer a series of questions Olson asked of him. The letter is significant not for what it reveals about Simons' Milwaukee period, but for what it shows of Simons' inability to explain his actions and ideas.

The standard bibliography for historians interested in American socialism is the second volume of *Socialism and American Life,* edited by Donald Drew Egbert and Stow Persons (Princeton: Princeton University Press, 1952). A number of important studies have appeared since its publication. Among them are Howard H. Quint, *The Forging of American Socialism: Origins of the Modern Movement* (Columbia: University of South Carolina Press, 1953); David Shannon, *The Socialist Party of America* (New York: Macmillan, 1955); Ira Kipnis, *The American Socialist Movement, 1897–1912* (New York: Columbia University Press, 1952); and, most recently, James Weinstein, *The Decline of Socialism in America, 1912–25* (New York: Monthly Review Press, 1967). Kipnis believes that the decline of the SP was due to its internal factionalism and to its expulsion in 1912 of the left wing of the party. Weinstein believes that the SP did not decline after 1912 but remained a broadly based, deeply rooted movement that grew in strength and popularity during World War I. He claims that after 1919 socialism no longer revolved around a single party but that a general movement, socialist in character, continued to exist until 1925.

David Shannon has challenged Kipnis' thesis in the former's book *The Socialist Party of America* and in his review of the Kipnis book in the *Journal of Southern History*, August 1953. In answer to Weinstein, Simons himself would point out that while the party's membership did indeed grow after 1917 the party's character changed greatly during those years. It became less "American," less related to the central concerns of American life, and less likely to stir the imagination or expectations of American reformers. Although Weinstein recognizes that only a few SP members defected because of the party's antiwar stand in 1917, those "few" were among the most capable and influential of the prewar Socialists.

An inevitable posthumous misfortune has befallen the American socialist movement. Historians, denied the opportunity to show the operations of socialist politics at the center of American public life, have concentrated upon the infighting, personal feuds, and quarreling over platforms and resolutions that marked the SP in its years of greatest promise. This can become dreary, and it can also be deceptive, for it is doubtful that any American political party subjected to similar scrutiny could be the object of admiration. It would probably be possible to "prove" the intellectual, moral, or ideological bankruptcy of any party by dwelling upon its backstage maneuvers.

For anyone, therefore, who seeks to get a sense of the real flavor of the movement, it is important to read contemporary accounts of the party conventions and leaders in the nonsocialist periodicals of the day. The memoirs of old Socialists are also essential in this regard: Oscar Ameringer, *If You Don't Weaken* (New York: Holt, 1940); Morris Hillquit, *Loose Leaves from a Busy Life* (New York: Macmillan, 1934); and Charles Edward Russell, *Bare Hands and Stone Walls* (New York: Scribner's, 1933), are good examples of the genre.

One of the most obvious problems connected with a biography of A. M. Simons is to explain why he, like so many of his socialist colleagues, traversed the vast ideological distance from left to right. It is, of course, a commonplace that men become more conservative as they grow older, but there seems to be no good explanation of why this should be so. Some tentative suggestions are made in James C.

Davies, *Human Nature and Politics* (New York: John Wiley, 1963), and in Lucian Pye, "Personal Identity and Political Ideology," in *Psychoanalysis and History,* ed. Bruce Mazlish (Englewood Cliffs, N.J.: Prentice-Hall, 1963). Insight into this phenomenon is also provided by Henry Bedford, *Socialism and the Workers in Massachusetts, 1886–1912* (Amherst: University of Massachusetts Press, 1966). Bedford points out that ambivalence was at the core of the socialist movement. "Impossibilism" and "opportunism" were not simply characteristics of different wings of the SP but were both present within individual members of the party.

When considering Simons' apostasy it is worth remembering that he was no mere summer soldier for the SP. He was nearly 50 years old when he broke with the movement, even though he was moving from left to right over the course of two decades. The relationship between Simons' socialist career and his later work as a management consultant and efficiency expert is illuminated by Samuel Haber in *Efficiency and Uplift* (Chicago: University of Chicago Press, 1964).

Many challenging tasks remain for historians of American socialism. Two recent bibliographical articles will aid the scholar interested in the subject. Gerald Friedberg's "Sources for the Study of Socialism in America, 1901–1919," *Labor History,* VI (Spring 1965), 159–65, is an excellent annotated bibliography of archival material on socialism and Socialists of that period. F. Gerald Ham's "Labor Manuscripts in the State Historical Society of Wisconsin," *Labor History,* VII (Fall 1966), 313–42, is a guide to the collections held by the society. Biographies of such important figures as Victor Berger, Charles Edward Russell, and Robert Hunter remain to be written. Comparative studies of socialism in America, Great Britain, Australia, and elsewhere would doubtless shed light on the characteristic responses made by each country's Socialists to the great forces—war, revolution, industrialization—that have agitated modern times. The Negro Revolution of the 1960s is now beset with factional strife not unlike that which plagued the socialist movement early in this century. Historians might well find that a comparative study of the two phenomena would yield new insights into both.

INDEX

Addams, Jane: on radicalism, 31; meets Upton Sinclair, 78; mentioned, 29, 32, 45
agricultural policy: Socialist, 57; of A. M. Simons, 59–60, 121, 122–26, 133–35; Marxist, 122, 124
Allen, Henry, 75
American Alliance for Labor and Democracy, 174–75
American College of Dentists, 211
American Dental Association, 211
American Federation of Labor: De-Leon's view of, 38; and Socialist rival, 42; political activities in 1906, 97–98
American Medical Association: and industrial medicine, 23; Simon works for, 211
American Railway Union, 107
American School, Chicago, 207, 210
American Socialist and Labor Mission, 1918, 178–91 *passim*
Americanization Committee, Milwaukee, 167–69
Ameringer, Oscar, 165
Anderson, Sherwood, 129
Appeal to Reason, 73, 75–76, 116
Associated Charities, Cincinnati, 17, 18–19
Athena literary society, 11
Ayres, Philip W., 17, 20

Beard, Charles Austin, 76, 166, 217
Bebel, August, 103
Belgium, socialism in, 50–52
Bemis, Edward, 69
Benson, Allan, 159
Berger, Victor: quoted on Gompers, 98; elected to National Executive Committee of Socialist party, 100; predicts electoral success in 1908, 109; and Socialist-labor alliance, 110; and Milwaukee *Leader*, 144–45; socialist organization of, 145–46; defeated for Congress, 155; convicted under Espionage Act, 169; mentioned, 86, 113, 114, 164, 178
Berlyn, Barney, 86
Bernstein, Eduard, 47, 52
bolshevism: Socialist party's response to, 193; Simons' view of, 194–95
Bourne, Randolph, 129
Brandeis, Louis, and Eastern Rate Case, 200
Bryan, William Jennings, 32, 108
Bureau of Medical Economics, 213–14
Burns, John, 180–81
Butchers' National Protective Association, 22

Call, Henry Laurens, 118
Camp, Anna, 68
Camp, Katherine, 68
charity organization movement: nature and functions of, 18, 19; Simons' evaluation of, 32
Chicago Bureau of Charities, 20
Chicago *Daily Socialist*, 93–94
Chicago *Record*, 14
Chicago Socialist party local, 85–86
Chicago stockyards: efficiency of, 22; labor in, 22–24, 25–26; conflicting views of, 22, 23; housing near, 23; Upton Sinclair visits, 77–79
Chicago teamsters' strike, 1905, 67
Cincinnati Social Settlement, 18
Cole, G. D. H., 181
Columbian Exposition, 20
Coman, Katherine, economic historian, 75
Coming Nation: purpose of, 116; changing character of, 127–30; and The *Masses*, 129–31; failure of, 139
Committee of Public Information (CPI), 166, 188